Masculinities in Organizations

Research on Men and Masculinities Series

Series Editor:
MICHAEL S. KIMMEL, SUNY Stony Brook

Contemporary research on men and masculinity, informed by recent feminist thought and intellectual breakthroughs of women's studies and the women's movement, treats masculinity not as a normative referent but as a problematic gender construct. This series of interdisciplinary, edited volumes attempts to understand men and masculinity through this lens, providing a comprehensive understanding of gender and gender relationships in the contemporary world. Published in cooperation with the Men's Studies Association, a Task Group of the National Organization for Men Against Sexism.

Volumes in this Series

1. Steve Craig (ed.)
   MEN, MASCULINITY, AND THE MEDIA
2. Peter M. Nardi (ed.)
   MEN'S FRIENDSHIPS
3. Christine L. Williams (ed.)
   DOING WOMEN'S WORK: Men in Nontraditional Occupations
4. Jane C. Hood (ed.)
   MEN, WORK, AND FAMILY
5. Harry Brod and Michael Kaufman (eds.)
   THEORIZING MASCULINITIES
6. Edward H. Thompson, Jr. (ed.)
   OLDER MEN'S LIVES
7. William Marsiglio (ed.)
   FATHERHOOD
8. Donald Sabo and David Frederick Gordon (eds.)
   MEN'S HEALTH AND ILLNESS
9. Cliff Cheng (ed.)
   MASCULINITIES IN ORGANIZATIONS

Masculinities in Organizations

Edited by
Cliff Cheng

Published in cooperation with the Men's Studies Association,
A Task Group of the National Organization for Men Against Sexism

SAGE Publications
International Educational and Professional Publisher
Thousand Oaks London New Delhi

For information address:

SAGE Publications, Inc.
2455 Teller Road
Thousand Oaks, California 91320
E-mail: order@sagepub.com

SAGE Publications Ltd.
6 Bonhill Street
London EC2A 4PU
United Kingdom

SAGE Publications India Pvt. Ltd.
M-32 Market
Greater Kailash I
New Delhi 110 048 India

Printed in the United States of America

Library of Congress Cataloging-in-Publication Data

Main entry under title:

Masculinities in organizations / editor, Cliff Cheng.
p. cm.—(Research on men and masculinities; vol. 9)
Includes bibliographical references and index.
ISBN 0-7619-0223-6 (alk. paper)).—ISBN 0-7619-0224-4 (pbk.: alk. paper)
1. Corporate culture. 2. Masculinity (Psychology) 3. Sex role in the work environment. 4. Control (Psychology) 5. Gender identity. I. Cheng, Cliff. II. Series: Research on men and masculinities series; 9.
HD58.7.M376 1996
302.3'5—dc20 96-10041

This book is printed on acid-free paper.

96 97 98 99 10 9 8 7 6 5 4 3 2 1

Sage Production Editor: Vicki Baker

Contents

Series Editor's Introduction

The publication of Rosabeth Kanter's pioneering study *Men and Women of the Corporation* in 1977, shook both the academic and business worlds, as social scientists and corporate managers came to understand the complex set of problems that women faced when entering formerly all-male institutions. Corporations were now perceived as sites of reproduction of a gendered order—that is, the homosocial reproduction of male dominance. Women entering such arenas were likely to face the twin dilemmas of tokenism: They were hypervisible as members of their group and invisible as individuals. This caused high levels of stress. Clearly, ending sex discrimination was not going to be easy.

It was more than a matter of numbers. Much of the research designed to integrate women into corporate culture was guided by what we might call the *Field of Dreams* assumptions, taken from an oft-repeated line in that weepy, favorite male film: "If you build it, they will come." If only we could build our corporations—that is, make it clear to women that they are welcome, without discrimination—then, naturally, they would flock to our corporate headquarters. So corporate reformers sought to build it right. Even Kanter had hoped that proportionality might alleviate the extraordinary burden on those intrepid women, so that future generations would find a welcome mat instead of a glass ceiling.

But recent research suggests that the increasing weight of numbers was more than counterbalanced by the gendered nature of the institutions themselves. The "field of dreams" fallacy was based on the assumption that when "they" arrived, they would act just like those who were already there: That is, once women were admitted, they would act just like men.

Corporate culture itself, as it turned out, was gendered—and that gender was masculine. Thus, for example, although women compose just under 50% of all law students at the University of Pennsylvania Law School, and most of them enter with grades comparable to, if not better than, their male counterparts, the institutional culture of legal education finds many of these women falling to the bottom of their class.

Surely, then, research needed to focus not only on the gender of the employees or managers but also on the gender of the institutions themselves. In this respect, however, the research from both management and business schools and the social scientific research on organizations suddenly fell mute. This volume is an effort to correct that silence, suggesting some of the complicated ways in which homosocial reproduction is constituted and how these gendered institutions remain "masculine."

Such an examination goes beyond the simple numbers games that many organizations play, deeper than the analysis of the glass ceiling that so many women face. A study of gendered organizations must look at the architecture of the building in its entirety, not simply at the composition of the ceiling or the gender of its inhabitants. Only by examining the organization as a whole can the possible entry points be identified and the possibilities of institutional transformation be assessed.

Masculinities in Organizations is the first volume to address these issues, exploring the ways in which gender is part of the organizing principle of organizational culture and the ways in which gender assumptions saturate corporate discourse. It seeks to generate significant discussion and dialogue on the question of masculinities and organizations.

This is the ninth volume in the **Sage Series on Research on Men and Masculinities.** The purpose of the series is to gather together the finest empirical research in the social sciences that focuses on the experiences of men in contemporary society.

Following the pioneering research of feminist scholars over the past two decades, social scientists have come to recognize gender as one of the primary axes around which social life is organized. Gender is now seen as equally central as class and race, both at the macrostructual level of the allocation and distribution of rewards in a hierarchical society and at the micropsychological level of individual identity formation and interpersonal interaction.

Social scientists distinguish gender from sex. *Sex* refers to biology, the biological dimorphic division of male and female; *gender* refers to the cultural meanings that are attributed to those biological differences. Although biological sex varies little, the cultural meanings of gender vary enormously. Thus, we speak of gender as socially constructed; the definitions of masculinity and femininity as the products of the interplay between a variety of social forces. In particular, we understand gender to vary spatially (from one culture to another), temporally (within any one culture over historical time), and longitudinally (through any individual's life course). Finally, we understand that different groups within any culture may define masculinity and femininity differently, according to subcultural definitions; race, ethnicity, age, class, sexuality, and region of the country all affect our different gender definitions. Thus, it is more accurate to speak of "masculinities" and "femininities" than positing a monolithic gender construct.

It is the goal of this series to explore the varieties of men's experiences, remaining mindful of specific differences among men and aware of the mechanisms of power that inform both men's relations with women and men's relations with other men. This volume helps us to understand those dynamics within the structure of gendered organizations.

MICHAEL S. KIMMEL
Series Editor

Men and Masculinities Are Not Necessarily Synonymous: Thoughts on Organizational Behavior and Occupational Sociology

CLIFF CHENG

Nearly 20 years have passed since Rosabeth Kanter's (1977) *Men and Women of the Corporation* studied women (and minorities) in a large American industrial corporation. Nearing the anniversary of this watershed effort, one that has yet to be surpassed despite numerous imitators, the current volume seeks to encourage the interdisciplinary, cross-cultural study of masculinities and men in organizations. As editor, my vision for this book is to create an interdisciplinary, international forum on masculinities and men in organizations in an effort to present as many viewpoints, theories, and methods as possible.

Having long admired Jay Lorsch's (1987) anthology, *Handbook of Organizational Behavior,* for the way he recruited the top writers in their respective niches to contribute to what has become an unsurpassed single volume overviewing this field, I asked him for his thoughts on how to make this book as high quality as his. His wise advice was to simply get the best authors, and quality would fall into place after that.

To some, the book may seem curious, as they may wonder, "Why study men? Isn't most of the literature in organizational studies about men already?" It is plainly observable that most of the literature in organizational studies has tacitly featured men, but not men as gendered.

First, this study of masculinities in organizations and occupations is not necessarily about men. It is about masculinities, a kind of gender that is socially constructed. Sex is biological. Gender is socially performed. The two are *not necessarily synonymous,* especially when race, class, sexual identity, colonialism, religion, and so on are considered.

Writing about masculinities need not be about the male sex. Masculinity can be and is performed by women. Women who are successful managers perform *hegemonic masculinity* (Baril, Elbert, Mahar-Porter, & Reavy, 1989). Hegemonic masculinity refers to the *currently dominant* form of masculinity as constructed *in relation* to (and, therefore, dependent on) femininities and subordinated, marginalized, and colonized masculinities (Connell, 1987, pp. 183-188; Kimmel, 1994). In their chapters within this volume, Jennifer Pierce looks at the occupational, hegemonically masculine, emotional labor of trial lawyers; Judi Addelston and Michael Stirratt write about hegemonic masculinity in the organizational culture of a military college. Masculinities also include nonhegemonic masculinities that have been just as subordinated, marginalized, and colonized as hegemonic masculinity. In my chapter, I examine how Asian and Asian American male candidates were rejected in an assessment center as possible selections for the position of team managers, because assessors perceived them as being "too feminine." The concept of different types of masculinities is again illustrated in Tomoko Hamada's chapter that studies how Euro-American males work for a Japanese transplant organization. Outside the organization, in the dominant group culture, the gender performance of these Euro-American males is hegemonic, but inside, their performance is marginalized and subordinated, because the dominant group has defined and reinforced another form of hegemonic masculinity. Our focus here is to examine how gender, in particular masculinities, are socially constructed in organizations and occupations.

Statements that treat sex and gender as synonymous are part of bipolar sex role theory, a theory that is naively reductionistic and theoretically uninformed, although it is an empirical construct. Measuring gender phenomena beyond role is difficult, given the constraints of positivism. The concept of role may be of some use when a more sophisticated, multivariate model is situated in interaction and the multiple aspect of diversity is taken into account.

The theory behind the notion that sex is biological and gender is socially constructed is ethnomethodology, referring to the following:

> The study of particular subject matter: the body of common-sense knowledge and the range of procedures and considerations by means of which the

> ordinary members of society make sense of, find their way about in, and act on circumstances in which they find themselves. (Heritage, 1984, p. 4)

Ethnomethodology studies the sense-making process that constructs a seemingly ready-made and meaningful social world. It studies "practices of common-sense reasoning and cognitive style through which we experience the social world as a factual object" (Leiter, 1980, p. 4). Kessler and McKenna's (1978) *Gender: An Ethnomethodological Approach,* one of those books that are as widely quoted as they are misunderstood, is cited as saying that gender is socially constructed. Yet precious few writers appreciate the theoretical realignment an ethnomethodological approach to gender would entail. Those who misunderstand Kessler and McKenna continue to make universal and monolithic statements about *all* women or *all* men, as if only biological sex categories mattered. In this book, however, we continuously ask what *type* of masculinity and femininity is being performed.

The key study that Kessler and McKenna cite heavily in their 1978 book is that of Garfinkel (1967/1992). Garfinkel's subject was Agnes, a biological man who wanted to have a sex change operation to become a female. Although psychologists wanted to know Agnes's motivation for wanting this operation, Garfinkel wanted to know how Agnes was going to successfully present herself as a female. Her femininity was a social *accomplishment.* The case of Agnes illustrates how the seemingly stable and orderly structure of sex is changed through the performance of gender. Heretofore, most gender writers have been unclear and tend to confuse sex with gender. In short, masculinities can be performed by both women *and* men. And femininities can be and are performed by both men *and* women.

Second, another important misconception is that masculinity is homogeneous. As the title of this book indicates, masculinit*ies* are plural. This is a *very* deliberate choice of a word. Most gender writers, especially those studying organizations, tend to treat *masculinity* as if it were homogeneous. To some, this is intentionally motivated by gender politics (Cheng, 1995a; hooks, 1984, pp. 67-76, 114). Gender writers who intentionally disregard diverse types of masculinities, especially marginalized, subordinated, and colonialized ones, are playing a zero-sum, hegemonically masculine game of "oppression Olympics" (Ely, 1996) that mistakenly assumes that acknowledging the oppression of other groups will detract from one's own oppressed group. Such intergroup conflict colludes with and strengthens the existing hegemonically masculine system.

Third, if valuing differences is to occur in organizations, then the differences presented by masculinities and men need to be studied. A similar situation has occurred with race. Euro-American males and those who bought into their dominant discourse have studied others but not themselves. Whiteness is a topic of inquiry (Alderfer, 1982, 1994; hooks, 1994). Masculinities and men in organizations cannot be privileged from inquiry, if valuing differences in organizations and occupations is to occur.

Fourth, it evident that women's experiences have been excluded from what is considered to be knowledge in most of the academic literature because of a hegemonically masculine bias. Their exclusion have not precluded most of the academic literature treating masculinities and men as homogeneous. Instead, they overgeneralize men and do not deal with the experience of masculinity. New men's studies do not have traditional hegemonically male bias (Brod, 1987, pp. 39-41). In fact, they identify the change target as *the institution of hegemonic masculinity* (patriarchy) and look at the behaviors of masculinities, for example, hegemonic or otherwise, instead of making sweeping, empirically unsupportable statements about *all* men.

Finally, work organizations are places in modern times where hegemonic masculinity has been used as an organizing principle and where it is contested for, achieved, and conferred. Therefore, studying masculinities should enable us to look at important and often overlooked aspects of human behavior in organizations.

Work and Masculine Identity

"Masculinity is accomplished, it is not something done to men or something settled beforehand. And masculinity is never static, never a finished product. Rather, men construct masculinities in specific social situations (although not in circumstances of their own choosing) in so doing, men reproduce (and sometimes change) social structure. . . . Masculinity must be viewed as structured action—what men do under specific constraints and varying degrees of power" (Messerschmidt, 1993, pp. 80, 81).

Masculine identity is socially constructed through work which is embedded in an occupation and often within an organization. Men's primary identification is with work (Elder, 1974; Miller, 1965; Veroff & Feld, 1970; Weiss, 1990) and as more women strive to become "successful" in hegemonically defined organizations, they too adopt a primary identification with work and hegemonic masculinity.

For Seidler (1991, pp. 111-113) masculine identity requires self-denial at work based on the Protestant ethic (Hoch, 1979, p. 78; Gradman, 1994, pp. 105-106). Work is self-sacrifice for the family not the self. Gradman's

(1994, p. 105) view is less self-sacrificing. He argues that for the hegemocially masculine identified male (or female), work provides an extrinsic reward of money and social status. The intrinsic rewards of self-expression and fulfillment are also derived from work. Work enables a self-concept of being powerful, self-reliant, competent (Gradman, 1994, p. 105). Work for the heterosexual male, particularly if he is "successful" (in hegemonically masculine terms), is a means to impress and "win" a mate. Since hegemonic masculinity is constructed in relation to femininity (Connell, 1987), men constructing this form of masculinity need women to validate their identity (Pleck, 1980, p. 416; Telford, in this volume).

Occupations and organizations traditionally have provided a homosocial context, an in-group devoid of women and femininity (Hantover, 1978; Spain, 1992, pp. 60-62, 70-72; Weber, 1922/1968, p. 371; 1978, pp. 144, 906-907). Men form a homosocial community with other men (Weiss, 1990). The in-group, despite idealizations, may not be filled with "male bonding," but instead with hegemonically masculine norms giving rise to man-to-man relationships in which "we [men] are automatically suspicious of other men, who are always potential competitors. We learn not to need anything from other men, because we fear this will give them power over us" (Seidler, 1991, p. 30).

Men's competition with one another results in men's friendships being "emotionally improvised" and overly dependent on women (Rubin, 1983, p. 135). "Men are raised in a culture with a mixed message: Strive for healthy, emotionally intimate friendships, but be careful—if you appear too intimate with another man you might be negatively labeled homosexual" (Nardi, 1992, p. 2).

While work is the primary source of hegemonically masculine identity, wage laborers are subject to firings and lay-offs which makes wage labor an unstable source of masculinity (Tolson, 1977). Retirement and unemployment make men deviate from the hemgeonically masculine standard (Gradman, 1994, p. 105). "Work and career dominate a man's identity, leaving him unprepared for the realities of retirement" (p. 104). Retirement "is often perceived as a vague and distant goal and a reward for hard labor" (p. 104).

Useful Knowledge

Organizational behavior (OB) as an applied social and behavioral science has a special contribution to make to the study of gender. First, it provides an empirical setting. Broadly, these are more than just business organizations. Other task groups are of interest, as well as studying the social and behavioral science implications of the integration of tasks and interactions in affect groups. Constructing gender has implications for getting power or becoming powerless. In organizational life, where most people spend their waking lives, gender constructions are part of the daily competition for personal and organizational power.

Second, OB-applied focus (at least at its inception) contributes to the gender studies literature by developing *useful knowledge:* "Knowledge which serves an actor's purpose, such as contributing to decision making, guiding behaviors, and solving problems. This implies that usability of information can only be determined relative to particular users and their purposes" (Mohrman, Cummings, & Lawler, 1983, p. 613). By calling for useful knowledge, I am most definitely *not* calling for functionalism that reinforces the hegemonically masculine gender system of modernistic organization or manipulative organizational humanism, although such knowledge is typically used to further that purpose. Rather, I am calling for the production of useful knowledge that benefits change agents, practicing managers and employees who are interested in changing the oppressive bipolar gender system of modernistic organizations that is built on rigid sex segregation and other forms of discrimination.

Two problems have made the knowledge that OB has produced unuseful. One is reductionism that, although increasing the methodological rigorousness of OB research, has the dysfunction of producing knowledge that only other academics can understand. A newer problem has resulted in their rebellion against positivism: Some OB professors have become too enamored with the critical theories of the humanities, to the point where they no longer consider it necessary to rigorously gather quantitative or qualitative empirical data and to base any analysis on empirical observations. Criticism for its own sake has replaced gathering and analyzing data based on the interaction of people, groups, and organizations and their multileveled interactions. There is a place, a small one, for criticism of the OB literature, but not to the point where organizational scientists turn into literary critics. These theories are perhaps best applied by analyzing rigorously collected empirical data.

Most academic research is not useful when it is based on four main criticisms (Mohrman, Cummings, & Lawler, 1983, p. 615):

1. The researcher's legitimacy, competency, and intent are questioned. Researchers are criticized by potential organizational users as being naive,

ignorant of the real world, biased by their own theories, and unaware of the trouble they cause.

2. Findings are discounted, because they are perceived as ambiguous, overly negative, or irrelevant to the particular organization.
3. The importance of the study is questioned, as researchers examine unimportant issues, ignore important variables, or merely discover the obvious.
4. The presentation of the findings is attacked as being boring, full of jargon, poorly written, or too technical.

Useful knowledge, on the other hand, has the following characteristics (Thomas & Tymon, 1982):

1. *Descriptive relevance* accurately captures practitioners in organizational settings and emphasizes external validity, the complexities of organizational settings, rather than internal validity.
2. *Goal relevancy* emphasizes applied rather than basic problems.
3. *Operational validity* emphasizes concrete variables that the practitioner can control and change.
4. *Nonobviousness* meets or exceeds *commonsense* theories of practitioners. Academic research often oversimplifies to prove certain hypotheses.
5. *Timeliness*—The theory must be available to practitioners so that they do not have to wait for all the facts to make decisions.

The call for the production of useful knowledge is not at the sacrifice of theoretical rigor. It is a call to extend rigorous theory, one that does not collude with the status quo, into practice (Argyris, 1968, 1970).

Overview

This volume represents an initial effort to stimulate thinking and, more important, empirical research on masculinities and men in organizations and organizations. Seeing that it requires a pioneering effort to create a single volume on the topic, this anthology attempts a broad overview of the field. It is too early to define, let alone anthologize, one specific point of view with a particular methodological commitment.

Part I deals with the performance of hegemonic masculinity. Jennifer Pierce explores how lawyers strategically use emotion to perform a "Rambo"-styled role (referring to the American action movie hero played by Sylvester Stallone) to win in litigation. James Messerschmidt examines how the fatal decision to launch the space shuttle *Challenger* was influenced by hegemonic masculinity. Judi Addelston and Michael Stirratt observe hegemonic masculinity at The Citadel, a state-supported military college that has recently been involved in high-profile litigation over its attempts to evade making its all-male student body coeducational.

Part II explores an underresearched aspect of the OB literature, the relationships between "Sex Segregation, Homosociality, and Hegemonic Masculinity." Sex segregation refers to the numerical dominance of men in a given occupation. When there is an absence of women altogether, male homosociality occurs. Rosemary Wright examines how hegemonically masculine occupational culture in the computing field creates sex segregation. Amy Wharton and Sharon Bird take us inside work teams to study the effects of gender demographics on homosociality. Martin Kilduff and Ajay Mehra explore hegemonically masculine identities and gendered interaction patterns among MBA students at an elite university.

Hegemonic masculinity, as Connell (1987) points out, has changed in history. In hierarchial relations, the upper strata are defined by and dependent on lower ones. Hegemonic masculinity is constructed relative to femininity and subordinated, marginalized, and colonized masculinities (Connell, 1987, pp. 183-188). In Part III, the marginalization of nonhegemonic forms of masculinities by hegemonic masculinity is addressed. Laurie Telford provides a unique application of the social verification literature, suggesting that nonhegemonic masculinities in organizations are not verified in the same way as the hegemonic type is. Tomoko Hamada explores how Euro-American men, whose form of masculinity dominates in American society, are no longer dominant when they work for a Japanese firm in the United States. Lastly, I extend the *good manager* line of research, whereby ideal managers perform hegemonic masculinity by adding race and culture (e.g., Asian and Asian American) into the picture.

References

Alderfer, C. P. (1982). Problems of changing white males' behavior and beliefs concerning race relations in the United States. In P. Goodman (Ed.), *Change in organizations* (pp. 122-165). San Francisco: Jossey-Bass.

Alderfer, C. P. (1994). A white perspective on unconscious processes within black-white race relations in the United States. In E. Trickett, R. J. Watts, & D. Birman (Eds.), *Human diversity: Perspective on people in context.* San Francisco: Jossey-Bass.

Argyris, C. (1968). Some unintended consequences of rigorous research. *Psychological Bulletin, 70,* 185-197.

Argyris, C. (1970). *Intervention theory and method: A behavioral science approach.* Reading, MA: Addison-Wesley.

Baril, G., Elbert, N., Mahar-Porter, S., & Reavy, G. (1989). Are androgynous managers really more effective? *Group & Organizational Studies, 14*(2), 234-249.

Brod, H. (1987). The case for men's studies. In H. Brod (Ed.), *Making of masculinities* (pp. 39-62). New York: Routledge.

Cheng, C. (1995a). Gender dialogues and gender ideologues: what happened to professorial responsibility to the profession of management? *Journal of Organizational Change Management, 8*(6), 67-73.

Cheng, C. (1995b). Experience, essentialism and essence: Changing organizations through personal work and gender stories. *Journal of Organizational Change Management, 8*(5), 3-7.

Connell, R. W. (1987). *Gender and power: Society, the person and sexual politics.* Stanford, CA: Stanford University Press.

Elder, G. H. (1974). *Children of the great depression: Social change in life experience.* Chicago: University of Chicago Press.

Ely, R. J. (1996). The role of dominant identity and experience in organizational work on diversity. In S. E. Jackson & M. Ruderman (Eds.), *Diversity in work teams: Research paradigms for a changing workplace.* Washington, DC: American Psychological Association.

Garfinkel, H. (1992). *Studies in ethnomethodology.* Englewood Cliffs, NJ: Prentice Hall. (Original work published 1967)

Gradman, T. J. (1994). Masculine identity from work and retirement. In E. H. Thompson (Ed.), *Older men's lives* (pp. 104-121). Newbury Park, CA: Sage.

Hantover, J. P. (1978). The Boy Scouts and the validation of masculinity. *Journal of Social Issues, 34*(1), 184-195.

Heritage, J. (1984). *Garfinkel & ethnomethodology.* Cambridge, UK: Polity.

Hoch, P. (1979). *White hero black beast.* London, UK: Pluto.

hooks, b. (1989). *Talking back: Thinking feminist, thinking black.* Boston: South End.

hooks, b. (1994). *Teaching to transgress.* New York: Routledge.

Kanter, R. M. (1977). *Men and women of the corporation.* New York: Basic Books.

Kessler, S. J., & McKenna, W. (1978). *Gender: An ethnomethodological approach.* New York: John Wiley.

Kimmel, M. S. (1994). Masculinities as homophobia: Fear, shame, and silence in the construction of gender identity. In H. Brod & M. Kaufman (Eds.), *Theorizing masculinities* (pp. 119-141). Thousand Oaks, CA: Sage.

Leiter, K. (1980). *A primer on ethnomethodology.* New York: Oxford University Press.

Lorsch, J. W. (Ed.). (1987). *Handbook of organizational behavior.* Englewood Cliffs, NJ: Prentice Hall.

Messerschmidt, J. W. (1993). *Masculinities and crime: Critique and reconceptualization of theory.* New York: Rowland & Littlefield.

Miller, S. J. (1965). The social dilemma of the ageing leisure participant. In W. A. Rose & W. A. Peterson (Eds.), *Older people and their social world* (pp. 77-92). Philadelphia, PA: F. A. Davis.

Mohrman, S. A., Cummings, T. G., & Lawler, E. E. (1983). Creating useful research with organization: Relationship and process issues. In Kilmann et al. (Eds.), *Producing useful knowledge for organizations* (pp. 613-624). New York: Praeger.

Nardi, P. M. (1992). "Seamless souls": An introduction to men's friendships. In P. M. Nardi (Ed.), *Men's friendships* (pp. 1-14). Newbury Park, CA: Sage.

Pleck, J. (1980). Men's power with women, other men, and society: A men's movement analysis. In E. Pleck & J. Pleck (Eds.), *The American man*. Englewood Cliffs, NJ: Prentice Hall.

Rubin, L. B. (1983). *Intimate strangers: Men and women together*. New York: Harper & Row.

Seidler, V. J. (1991). *Recreating sexual politics: Men, feminism and politics*. London, UK: Routledge.

Spain, D. (1992). Spatial foundations of men's friendships and men's power. In P. M. Nardi (Ed.), *Men's friendships* (pp. 59-73). Newbury Park, CA: Sage.

Thomas, K., & Tymon, W. (1982). Necessary properties of relevant research: Lessons from recent critics of the organizational sciences. *Academy of Management Review, 7,* 345-353.

Tolson, A. (1977). *Limits of masculinity: Male identity and women's liberation*. New York: Harper & Row.

Veroff, J., & Feld, S. (1970). *Marriage and work in America: A study of motives and roles*. New York: Van Nostrand Reinhold.

Weber, M. (1968/1922). *Economy and society* (Vol. 1). (G. Roth & K. Wittich, Trans.) New York: Bedminster.

Weber, M. (1978). *Economy and society* (Vol. 2). In G. Roth & C. Wittich (Eds). Berkeley: University of California Press.

Weiss, R. S. (1990). *Staying the course: The emotional and social lives of men who do well at work*. New York: Free Press.

Acknowledgments

No editor can function without reviewers and colleagues. The way to produce good quality is for the editor to play detective and find the most creative writers. Detectives are always dependent on tipsters. My special thanks to Clay Alderfer, Frank Barrett, Dave Berg, Marty Chemers, Bob Connell, Bob Dennehy, Ellen Fagenson, Gary Fine, Sissel Froberg, Jack Gabbarro, Silvia Gherardi, Bob Golembiewski, Barbara Gutek, Arlie Hochchild, Deborah Kerfoot, Martin Kilduff, Toni King, Pat Lin, Judith Lorber, Jay Lorsch, Lisa Mainero, Richard Majors, Dan Martin, Patricia Yancey Martin, Bob Marx, Jim McKay, Ajay Mehra, Mark Meir, Michael Messner, Albert Mills, Lynda Moore, David Morand, Ann Morrison, Peter Nardi, Howard Schwartz, Ralph Stablein, Don Szabo, Laurie Telford, Stephen Whitehead, and many others. Above all, I greatly appreciate the contributions that the authors have made to this volume. Their bravery for venturing into this new area is remarkable.

To Michael Kimmel, I am grateful for this chance to be part of the **Sage Series on Research on Men and Masculinities.** I can think of no better way to help open up masculinities and men to organizational inquiry. There is no better series editor than Michael in this area. To Peter Labella at Sage, my thanks for making this a fun experience and thanks to Frances Borghi, Sharrise Purdum, Vicki Baker, Anton Diether, and Lisa Bright at Sage for their contributions to this project. I am also grateful to Harry Brod for connecting me with Michael Kimmel.

Last, I would like to honor all the men with whom I have been in men's groups since the early 1980s. They not only have taught me much about myself and how I interact act with others, but they have influenced me to study organizational behavior and help groups and organizations change in a prosocial manner through the use of process consultation.

PART I

OCCUPATIONAL AND ORGANIZATIONAL HEGEMONIC MASCULINITY

1

Rambo Litigators

Emotional Labor in a Male-Dominated Occupation

JENNIFER PIERCE

> Litigation is war. The lawyer is a gladiator and the object is to wipe out the other side.
>
> —Cleveland lawyer
> quoted in the *New York Times*

A recent spate of articles in the *New York Times* and a number of legal dailies characterized some of America's more flamboyant and aggressive trial lawyers as "Rambo litigators."[1] This hypermasculine, aggressive image is certainly not a new one. In popular culture and everyday life, jokes and stories abound that characterize lawyers as overly aggressive, manipulative, unreliable, and unethical individuals.[2] What jokes, as well as the popular press, fail to consider is that such behavior is not simply the result of individual failings but is actually required and reinforced by the legal profession itself.

Legal scholar Carrie Menkel-Meadow (1985) suggests that the adversarial model with its emphasis on "zealous advocacy" and "winning" encourages a "macho ethic" in the courtroom (pp. 51-54). Lawyers and teachers of trial lawyers argue that the success of litigators depends on their ability to manipulate people's emotions (Brazil, 1978; Turow, 1987). Trial lawyers must persuade judges and juries, as well as intimidate witnesses and opposing counsel in the courtroom, in deposition, and in negotiations. The National Institute of Trial Advocacy, for example, devotes a 3-week training seminar to teaching lawyers to hone such emotional skills, thereby improving their success in the courtroom (Rice, 1989). This chapter makes this aspect of lawyering explicit by examining the emotional dimension of legal work in a particular specialty of law—litigation. Sociological studies of the legal profession have yet to seriously examine the emotional dimension of lawyering.[3] Although a few studies make reference to the emotional dimension of work, it is not the central focus of their research.[4] For example, Nelson (1988) reduces lawyering to three roles—"finders, minders and grinders," meaning "lawyers who seem to bring in substantial clients . . . lawyers who take care of the clients who are already here and there are the grinders who do the work" (senior partner quoted in Nelson, 1988, pp. 69). Nelson's reduction of these roles to their instrumental and intellectual dimensions neglects the extent to which instrumental tasks may also contain emotional elements.

The sparse attention other sociological studies have given to this dimension of lawyering is contradicted by my 15 months of field research (from 1988 to 1989) at two large law firms in San Francisco—6 months at a private firm (Lyman, Lyman and Portia) and 9 months in the legal department of a large corporation (Bonhomie Corporation).[5] Litigators make use of their emotions to persuade juries, judges, and witnesses in the courtroom and in depositions, in communications with opposing counsel, and with clients. However, in contrast to the popular image, intimidation and aggression constitute only one component of the emotional labor required by this profession. Lawyers also make use of strategic friendliness, that is, the use of charm or flattery to manipulate others. Despite the apparent differences in these two types of emotional labor, both use the manipulation of others for a specific end—winning a case. Although other jobs require the use of manipulation to achieve specific ends, such labor may serve different purposes and be embedded in a different set of relationships. Flight attendants, for example, are friendly and reassuring to passengers so as to alleviate their anxiety about flying

(Hochschild, 1983). However, flight attendants' friendliness takes the form of deference: Their relationship to passengers is supportive and subordinate. By contrast, in litigation, the goal of strategic friendliness is to *win over* or dominate another. As professionals who have a monopoly over specialized knowledge, attorneys hold a superordinate position with respect to clients, witnesses, and jurors and a competitive one with other lawyers. If trial lawyers want to win their cases, they must be able to successfully manipulate and ultimately dominate others for their professional ends.

By doing whatever it takes within the letter of the law to win a case, lawyers effectively fulfill the goal of zealous advocacy: persuading a third party that the client's interests should prevail. In this way, intimidation and strategic friendliness serve to reproduce and maintain the adversarial model. At the same time, by exercising dominance and control over others, trial lawyers also reproduce gender relations. The majority of litigators who *do dominance* are men (88% of litigators are male) and those who defer are either female secretaries and paralegals,[6] other women, or men who become feminized in the process of losing. In addition to creating and maintaining a gendered hierarchy, the form such emotional labor takes is gendered. It is a masculinized form of emotional labor, not only because men do it but because dominance is associated with masculinity in our culture. West and Zimmerman (1987) argue, for example, that displays of dominance are ways for men to "do gender."[7] Similarly, psychoanalytic feminists equate masculinity with men's need to dominate women (Benjamin, 1988; Chodorow, 1978). In the case of trial lawyers, the requirements of the profession deem it appropriate to dominate women as well as other men. Such *conquests* or achievements at once serve the goals of effective advocacy and become the means for the trial lawyer to demonstrate a class specific form of masculinity.

Gamesmanship and the Adversarial Model

Popular wisdom and lawyer folklore portray lawyering as a game, and the ability to play as gamesmanship (Spence, 1988). As one of the trial attorneys I interviewed said,

> The logic of gamesmanship is very interesting to me. I like how you make someone appear to be a liar. You know, you take them down the merry path and before they know it, they've said something pretty stupid. The challenge is getting them to say it without violating the letter of the law.

Lawyering is based on gamesmanship—legal strategy, skill, and expertise. But trial lawyers are much more than chess players. Their strategies are not simply cerebral, rational, and calculating moves but highly emotional, dramatic, flamboyant, and shocking presentations that invoke sympathy, distrust, or outrage. In my redefinition of the term, *gamesmanship* involves the utilization of legal strategy through a presentation of an emotional self designed specifically to influence the feelings and judgment of a particular legal audience—the judge, the jury, the witness, or opposing counsel. Furthermore, in my definition, the choices litigators make about selecting a particular strategy are not simply individual, they are institutionally constrained by the structure of the legal profession, formal and informal professional norms such as the American Bar Association's (1982) *Model Code of Professional Responsibility* and training in trial advocacy through programs sponsored by the National Institute of Trial Advocacy.

The rules governing gamesmanship derive from the adversarial model that underlies the basic structure of our legal system. This model is a method of adjudication that involves two advocates (e.g., the attorneys) presenting their case to an impartial third party (i.e., the judge and the jury) who listens to evidence and argument and declares one party the winner (Luban, 1988; Menkel-Meadow, 1985). As Menkel-Meadow (1985) observes, the basic assumptions that underlie this set of arrangements are "advocacy, persuasion, hierarchy, competition and binary results (win or lose)." She writes, "The conduct of litigation is relatively similar . . . to a sporting event—there are rules, a referee, an object to the game, and a winner is declared after play is over" (p. 51).

Within this system, the attorney's main objective is to persuade the impartial third party that his client's interests should prevail (American Bar Association, 1982, p. 34). However, clients do not always have airtight, defensible cases. How, then, does the *zealous advocate* protect his clients interests and achieve the desired result? When persuasion by appeal to reason breaks down, an appeal to emotions becomes tantamount (Cheatham, 1955, pp. 282-283). As legal scholar John Buchan (1939) writes, "The root of the talent is simply the *power to persuade*" [italics added] (pp. 211-213). By appealing to emotions, the lawyer becomes a "con man."[8] He acts "as if" he has a defensible case; he puffs himself up, he bolsters his case. Thus, the successful advocate must not only be smart, but as famous turn-of-the-century trial lawyer Francis Wellman (1903/1986, p. 13) observes, he must also be a "good actor." In his book, *The Art of Cross-Examination,* first published in 1903 and reprinted to the present,

Wellman describes how carefully the litigator must present himself to the judge and jury:

> The most cautious cross-examiner will often elicit a damaging answer. Now is the time for the greatest self-control. If you show by your face how the answer hurt, you may lose by that one point alone. How often one sees a cross-examiner fairly staggered by such an answer. He pauses, blushes . . . [but seldom regains] control of the witness. With the really experienced trial lawyer, such answers, instead of appearing to surprise or disconcert him, will seem to come as a matter of course, and will fall perfectly flat. He will proceed with the next question as if nothing happened, or else perhaps give the witness an incredulous smile, as if to say, "Who do you suppose would believe that for a minute." (pp. 13-14)

More recently, teacher and lawyer David Berg (1987) advises lawyers to think of themselves as actors, and the jury, an audience. He writes,

> Decorum can make a difference, too. . . . *Stride* to the podium and *exude confidence,* even if there is a chance that the high school dropout on the stand is going to make you look like an idiot. *Take command* of the courtroom. Once you begin, do not grope for questions, shuffle through papers, or take breaks to confer with co-counsel. Let the jury know that you are prepared, that you do not need anyone's advice, and that *you care* about the case . . . because if *you don't care, the jurors won't care.* (1987, p. 28, italics added)

Wellman (1903/1986) and Berg (1987) make a similar point: Trials are the enactment of a drama in the courtroom, and attorneys are the leading actors. Appearance and demeanor are of utmost importance. The lawyer's manner, his tone of voice, his facial expressions are all means to persuade the jury that his client is right. Outrageous behavior is acceptable, as long as it remains within the letter of the law. Not only are trial lawyers expected to act but with a specific purpose in mind: to favorably influence feelings of the jurors. As Berg points out, "if you don't show you care, the jurors won't care."

This emphasis on acting is also evident in the courses taught by the National Institute for Trial Advocacy (NITA) where neophyte litigators learn the basics in presenting a case for trial. NITA's emphasis is on "learning by doing" (Kilpatrick, quoted in Rice, 1989). Attorneys do not simply read about cases but practice presenting them in a simulated courtroom with a judge, a jury, and witnesses. In this case, doing means acting. As one of the teacher-lawyers said on the first day of class, "Being a good trial lawyer means being a good actor. . . . Trial attorneys love to perform." Acting, in sociological terms, translates into emotional labor, that is, inducing or suppressing feelings in order to produce an outward countenance that influences the emotions of others. Teacher-lawyers discuss style, delivery, presentation of self, attitude, and professionalism. Participants, in turn, compare notes about the best way to "handle" judges, jurors, witnesses, clients, and opposing counsel. The efforts of these two groups constitute the teaching and observance of "feeling rules" or professional norms that govern appropriate lawyerlike conduct in the courtroom.

The 3-week course I attended[9] took students through various phases of a hypothetical trial—jury selection, opening and closing statements, and direct and cross-examination. Each stage of the trial has a slightly different purpose. For example, the objective of jury selection is to uncover the biases and prejudices of the jurors and to develop rapport with them. On the other hand, an opening statement sets the theme for the case, whereas a direct examination lays the foundation of evidence for the case. Cross-examination is intended to undermine the credibility of the witness, whereas closing represents the final argument. Despite the differing goals that each of these phases has, the means to achieve them is similar in each case, that is, the attempt to persuade a legal audience favorably to one's client through a particular emotional presentation of self.

In their sessions on direct and cross-examination, students were given primarily stylistic, as opposed to substantive, responses on their presentations. They were given finer legal points on the technicalities of their objections—the strength or weakness of their arguments. But in the content analysis of my field notes, I found that 50% to 80% of comments were directed toward the attorney's particular style. These comments fell into five categories: (a) personal appearance, (b) presentation of self (nice, aggressive, or sincere manner), (c) tone and level of voice, (d) eye contact, and (e) rapport with others in the courtroom.

For example, in one of the sessions, Tom, a young student-lawyer in the class, did a direct examination of a witness to a liquor store robbery. He solemnly questioned the witness about his work, his special training in enforcing liquor laws, and how he determined whether someone was intoxicated. At one point when the witness provided a detail that Tom had not expected, rather than expressing surprise, Tom appeared nonchalant and continued with his line of questions. At the end of his direct, the teacher-lawyer provided the following feedback:

> Good background development of witness. Your voice level was appropriate but try modulating it a bit more for emphasis. You also use too many thank you's to the judge. You should ingratiate yourself with the judge but not

> overly so. You also made a good recovery when the witness said something unexpected.

When Patricia, a young woman attorney, proceeded nervously through the same direct examination, opposing counsel objected repeatedly to some of her questions, which flustered her. The teacher-lawyer told her,

> You talk too fast. And you didn't make enough eye contact with the judge. Plus, you got bogged down in the objections and harassment from opposing counsel. You're recovery was too slow. You've got to be more forceful.

In both these examples, as in most of the sessions that I observed, the focus of the comments was not on the questions asked but on *how* the questions were asked. Tom was told to modulate his voice; Patricia was told not to talk so fast. In addition, the teacher-lawyer directed their attention to rapport with others in the courtroom. Tom was encouraged not to be overly ingratiating with the judge, whereas Patricia was told to pay more attention to the judge. Moreover, the teacher commended Tom for his "recovery," that is, regaining self-composure and control of the witness. He criticized Patricia, on the other hand, for not recovering well from an aggressive objection made by opposing counsel.[10]

In my fieldwork at NITA and in the two law offices, I found two main types of emotional labor: intimidation and strategic friendliness. Intimidation entails the use of anger and aggression, whereas strategic friendliness uses politeness, friendliness, or playing dumb. Both forms are related to gamesmanship. Each involves an emotional presentation of self that is intended to favorably influence the feelings of a particular legal audience toward one's client. Many jobs appear to require strategic friendliness and intimidation. Domestic workers, for example, sometimes "play dumb" so as not to alienate their white female employers (Rollins, 1985). For domestic workers, however, this strategy is a means for someone in a subordinate position to survive a degrading job. By contrast, for litigators, strategic friendliness, like intimidation, is a means for an individual with professional status to control and dominate others in an effort to win one's case. Although both the litigator and the domestic worker may play dumb, in each job, the behavior serves different goals that are indicative of their divergent positions in relationship to others.

Intimidation and strategic friendliness not only serve the goals of the adversarial model, but they exemplify a masculine style of emotional labor. They become construed as masculine for several reasons. First, emotional labor in the male-dominated professional strata of the gendered law firm is interpreted as masculine, simply because men do it. Ruth Milkman (1987), for example, suggests that "idioms of sex-typing can be applied to whatever women and men happen to be doing" (p. 50). Male trial attorneys participate in shaping this idiom by describing their battles in the courtroom and with opposing counsel as "macho," "something men get into," and "a male thing." In addition, by treating women lawyers as outsiders and excluding them from professional networks, they further define their job as exclusively male.

In addition, the underlying purpose of gamesmanship itself, that is, the control and domination of others through manipulation, reflects a particular cultural conception of masculinity. Connell (1987), for example, describes a hegemonic form of masculinity that emphasizes the domination of a certain class of men—middle to upper-middle class—over other men and over women. Connell's cultural conception of masculinity dovetails neatly with feminist psychoanalytic accounts that interpret domination as a means of asserting one's masculinity (Benjamin, 1988; Chodorow, 1978). The lawyers I studied also employed a ritual of degradation and humiliation against other men and women who were witnesses or opposing counsel. The remainder of this chapter describes the two main components of emotional labor—intimidation and strategic friendliness—the purpose of each, and shows how these forms becomes construed as masculine. These forms of emotional labor are explored in practices, such as cross-examination, depositions, jury selection, and in opening and closing statements.

Intimidation

The first and most common form of emotional labor associated with lawyers is intimidation. In popular culture, the tough, hard-hitting, and aggressive trial lawyer is portrayed in television shows, such as *L.A. Law* and *Perry Mason* and in movies, such as *The Firm, A Few Good Men,* and *Presumed Innocent.* The news media's focus on famous trial attorneys such as Arthur Liman, the prosecutor of Oliver North in the Iran-Contra trial, also reinforce this image. Law professor Wayne Brazil (1978) refers to this style of lawyering as the *professional combatant.* Others have used terms such as *Rambo litigator, legal terrorists,* and *barbarians of the bar* (Margolick, 1988; Miner, 1988; Sayler, 1988). Trial attorneys themselves call litigators from large law firms "hired guns" (Spangler, 1986). The central figure that appears again and again in these images is not only intimidating but strongly masculine. In the old West, hired guns were sharpshooters, men who were hired to kill other men. The strong, silent movie character Rambo is emblematic of a highly stylized, super masculinity. Finally, most of the actors who play tough, hard-hitting lawyers in the television shows and movies mentioned above are men. Thus, intimidation is not simply a form of emotional labor associated with trial lawyers, it is a masculinized form of labor.

Intimidation is tied to cultural conceptions of masculinity in yet another way. In a review of the literature on occupations, Connell (1987) observes that the cult of masculinity in working-class jobs centers on physical prowess and sexual contempt for men in managerial or office positions (p. 180). Like the men on the shop floor in Michael Burawoy's (1979) study who brag about how much they can lift or produce, lawyers in this study boast about "destroying witnesses," "playing hardball," "taking no prisoners," and about the size and amount of their "win." In a middle-class job such as the legal profession, however, intimidation depends not on physical ability but on mental quickness and a highly developed set of social skills. Thus, masculinizing practices, such as aggression and humiliation, take on an emotional and intellectual tone specific to middle-class occupations and professions.

This stance is tied to the adversarial model's conception of the "zealous advocate" (American Bar Association, 1982). The underlying purpose of this strategy is to intimidate, scare, or emotionally bully the witness or opposing counsel into submission. A destructive cross-examination is the best example.[11] Trial attorneys are taught to intimidate the witness in cross-examination, "to control the witness by never asking a question to which he does not already know the answer and to regard the impeachment of the witness as a highly confrontational act" (Menkel-Meadow, 1985, p. 54). Wellman (1903/1986) describes cross-examination in this way:

> It requires the greatest ingenuity; a habit of logical thought; clearness of perception; infinite patience and self-control; the power to read men's minds intuitively, to judge of their characters by their faces, to appreciate their motives; ability to act with force and precision; a masterful knowledge of the subject matter itself; an extreme caution; and, above all *the instinct to discover the weak point in the witness under examination* . . . It is a *mental duel* between counsel and witness. (p. 8, italics added)

Berg (1987) echoes Wellman's words when he begins his lecture on cross-examination by saying, "The common denominator for effective cross-examination is not genius, however. It's a combination of preparation and an instinct for the jugular" (p. 27). Again, cross-examination involves not only acting mean but creating a specific impression on the witness.

In the sections on cross-examination at NITA, teachers trained lawyers how to *act mean.* The demonstration by the teachers on cross-examination best exemplified this point. Two male instructors reenacted an aggressive cross-examination in a burglary case. The prosecutor relentlessly hammered away, until the witness couldn't remember any specific details about what the burglar looked like. At its conclusion, the audience clapped vigorously. Three male students who had been asked to comment on the section responded unanimously and enthusiastically that the prosecutor's approach had been excellent. One student commentator said, "He kept complete control of the witness." Another remarked, "He blasted the witness's testimony." And the third added, "He destroyed the witness's credibility." The fact that a destructive cross-examination served as the demonstration for the entire class underlines the desirability of aggressive behavior as a model for appropriate lawyerlike conduct in this situation. Furthermore, the students' praise for the attorney's tactics collectively reinforce the norm for such behavior.

Teachers emphasized the importance of using aggression on an individual level as well. Before a presentation on cross-examination, Tom, one of the students, stood in the hallway with one of the instructors trying to "psyche himself up to get mad." He repeated over and over to himself, "I hate it when witnesses lie to me, it makes me so mad!" The teacher coached him to concentrate on that thought, until Tom could actually evoke the feeling of anger. He said to me later in an interview, "I really felt mad at the witness when I walked into the courtroom." In the actual cross-examination, each time the witness made an inconsistent statement, Tom became more and more angry: "First, you told us you could see the burglar, now you say your vision was obstructed! So, which is it, Mr. Jones?" The more irate he became, the more intimidated and confused the witness became, until he completely backed down and said, "I don't know," in response to every question. The teacher characterized Tom's performance as "the best in the class," because it was the "the most forceful" and "the most intimidating." Students remarked that he deserved to "win the case."

NITA's teachers also used mistakes to train students in the rigors of cross-examination. For example, when Laura cross-examined the same witness in the liquor store case, a teacher commented on her performance:

> Too many words. You're asking the witness for information. Don't do that in cross-examination. You tell them what the information is. You want to be

> destructive in cross-examination. When the other side objects to an answer, *you were too nice. Don't be so nice!* [italics added]. Next time, ask to talk to the judge, tell him, "This is crucial to my case." You also asked for information when you didn't know the answer. Bad news. You lost control of the witness.

By being nice and losing control of the witness, Laura violated two norms underlying the classic confrontational cross-examination. A destructive cross-examination is meant to impeach the witness's credibility, thereby demonstrating to the jury the weakness in opposing counsel's case. In situations that call for such an aggressive cross-examination, being nice implies that the lawyer likes the witness and agrees with his or her testimony. By not being aggressive, Laura created the wrong impression for the jury. Second, Laura lost control of the witness. Rather than guiding the witness through the cross with leading questions[12] that were damaging to opposing counsel's case, she allowed the witness to make his own points. As we will see in the next section of the chapter, being nice can also be used as a strategy for controlling a witness; however, such a strategy is not effective in a destructive cross-examination.

Laura's violation of these norms also serves to highlight the implicitly masculine practices used in cross-examination. The repeated phrase, "keeping complete control of the witness," clearly signals the importance of dominating other women and men. Furthermore, the language used to describe obtaining submission—"blasting the witness," "destroying his credibility," or pushing him to "back down"—is quite violent. In addition, the successful control of the witness often takes on the character of a sexual conquest. One brutal phrase used repeatedly in this way is "raping the witness." Within this discursive field, men who "control," "destroy," or "rape" the witness are seen as "manly," whereas those who lose control are feminized as "sissies" and "wimps" or, in Laura's case, as "too nice."

The combative aspect of emotional labor carries over from the courtroom to other lawyering tasks, such as depositions. Attorneys not only "shred" witnesses in the courtroom but in depositions as well. When I worked at the private firm, Daniel, one of the partners, employed what he called his "cat and mouse game" with one of the key witnesses, Jim, in a deposition that I attended. During the deposition, Daniel aggressively cross-examined Jim. "When did you do this?" "You were lying, weren't you?" Jim lost his temper in response to Daniel's hostile form of interrogation—"You hassle me, man! You make me mad!" Daniel smiled and said, "I'm only trying to get to the truth of the situation." Then, he became aggressive again and said, "You lied to the IRS about how much profit you made, didn't you, Jim!" Jim lost his temper again and started calling Daniel a liar. A heated interchange between Daniel and opposing counsel followed, in which opposing counsel objected to Daniel's "badgering the witness." The attorneys decided to take a brief recess.

When the deposition resumed, Daniel began by accusing John, the other attorney, of withholding crucial documents to the case, while pointing his index finger at him. Opposing counsel stood up and started yelling in a high-pitched voice, "Don't you ever point your finger at me! Don't you ever do that to me! This deposition is over . . . I'm leaving." With that he stood up and began to cram papers into his briefcase in preparation to leave. Daniel immediately backed down, apologized, and said, "Sit down, John, I promise I won't point my finger again." He went on to smooth the situation over and proceeded to tell John in a very calm and controlled voice what his objections were. John made some protesting noises, but he didn't leave. The deposition continued.

In this instance, the deposition, rather than the courtroom, became the *stage* and Daniel took the leading role. His cross-examination was confrontational and his behavior with the witness and opposing counsel was meant to intimidate. After the deposition, Daniel boasted to me and several associates about how mad he had made the witness and how he had "destroyed his credibility." He then proceeded to reenact the final confrontation by imitating John standing up and yelling at him in a falsetto voice. In the discussion that followed, Daniel and his associates gave the effects of his behavior on the "audience" utmost consideration. Hadn't Daniel done a good job forcing the witness to lose control? Hadn't he controlled the situation well? Didn't he make opposing counsel look like a "simpering fool?"

The reenactment and ensuing discussion reveal several underlying purposes of the deposition. First, it suggests that the deposition was not only a fact-finding mission for the attorney but a show designed to influence a particular audience—the witness. Daniel effectively flustered and intimidated the witness. Second, Daniel's imitation of John with a falsetto voice, "as if" he were a woman, serves as a sort of "degradation ceremony" (Garfinkel, 1956). By reenacting the drama, he ridicules the man on the other side before an audience of peers, further denigrating him by inviting collective criticism and laughter from colleagues. Third, the discussion of the strategy builds up and elevates Daniel's status as an attorney for his aggressive, yet rational control of the witness and the situation. Thus, the discussion creates a space for collectively reinforcing Daniel's intimidation strategy.

In addition to highlighting the use of intimidation in depositions, this example also illustrates the way aggression as legal strategy or rule-governed aggression (Benjamin, 1988; Lyman, 1987) and masculinity become conflated, whereas aggression, which is not rule governed, is ridiculed as feminine. John shows his anger, but it is deemed inappropriate, because he loses control of the situation. Such a display of hostility does not serve the interests of the legal profession, because it does not achieve the desired result—a win for the case. As a result, Daniel and his associate regard John's behavior—his lack of control, his seeming hysteria and high voice with contempt. This contempt takes on a specific sexual character. Just as the working class "lads" in Paul Willis's (1977) book, *Learning to Labor,* denigrate the "earholes" or sissies for their feminine attributes, Daniel and his colleagues ridicule John for his femalelike behavior. Aggression as legal strategy or maleness is celebrated; contempt is reserved for aggression (or behavior) that is not rule governed and behavior that is also associated with the opposite sex.

Attorneys also used the confrontational approach in depositions at Bonhomie Corporation. In a deposition I sat in on, Mack, a litigator, used an aggressive cross-examination of the key witness.

Q: What were the names of the people that have migrated from one of the violators, as you call it, to Bonhomie Corporation?

A: I don't remember as of now.

Q: Do you have their names written down?

A: No.

Q: Well, if you don't remember their names and they're not written down, how can you follow their migration from one company to another?

A: You can consider it in the process of discovery that I will make some inquiring phone calls.

Q: Did you call anyone to follow their migration?

A: Well, I was unsuccessful as of yet to reach other people.

Q: Who have you attempted to call?

A: I can't tell you at this time. I have a list of processes in my mind to follow.

Q: Do you recall who you called and were not able to reach?

A: No.

Q: What's the list of processes in your mind to follow?

A: It's hard to describe.

Q: In other words, you don't have a list?

A: [quietly] Not really.

Q: Mr. Jensen, instead of wasting everyone's time and money, answer the question yes or no!

Opposing Counsel: Don't badger the witness.

Q: Answer the question, Mr. Jensen, yes or no!

Opposing Counsel: I said, don't badger the witness.

Q: Mr. Jensen, you are still required to answer the question!

A: [quietly] No.

In this case, Mack persisted in badgering the witness, who provided incoherent and vague answers. In response to the question, "Well, if you don't remember their names and they're not written down, how can you follow their migration from one company to another?" the witness gave the vague reply: "You can consider it in the process of discovery that I will make some inquiring phone calls." As the witness became more evasive, the attorney became more confrontational, "Answer the question, yes or no, Mr. Jensen!" By using this approach, the lawyer succeeded in making the witness appear even more uncooperative than he actually was and eventually pushed him to admit that he didn't have a list.

Later, in the same deposition, the attorney's confrontational tactics extended to opposing counsel.

Q: Let's change the subject. Mr. Jensen, can you tell me what representations were made to you about the reliability of the Bonhomie Corporation's spider system?

A: Nancy, the saleslady, said they use it widely in the United States, and could not be but very reliable. And, as we allege, fraudulent, and as somebody referred to it, was the, they wanted to give us the embrace of death to provide us more dependency, and then to go on and control our operation totally [sic].

Q: Who said that?

A: My attorney.

Q: When was that?

Opposing Counsel: Well, I . . .

Mack: I think he's already waived it. All I want to know is when it was supposedly said.

A: Well . . .

Opposing Counsel: I do use some great metaphors.

Mack: Yes, I know, I have read your complaint.

Opposing Counsel: Sorry?

Mack: I have read your complaint. That will be all for today, Mr. Jensen.

Here, the attorney did not stop with badgering the witness. When the witness made the statement about the "embrace of death," Mack was quick to find out who said it. And when opposing counsel bragged about his "great metaphors," Mack parried back with a sarcastic retort, "Yes, I know, I have read your complaint." Having had the final word, he abruptly ended the deposition. Like the other deposition, this one was not only an arena for intimidating the witness but for ridiculing the attorney on the other side. In this way, intimidation was used to control the witness and sarcasm to dominate opposing counsel. In doing so, Mack had achieved the desired result—the witness's submission to his line of questioning and a victory over the other side. Furthermore, in his replay of the deposition to his colleagues, he characterized his victory as a "macho blast against the other side," thereby underscoring the masculine character of his intimidation tactics.

Strategic Friendliness

Mr. Choate's appeal to the jury began long before final argument. . . . His manner to the jury was that of a *friend* [italics added], a friend solicitous to help them through their tedious investigation; never an expert combatant,

> intent on victory, and looking upon them as only instruments for its attainment. (Wellman, 1903/1986, pp. 16-17)

The lesson implicit in Wellman's anecdote about famous 19th-century lawyer Rufus Choate's trial tactics is that friendliness is another important strategy the litigator must learn and use to be successful in the courtroom. Like the use of aggression, the strategic use of friendliness is another feature of gamesmanship and, hence, another component of emotional labor. As Richard, one of the attorney-teachers at NITA stated, "Lawyers have to be able to vary their styles, they have to be able to have multiple speeds, personalities and style." In his view, intimidation did not always work and he proposed an alternative strategy, what he called "the toe-in-the-sand, aw shucks routine." Rather than adopting an intimidating stance vis-à-vis the witness, he advocated "playing dumb and innocent." "Say to the witness, 'Gee, I don't know what you mean. Can you explain it again?' until you catch the witness in a mistake or an inconsistent statement." Other litigators, such as Leonard Ring (1987), call this the "low-key approach." As an illustration of this style, Ring describes how opposing counsel delicately handled the cross-examination of a child witness.

> The lawyer for the defendant . . . stood to cross-examine. Did he attack the details of her story to show inconsistencies? Did he set her up for impeachment by attempting to reveal mistakes, uncertainties and confusion? I sat there praying that he would. But no, he did none of the things a competent defense lawyer is supposed to do. He was old enough to be the girl's grandfather . . . the image came through. He asked her very softly and politely: "Honey, could you tell us again what you saw?" She told it exactly as she had on my direct. I felt relieved. He still wasn't satisfied. "Honey, would you mind telling us again what you saw?" She did again exactly as she had before. He still wasn't satisfied. "Would you do it once more?" She did. She repeated, again, the same story—the same way, in the same words. By that time I got the message. The child had been rehearsed by her mother the same way she had been taught "Mary Had a Little Lamb." I won the case, but it was a very small verdict. (pp. 35-36)

Ring concludes that a low-key approach is necessary in some situations and advises against adhering rigidly to the prototypical combative style.

Similarly, Scott Turow (1987), lawyer and novelist, advises trying a variety of approaches when cross-examining the star witness. He cautions against adopting a "guerrilla warfare mentality" in cross-examination and suggests that the attorney may want to create another impression with the jury:

> Behaving courteously can keep you from getting hurt and, in the process, smooth the path for a win. [In one case I worked on] the cross examination was conducted with a politesse appropriate to a drawing room. I smiled to show that I was not mean-spirited. The chief executive officer smiled to show that he was not beaten. The commissioners smiled to show their gratitude that everybody was being so nice. And my client won big. (pp. 40-42)

Being nice, polite, welcoming, playing dumb, or behaving courteously are all ways that a trial lawyer can manipulate the witness to create a particular impression for the jury. I term this form of gamesmanship *strategic friendliness.* Rather than bully or scare the witness into submission, this tactic employs the opposite—friendliness, politeness, and tact. Despite this seeming difference, it shares with the former an emphasis on the emotional manipulation of another person for a strategic end—winning one's case. For instance, the attorney in Ring's account is gentle and considerate of the child witness for two strategic reasons. First, by making the child feel comfortable, he brings to light the fact that her testimony has been rehearsed. Second, by playing the polite, gentle grandfatherly role, he has created a favorable impression of himself with the jury. Thus, he simultaneously demonstrates to the jury that the witness has been rehearsed and that he, as opposing counsel, is a nice guy. In this way, he improves his chances for winning. And, in fact, he did. Although he didn't win the case, the verdict for the other side was "small."

Although strategic friendliness may appear to be a softer approach than intimidation, it carries with it a strongly instrumental element. Consider the reasoning behind this particular approach. Ring's attorney is nice to the child witness not because he's altruistically concerned for her welfare. He utilizes gentility as a strategy to achieve the desired result—a big win in the courtroom. It is simply a means to an end. Although this approach may be less aggressive than intimidation, it is no less manipulative. Like the goal of intimidation, the central goal of this component of gamesmanship is to dominate and control others for a specific end. This end is best summed up by litigator Mark Dombroff (1989) who writes, "So long as you don't violate the law, including the rules of procedure and evidence or do violence to the canons of ethics, winning is the only thing that matters" (p. 13).

This emphasis on winning is tied to hegemonic conceptions of masculinity and competition. Sociologist Mike Messner (1989) argues that achievement in sporting competitions, such as football, baseball, and basketball, serve as a measure of men's self-worth and their masculinity. This can also be carried over into the workplace. For example, in her research on men in sales, Leidner (1993) finds that defining the jobs as competition becomes a means for construing the work as masculine.

For litigators, comparing the number of wins in the courtroom and the dollar amount of damages or settlement awards allows them to interpret their work as manly. At Bonhomie Corporation and at Lyman, Lyman and Portia, the first question lawyers often asked others after a trial or settlement conference was "Who won the case?" or "How big were the damages?" Note that both Ring and Turow also conclude their pieces with descriptions of their win—"I won the case, but the verdict was small" and "I won big." Trial attorneys who did not "win big" were described as "having no balls," "geeks," or "wimps." The fact that losing is associated with being less than a man suggests that the constant focus on competition and winning is an arena for proving one's masculinity.

One important area that calls for strategic friendliness and focuses on winning is jury selection or *voir dire*. The main purpose of *voir dire* is to obtain personal information about prospective jurors to determine whether they will be fair, "favorably disposed to you, your client, and your case, and will ultimately return a favorable verdict" (Mauet, 1980, p. 31). Once an attorney has made that assessment, biased jurors can be eliminated through challenges for cause and peremptory challenges. In an article on jury selection, attorney Peter Perlman (1988) maintains that the best way to uncover the prejudices of the jury "is to conduct *voir dire* in an atmosphere that makes prospective jurors comfortable about disclosing their true feelings" (p. 5). He provides a check list of strategies for lawyers to use that enable jurors to feel more comfortable. Some of these include the following:

- Given the initial intimidation that jurors feel, try to make them feel as comfortable as possible; approach them in a *natural, unpretentious, and clear manner.*
- Because jurors don't relate to "litigants" or "litigation," humanize the client and the dispute.
- *Demonstrate the sincere* desire to learn of the jurors's feelings. (pp. 5-9, italics added)

Perlman's account reveals that the underlying goal of jury selection is to encourage the jury to open up so that the lawyer can eliminate the jurors he doesn't want and develop a positive rapport with the ones who appear favorable to his case. This goal is supported not only by other writings on jury selection (Blinder, 1978; Cartwright, 1977; Mauet, 1980; Ring, 1983) but also through the training offered by NITA. As a teacher-judge said after the class demonstration on jury selection, "Sell your personality to the jury. Try to get liked by the jury. You're not working for a fair jury but one favorable to your side."

At NITA, teachers emphasized this point on the individual level. In their sessions on *voir dire,* students had to select a jury for a case that involved an employee who fell down the steps at work and severely injured herself. (Jurors in the class were other students, in addition to myself.) Mike, one of the students, proceeded with his presentation. He explained that he was representing the wife's employer. He then went on to tell the jury a little bit about himself, "I grew up in a small town in Indiana." Then, he began to ask each of the jurors where they were from, whether they knew the witness or the experts, whether they played sports, had back problems, suffered any physical injuries, and ever had physical therapy. The instructor gave him the following comments:

> The personal comments about yourself seem forced. Good folksy approach, but you went overboard with it. You threw stuff out and let the jury nibble and you got a lot of information. But the main problem is that you didn't find out how people *feel* about the case or about their relatives and friends.

Another set of comments:

> Nice folksy approach but a bit overdone. Listen to what jurors say, don't draw conclusions. Don't get so close to them, it makes them feel uncomfortable. Use body language to give people a good feeling about you. Good personality, but don't cross certain lines. Never ask someone about their ancestry. It's too loaded a question to ask. Good sense of humor, but don't call one of your prospective jurors a "money man." And don't tell the jury jokes! You don't *win them over* [italics added] that way.

The sporting element to *voir dire* becomes "winning over the jury." This theme also became evident in discussions student lawyers had before and after jury selection. They discussed at length how best "to handle the jurors," "how to get personal information out of them," "how to please them," "how to make them like you," and "how to seduce them to your side." The element of sexual seduction is no more apparent than in the often used phrase, "getting in bed with the jury." The direct reference to sexual seduction and conquest suggests, as it did with the intimidation strategy used in cross-examination, that "winning over the jury" is also a way to prove one's masculinity. Moreover, the desired result in both strategic friendliness and intimidation is similar: obtaining the juror's submission and winning.

Strategic friendliness is used not only in jury selection but in the cross-examination of sympathetic witnesses. In one of NITA's hypothetical cases, a husband's spouse dies of an illness related to her employment. He sues his deceased wife's former employer for her medical bills, her lost wages, and "lost companionship." One of the damaging facts in the case that could hurt his claim for lost companionship was the fact that he had a girlfriend long before his wife died. In typical combative adversarial style, some of the student lawyers tried to bring this fact out in cross-examination to discredit his relationship with his wife. The teacher-judge told one lawyer who presented such an aggressive cross-examination,

> It's too risky to go after him. Don't be so confrontational. And don't ask the judge to reprimand him for not answering the question. This witness is too sensitive. Go easy on him.

The same teacher gave the following comments to another student who had "come on too strong":

> Too stern. Hasn't this guy been through enough already! Handle him with kid gloves. And don't cut him off. It generates sympathy for him from the jury when you do that. It's difficult to control a sympathetic witness. It's best to use another witness's testimony to impeach him.

And to yet another student:

> Slow down! This is a dramatic witness. Don't lead so much. He's a sympathetic witness—the widower—let him do the talking. Otherwise you look like an insensitive jerk to the jury.

In the cross-examination of a sympathetic witness, teachers advised students not to be aggressive but to adopt a gentler approach. Their concern, however, is not for the witness's feelings but how their treatment of the witness appears to the jury. The jury already thinks the witness is sympathetic, because he is a widower. As a result, the lawyers were advised not to do anything that would make the witness appear more sympathetic and them less so. The one student who did well on this presentation demonstrated great concern for the witness. She gently asked him about his job, his marriage, his wife's job, and her illness. Continuing with this gentle approach, she softly asked him whether anyone had been able to provide him comfort during this difficult time. By doing so, she was able to elicit the testimony about the girlfriend in a sensitive manner. By extracting the testimony about the girlfriend, she decreased the jury's level of sympathy for the bereaved widower. How much companionship did he lose, if he was having an affair? At the same time, because she did so in a gentle manner, she increased the jury's regard for her. She presented herself as a nice person. Her approach is similar to Laura's in using "niceness" as a strategy. However, in Laura's case, being nice was not appropriate to a destructive cross-examination. In the case of cross-examining a sympathetic witness, such an approach is necessary.

Opening statements also provide an opportunity for using the nonconfrontational approach. NITA provided a hypothetical case called *BMI v. Minicom,* involving a large corporation that sues a small business for its failure to pay on a contract. Minicom signed a contract for a $20,000 order of computer parts from BMI. BMI shipped the computer parts through UPS to Minicom, but they never arrived. According to the law in the case, the buyer bears the loss, typically through insurance, when the equipment is lost in mail. Mark gave an opening statement that portrayed Minicom as a small business started by ambitious, hard-working college friends "on their way to the big league in business." He played up the difficulties that small businesses face in trying to compete with giant corporations. And at a dramatic moment in the opening, he asked the jury to "imagine a world where cruel giants didn't squeeze out small companies like Minicom." The teacher provided the following comments:

> Good use of evocative imagery. BMI as cruel giant. Minicom squeezing in between the cracks. Great highlighting of the injustice of the situation.

The lawyer for Minicom attempted to gain sympathy from the jury by playing up the underdog role of his client—the small company that gets squeezed between the cracks of the cruel, dominating giant.

In his attempt to counter this image, Robert, the lawyer for BMI, used a courteous opening statement. He attempted to present himself as a nice guy. He took off his jacket, loosened his tie, smiled at the jury, and said, in a friendly conversational tone, "This case is about a broken contract. BMI fulfilled their side of the contract. Mr. Blakey, my client, worked round the clock to get the shipment ready for Minicom. He made phone call after phone call to inventory to make sure the parts got out on time. He checked and rechecked the package before he sent it to Minicom." He paused for dramatic emphasis and, looking sincere and concerned, said, "It's too bad UPS lost the shipment, but that's not BMI's fault. And now, BMI is out $20,000." He received the following comments from the teacher:

> Great use of gestures and eye contact. Good use of voice. You made the case sound simple but important. You humanized yourself and the people at BMI. Good building of sequence.

Here, the attorney for BMI tried to play down his client's impersonal, corporate image by presenting himself as a nice guy. Before he began his opening statement, he took off his jacket and loosened his ties to suggest a more casual and ostensibly less corporate image. He smiled at the jury to let them know that he was friendly—not the cruel giant depicted by opposing counsel. He used a friendly conversational tone to begin his opening statement. And he even admitted that it was not fair that the other side didn't get their computer parts. As the teacher's comments suggest, this strategy was most effective for this particular kind of case.

This approach can also be used in closing statements. In a hypothetical case, during which an insurance company alleged that the claimant set fire to his own business, the lawyer for the store owner tried to defuse the insurance company's strategy with a highly dramatic closing statement:

> Visualize Elmwood Street in 1952. The day Tony Rubino came home from the Navy. His father took him outside to show him a new sign he had made for the family business. It read "Rubino & Son." Standing under the sign "Rubino & Son" with his father was the happiest day of his life. [Pause] The insurance company wants you to believe, ladies and gentlemen of the jury, that Tony set fire to this family jewel. "I'll carry on," he told his father, and he did. . . . [With tears in her eyes, the lawyer concludes] You don't set fire to your father's dream.

The teacher's comments for Janine's closing statement were effusive:

> Great! Well thought out, sounded natural. Good use of details and organization. I especially liked "I don't know what it's like to have a son, but I know what it's like to have a father." And you had tears in your eyes! Gave me the closing-argument goose bumps. Pitched emotion felt real, not phony.

Janine's use of sentimental and nostalgic imagery, the son returning home from the Navy, the beginning of a father and son business, the business as the "family jewel" is reminiscent of a Norman Rockwell painting. It also serves to counter the insurance company's allegation that Tony Rubino set fire to his own store. With the portrait the lawyer paints and the concluding line, "You don't set fire to your father's dream," she rallies the jury's sympathy for Tony Rubino and their antipathy for the insurance company's malicious claim against them. Moreover, her emotional presentation of the story is so effective that the instructor thought it "sounded natural" and "felt real, not phony." The great irony here is that this is not a real case—it is a hypothetical case with hypothetical characters. There is no Tony Rubino, no family store, and no fire. Yet Janine's "deep acting" was so convincing that the teachers believed it was true—it gave him "the closing-argument goose bumps."

Strategic friendliness carries over from the courtroom to depositions. Before deposing a particularly sensitive or sympathetic witness, Joe, one of the attorneys in the private firm, asked me whether "there is anything personal to start the interview with—a sort of warm up question to start things off on a personal note?" I had previously interviewed the woman over the phone, so I knew something about her background. I told him that she was a young mother who had recently had a very difficult delivery of her first child. I added that she was worried about the baby's health, because he had been born prematurely. At the beginning of the deposition later that afternoon, Joe said in a concerned voice that he understood the witness had recently had a baby and was concerned about its health. She appeared slightly embarrassed by the question, but with a slow smile and lots of encouragement from him, she began to tell him all about the baby and its health problems. By the time Joe began the formal part of the deposition, the witness had warmed up and gave her complete cooperation. Later, the attorney bragged to me and one of the associates that he had the witness "eating out of his hand."

After recording these events in my field notes, I wrote the following impressions:

> On the surface, it looks like social etiquette to ask the witness these questions, because it puts her at ease. It lets her know he takes her seriously. But the "personal touch" is completely artificial. He doesn't give a shit about the witness as a person. Or, I should say, only insofar as she's *useful* to him.

Thus, something as innocuous as a personal remark becomes another way to create the desired impression with a witness and thereby manipulate him or her. Perhaps what is most ironic about strategic friendliness is that it requires a peculiar combination of sensitivity to other people and, at the same time, ruthlessness. The lawyer wants to appear kind and understanding, but that is merely a cover for the ulterior motive—winning. Although the outward presentation of self for this form of emotional labor differs from intimidation, the underlying goal is the same: the emotional manipulation of the witness for a favorable result.

Conclusion

In this chapter, I have redefined gamesmanship as the utilization of legal strategy through a presentation of emotional self designed specifically to influence the feelings and judgments of a particular legal audience, such as the judge, the jury, opposing counsel, or the witness. Gamesmanship as emotional labor constitutes two main components—intimidation and strategic friendliness. Despite their apparent differences, both share an emphasis on the manipulation of others toward a strategic end, that is, winning a case. Whereas, the object of intimidation is to "wipe out the other side," playing dumb and being polite represent strategically friendly methods for controlling legal audiences and bringing about the desired "win." Furthermore, I have shown that the attempt to dominate and control judges, juries, and opposing counsel not only serves the goals of the adversarial model but also becomes a means for trial lawyers to assert a hegemonic form of masculinity. Lawyers who gain the other side's submission characterize their efforts as a "macho blast," "a male thing," or "something men get into," whereas those who do not are regarded as "sissies" and "wimps." Thus, it is through their very efforts to be successful litigators that emotional labor in this male-dominated profession is masculinized.

This chapter also suggests many questions for future research on the role of masculinity and emotions in organizations. Masculinity is often a taken-for-granted feature of organizational life. Yet the masculinization of occupations and professions has profound consequences for workers located within them. Not only do male litigators find themselves compelled to act in ways they may find morally reprehensible, but women working in these jobs[13] are increasingly marginalized—facing sex discrimination and sexual harassment (Rhode, 1988; Rosenberg, Perlstadt, & Phillips, 1993). At the same time, because of its informal and seemingly invisible nature, emotional labor too is often unexamined and unquestioned (Fineman, 1993). Given that organizations often intrude on emotional life means that the line between the individual and the job becomes a murky one. The litigator who refuses to play Rambo may not only be unsuccessful, he may find himself without a job. Thus, many questions still require our attention. Is emotional labor gendered in other jobs? Under what conditions? When does emotional labor take on racialized or classed dimensions? When is it exploitative and when is it not? And finally, what role, if any, should emotions play in the workplace?

Notes

1. For examples, see Goldberg (1987), Margolick (1988), Miner (1988), and Sayler (1988).
2. For example, see the *National Law Journal's* (1986) article, "What America Really Thinks About Lawyers."
3. Classic studies on the legal profession have typically focused on the tension between professionalism and bureaucracy. For examples, see Smigel (1969) Carlin (1962), Spangler (1986), and Nelson (1988).
4. For example, in their classic book, *Lawyers and Their Work,* Johnstone and Hopson (1967) describe 19 tasks associated with the lawyering role. In only 2 of these 19 tasks do Johnstone and Hopson allude to the emotional dimension of lawyering—"emotional support to client" and "acting as a scapegoat" (pp. 119-120).
5. In addition to my field research, I also conducted 60 interviews with lawyers, paralegals, and secretaries, as well as 8 interviews with personnel directors from some of San Francisco's largest law firms. Field work and interviews were also conducted at the National Institute of Trial Advocacy where I spent 3 weeks with litigators during a special training course on trial preparation. These methodological decisions are fully discussed in the introductory chapter to my book, *Gender Trials* (Pierce, 1995). Please note, names of organizations and individuals have been changed throughout to protect confidentiality.
6. See Chapter 4, "Mothering Paralegals: Emotional Labor in a Feminized Occupation," in *Gender Trials* (Pierce, 1995).
7. West and Zimmerman (1987) conceptualize gender as "a routine accomplishment embedded in everyday interaction" (p. 1)
8. Blumberg (1967) describes lawyers as practicing a "confidence game." In his account, it is the client who is the "mark" and the attorney and other people in the court

who collude in "taking him out." In my usage, litigators "con" not only their clients but juries, judges, and opposing counsel as well.

9. Special thanks to Laurence Rose, Lou Natali, and the National Institute of Trial Advocacy for allowing me to attend and observe NITA's special 3-week training seminar on trial advocacy. All interpretations of NITA and its practices are my own and are *not* intended to reflect the goals or objectives of that organization.

10. Women were much more likely to be criticized for being "too nice." The significance of women being singled out for these kinds of "mistakes" is examined in Chapter 5, "Women and Men as Litigators," in *Gender Trials* (Pierce, 1995).

11. Mauet describes two approaches to cross-examination. In the first, the purpose is to elicit favorable testimony by getting the witness to agree with the facts that support one's case. On the other hand, a destructive cross-examination "involves asking questions which will discredit the witness or his testimony" (1980, p. 240).

12. The proper form of leading questions are allowed in cross-examination but *not* in direct examination. Mauet (1980) defines a leading question as "one which suggests the answer" and provides examples, such as "Mr. Doe, on December 13, 1977, you owned a car, didn't you?" (p. 247). In his view, control comes by asking "precisely phrased leading questions that never give the witness an opening to hurt you" (p. 243).

13. Women trial lawyers negotiate the masculinized norms of the legal profession in a variety of ways. See Chapter 5, "Women and Men as Litigators," in *Gender Trials* (Pierce 1995).

References

American Bar Association. (1982). *Model code of professional responsibility and code of judicial conduct.* Chicago: National Center for Professional Responsibility and ABA.

Benjamin, J. (1988). *The bonds of love: Psychoanalysis, feminism and the problem of domination.* New York: Pantheon.

Berg, D. (1987). Cross-examination. *Litigation: Journal of the Section of Litigation, American Bar Association, 14*(1), 25-30.

Blinder, M. (1978). Picking juries. *Trial Diplomacy, 1*(1), 8-13.

Blumberg, A. (1967). The practice of law as confidence game: Organizational co-optation of a profession. *Law and Society Review, 1*(2), 15-39.

Brazil, W. (1978). The attorney as victim: Toward more candor about the psychological price tag of litigation practice. *Journal of the Legal Profession, 3,* 107-117.

Buchan, J. (1939). The judicial temperament. In J. Buchan, *Homilies and recreations* (3rd ed.). London: Hodder & Stoughton.

Burawoy, M. (1979). *Manufacturing consent.* Chicago: University of Chicago Press.

Carlin, J. (1962). *Lawyers on their own.* New Brunswick, NJ: Rutgers University Press.

Cartwright, R. (1977, June). Jury selection, *Trial, 28,* 13.

Cheatham, E. (1955). *Cases and materials on the legal profession* (2nd ed.). Brooklyn, NY: Foundation.

Chodorow, N. (1978). *The reproduction of mothering: Psychoanalysis and the sociology of gender.* Berkeley & Los Angeles: University of California Press.

Connell, R. W. (1987). *Gender and power: Society, the person and sexual politics.* Stanford, CA: Stanford University Press.

Dombroff, M. (1989, September 25). Winning is everything! *National Law Journal,* p. 13, col. 1.

Fineman, S. (Ed.). (1993). *Emotions in organizations.* Newbury Park, CA: Sage.

Garfinkel, H. (1956). Conditions of successful degradation ceremonies. *American Journal of Sociology, 61*(11), 420-424.

Goldberg, D. (1987, July 1). Playing hardball. *American Bar Association Journal,* p. 48.

Hochschild, A. (1983). *The managed heart: Commercialization of human feeling.* Berkeley & Los Angeles: University of California Press.

Johnstone, Q., & Hopson, D., Jr. (1967). *Lawyers and their work.* Indianapolis, IN: Bobbs-Merrill.

Leidner, R. (1993). *Fast food, fast talk: Service work and the routinization of everyday life.* Berkeley: University of California Press.

Luban, D. (1988). *Lawyers and justice: An ethical study.* Princeton, NJ: Princeton University Press.

Lyman, P. (1987). The fraternal bond as a joking relationship: A case study of sexist jokes in male group bonding. In M. Kimmel (Ed.), *Changing men: New directions in research on men and masculinity* (pp. 148-163). Newbury Park, CA: Sage.

Margolick, D. (1988, August 5). At the bar: Rambos invade the courtroom. *New York Times,* p. B5.

Mauet, T. (1980). *Fundamentals of trial techniques.* Boston: Little, Brown.

Menkel-Meadow, C. (1985, Fall). Portia in a different voice: Speculations on a women's lawyering process. *Berkeley Women's Law Review,* pp. 39-63.

Messner, M. (1989). Masculinities and athletic careers. *Gender & Society, 3*(1), 71-88.

Milkman, R. (1987). *Gender at work.* Bloomington: University of Indiana Press.

Miner, R. (1988, December 19). Lawyers owe one another. *National Law Journal,* pp. 13-14.

Nelson, R. (1988). *Partners with power.* Berkeley & Los Angeles: University of California Press.

Perlman, P. (1988). Jury selection. *The Docket: Newsletter of the National Institute for Trial Advocacy, 12*(2), 1.

Pierce, J. L. (1995). *Gender trials: Emotional lives in contemporary law firms.* Berkeley & Los Angeles: University of California Press.

Rhode, D. (1988). Perspectives on professional women. *Stanford Law Review, 40,* 1163-1207.

Rice, S. (1989, May 24). Two organizations provide training, in-house or out. *San Francisco Banner,* p. 6.

Ring, L. (1983, July). *Voir dire:* Some thoughtful notes on the selection process. *Trial, 19,* 72-75.

Ring, L. (1987). Cross-examining the sympathetic witness. *Litigation: Journal of the Section of Litigation, American Bar Association, 14*(1), 35-39.

Rollins, J. (1985). *Between women: Domestics and their employers.* Philadelphia: Temple University Press.

Rosenberg, J., Perlstadt, H., & Phillips, W. (1993). Now that we are here: Discrimination, disparagement and harassment at work and the experience of women lawyers. *Gender & Society, 7*(3), 415-433.

Sayler, R. (1988, March 1). Rambo litigation: Why hardball tactics don't work. *American Bar Association Journal,* p. 79.

Smigel, E. (1969). *The Wall Street lawyer: Professional or organizational man?* (2nd ed.). New York: Free Press.

Spangler, E. (1986). *Lawyers for hire: Salaried professionals at work.* New Haven, CT: Yale University Press.

Spence, G. (1988). *With justice for none.* New York: Times Books.

Turow, S. (1987). Crossing the star. *Litigation: Journal of the Section of Litigation, American Bar Association, 14*(1), 40-42.

Wellman, F. (1986). *The art of cross-examination: With the cross-examinations of important witnesses in some celebrated cases* (4th ed.). New York: Collier. (Original work published 1903)

West, C., & Zimmerman, D. (1987). Doing gender. *Gender & Society, 1*(2), 125-151.

What America really thinks about lawyers. (1986, October). *National Law Journal,* p. 1.

Willis, P. (1977). *Learning to labor.* Farnborough, UK: Saxon House.

2

Managing to Kill

Masculinities and the Space Shuttle *Challenger* Explosion

JAMES W. MESSERSCHMIDT

It has been 10 years since the Space Shuttle *Challenger* exploded in midair, just 73 seconds into flight, killing all seven crew members. The President's Commission (1986) investigating the explosion concluded that the loss of *Challenger* was due to a failure in the joint between two segments of the right solid rocket booster (SRB). O-rings—intended to prevent hot gases from escaping through the joint during the propellant burn of the rocket engine—failed to seal properly because of the extremely cold temperature at launch time (29° F). More specifically, the cold temperature impaired O-ring resiliency, allowing the hot gases to escape, ignite, and within seconds penetrate the External Tank.[1]

The President's Commission (1986) further concluded that problems with the O-ring design were well-documented—and, therefore, well-known—by both government (NASA) and corporate (Morton Thiokol, Inc.) officials years before that fateful day. Indeed, the Commission concluded that the explosion was "rooted in history" and that a "flawed decision-making process" led to the launch (p. 82).

In addition to the President's Commission, criminological investigations of the explosion have appeared in recent years, focusing primarily

AUTHOR'S NOTE: This chapter is a slightly revised version of an article published in *masculinties* 3(4), and reprinted by permission of the editor.

on the organizational context within which the "flawed decision" to launch was reached (Kramer, 1992; Vaughan, 1989, 1994). This chapter contributes to this evolving reexamination of the explosion by considering the fact—that previous investigations ignore—that those involved in the decision to launch *Challenger* were all men; my interest is the gendered character of the events and decisions leading to the *Challenger* explosion. Indeed, such an investigation opens a window to corporate decision making, generating new insights into corporate masculinities and corporate crime.[2]

Maier's (1993) account is the sole examination of the explosion that considers gender; unfortunately, it relies on David and Brannon's (1976) outdated sex role theory. Although I have criticized sex role theory elsewhere [there is no point in repeating that critique here (Messerschmidt, 1993, pp. 25-29)], it should be pointed out that such analysis ultimately homogenizes men by reducing all masculinities to one normative standard type, therefore, unable to account for human agency and the social construction of differing masculinities. Gender is conceptualized here not in this traditional sociological sense but, rather, as an active, behavior-based, situational accomplishment (Connell, 1987, 1995a; Messerschmidt, 1993; Thorne, 1993; West & Fenstermaker, 1993; West & Zimmerman, 1987). Conceptualizing gender in terms of social situation and structured action permits a deeper formulation, not only of what has been visible but what previously has been hidden—such as masculinit*ies* (Connell, 1995a; Messerschmidt, 1993). This newly emerging feminist perspective, outlined below, is used to examine the relationship between the differentiation of corporate masculinities (managers versus engineers) and the Space Shuttle *Challenger* explosion.

Gender as Structured Action[3]

Candace West and Don Zimmerman (1987) argue that in Western industrialized societies, there exist but two "sex categories," and that individuals are assigned at birth to one or the other. Moreover, in all social situations, we attempt to adorn ourselves with culturally appropriate "female" or "male" fashion; and in every interaction, we consistently engage in gender attribution—identifying and categorizing people by appropriate sex category while simultaneously categorizing ourselves to others (see also Kessler & McKenna, 1978).

Nevertheless, as West and Zimmerman (1987) argue, *gender* entails considerably more than the social signs of a sex category. Rather, gender involves a situated accomplishment: "the activity of managing situated conduct in light of normative conceptions, attitudes, and activities appropriate to one's sex category" (p. 127). And because gender is the outcome of social practices in specific settings, it serves to inform such practices in reciprocal relation. Thus, although sex category defines social identification as woman or man, gender systematically corroborates that identification through social interaction: We coordinate our activities to "do" gender in situational ways.

Crucial to conceptualization of gender as situated accomplishment is the notion of "accountability." Because individuals realize their behavior is accountable to others, they configure and orchestrate their actions in relation to how they might be interpreted by others in the particular social context in which they occur. In other words, in their daily activities, individuals attempt to become socially identified as female or male. Accountability, thus, "allows individuals to conduct their activities in relation to their circumstances" (West & Fenstermaker, 1993, p. 156) and thereby highlights the possibility that gender varies by social situation and circumstance. Within every interaction, then, we encourage and expect others to attribute a particular sex category to us. We facilitate the ongoing task of accountability by demonstrating that we are "male" or "female" through concocted behaviors that may be interpreted as such. In this way we do masculinity or femininity differently, depending on the social situation and the social circumstances we encounter. Thus, "doing gender" renders social action accountable in terms of normative conceptions, attitudes, and activities appropriate to one's sex category in the specific social situation in which one acts (p. 157).

In this view, then, masculinity is accomplished systematically, not imposed on men or settled beforehand. Although early in life, we develop relatively fixed individual identities as a member of one sex category, masculinity is never a static or a finished product. Rather, men construct masculinities in specific social situations. In other words, men participate in self-regulating conduct, whereby they monitor their own and other's gendered conduct.

Although masculinity is "made," so to speak, through the unification of self-regulated practices, these practices do not occur in a vacuum. Instead, they are influenced by the social structural constraints we experience. Following Connell (1987, 1995a) and outlined elsewhere (Messerschmidt, 1993), three specific social structures—gender division of labor, gender relations of power, and sexuality—underlie relations between women and men. These social structures are not external to social actors or simply and solely constraining; on the contrary, structure is realized only through social action, and social action requires structure as its condition. Moreover, women and men do gender in specific social situations, thereby reproducing and sometimes changing social structures. And given that men reproduce masculine ideals in socially structured specific practices, there are a variety of ways to do masculinity. Although masculinity is always individual and personal, specific forms of masculinity are available, encouraged, and permitted, depending on one's social situation, class, race, and sexual orientation. Accordingly, masculinity must be viewed as *structured action*—what men do under specific social structural constraints.

In this way, then, social relations (such as class, race, and gender) link each of us in a common relationship to others: We share structural space. Consequently, common or shared blocks of knowledge evolve through interaction, in which particular masculine ideals and activities play a part. Through such interaction, masculinity is institutionalized, permitting men to draw on such existing, but previously formed, masculine ways of thinking and acting to construct a masculine identity for specific settings. The particular criteria of masculine identities are embedded in the social situations and recurrent practices whereby social relations are structured (Giddens, 1989, p. 285).

Thus, we must recognize, first, that men are positioned differently throughout society and that, therefore, they share with other men the construction of masculinities peculiar to their position in society. We must accept also that socially organized power relations among men are constructed historically on the basis of class, race, sexual preference, and specific social situations; that is, in specific contexts (such as organizations), some men have greater power than other men. In this sense, then, masculinity can be understood only as a relational construct.

Connell's (1987, 1995a) notion of "hegemonic masculinity" is relevant here. Hegemonic masculinity is the culturally idealized form of masculinity in a given historical setting. It is culturally honored, glorified, and extolled at the symbolic level in the mass media. In Western industrialized societies, hegemonic masculinity is characterized by work in the paid labor market, the subordination of women, and heterosexism. Hegemonic masculinity, as the culturally dominant ideal, influences but does not determine masculine behavior. As Barrie Thorne (1993) notes, "Individuals and groups develop varied forms of accommodation, reinterpretation, and resistance to ideologically hegemonic patterns" (p. 106). Although men attempt to express hegemonic masculinity through speech, dress, physical appearance, activities, and relationships with others, these social signs of masculinity accommodate to the specific context of one's actions and are self-regulated within that context. Thus, masculinity is based on a social construct that reflects unique circumstances and relationships—a social construction that is renegotiated in each particular context. In other words, social actors self-regulate their behavior and make specific choices in specific contexts. As Connell (1987) points out, everyday masculine practices draw on the cultural ideals of hegemonic masculinity, but they do not necessarily correspond to actual masculinities as they are lived. What most men support is not necessarily what they are (p. 186). In this way, then, men construct varieties of masculinities through specific practices. By emphasizing diversity in gender constructions, a more fluid and situated approach to gender is realized.

Taking this approach permits us to conceptualize gender and crime in new ways, ways that enable us to explore how and in what respect masculinity is constituted in certain settings at certain times, and how that construct relates to crime. For example, as discussed earlier, work in the paid labor market is central to hegemonic masculinity and, therefore, to the lives of most men. Indeed, "the job" is a major basis of identity and what it means to be a man. For criminology, however, the association among masculinity, work and crime historically has been explored only in the case of *unemployed* men engaged in street crime. And routinely at issue here is not the unemployed male's relationship to work per se but, rather, his limited or lack of access to the paid labor market. What is missing in the criminological and gender studies literature is a full consideration of gender and crime within the context of work and, especially, in the setting of white-collar work. This chapter attempts to fill that void by examining the relationship between masculinity and crime involving male managers and engineers in a particular corporate organizational setting.

The focus of the remaining sections, then, explores the differentiation of corporate masculinities by observing the work and product of their construction in a specific setting and through certain practices. I examine such masculinities not in terms of relations between women and men but as they are reproduced among men in corporations. A review of the empirical evidence on the Space Shuttle *Challenger* explosion, with an eye to the social context in which both gender and corporate crime are accomplished, reveals that gender is a critical structural tool in corporations. Indeed, the definition and interpretation of the boundaries between masculinities—and thus the hierarchical separation of some men from other men—are critical organizational bases in corporate bureaucracies. Accordingly, the specific masculine meanings constructed through particular occupations and the ways in which corporate crime is related to those meanings and occupations must be analyzed thoroughly. As such, I argue that only through an analysis of corporate masculinities can we make coherent sense of the Space Shuttle *Challenger* explosion.[4]

Although men are always doing masculinity, the significance of masculine accomplishment is socially situated and, thus, is an intermittent matter. That is, certain occasions present themselves as more intimidating for demonstrating and affirming masculinity. In such settings, sex category is particularly salient; it is, as David Morgan (1992) puts it, "more or less explicitly put on the line" (p. 47)—a time when doing masculinity requires extra effort. Under such conditions in corporations, corporate crime may be invoked as a practice for doing masculinity and distinguishing masculinities from one another. The Space Shuttle *Challenger* explosion provides an excellent case study of how in the same social situation one type of masculinity (manager) was constructed through the commission of corporate crime, while contemporaneously another type of masculinity (engineer) was constructed through resisting that crime.

Risky Technology

The National Aeronautics and Space Administration (NASA) had long been interested in frequent, economical access to space, and in 1970, the White House declared that funding on the order of previous NASA projects—such as *Gemini* and *Apollo*—was no longer possible (President's Commission, 1986, p. 2). Thus, to obtain funding from Congress, NASA had to guarantee a program with low development costs and dependable routine operations. To accomplish this, NASA proposed a Space Shuttle that would be both reusable and cost-effective in design.[5] Moreover, the Shuttle was to be economically self-sufficient through satellite launchings and commercially supported in-flight research. It was in the increasingly austere fiscal environment of the early 1970s, then, that the Shuttle was born (p. 4).

Morton Thiokol, Inc. (MTI) was selected on November 20, 1973, to receive the NASA contract to design and build the SRBs. Not surprisingly, costs were the primary concern of NASA's selection board.[6] Although the board noted several problems with the MTI proposal, they were deemed "technical in nature" and "the costs to correct did not negate the MTI cost advantage." Furthermore, the dual O-ring feature was especially noteworthy to the selection board.[7] Thus, a cost-plus-award-fee contract, worth approximately $800 million, was awarded to MTI (p. 121).

However, from the beginning there were problems with MTI's dual O-ring design, all of which were well documented by both NASA and MTI.[8] Despite consistent evidence of the hazardous nature of the O-ring design, Shuttle missions were not halted to correct the anomalies. In fact, as the President's Commission (p. 5) points out, with the landing of the fourth test flight, "the orbital flight test program came to an end [and remarkably] NASA declared the Space Shuttle 'operational.' " Initially, managers and engineers at both NASA's Marshall Space Flight Center in Huntsville, Alabama—which has authoritative responsibility for the orbiter's main engine, the External Tank, and the solid rocket booster—and at MTI incessantly rationalized that after some initial erosion, the O-rings would ultimately seal intact; if the primary O-ring failed to seal the joint, the secondary O-ring would act as a backup. Flight after flight was approved by both organizational managers and engineers, "accepting the possibility of some O-ring erosion due to hot gas impingement" and the belief that redundancy would prevail (p. 132).[9]

By January 24, 1985, however, when the 15th Shuttle flight was launched, the temperature of the O-rings at lift-off was 53° F, the coldest launch temperature to that date. On that flight, O-ring erosion occurred in both SRBs, as well as in both primary and secondary O-rings. Accordingly, several MTI *engineers* became much more concerned and reported to Marshall that this launch occurred during the "worst case temperature change in Florida history" and that "low temperature enhanced the probability of erosion" (p. 136). Although previously MTI engineers felt the possibility existed for significant reduction of the erosion problem and a belief in redundancy, the results of this flight clearly indicated the anomalies needed to be corrected immediately. As Roger Boisjoly (1987), the leading engineering specialist at MTI, stated in a letter to MTI management,

> This letter is written to insure that management is fully aware of the seriousness of the current O-ring erosion problem in the SRB joints from an engineering standpoint. . . . It is my honest and very real fear that if we do not take immediate action to dedicate a team to solve the problem, with the field joint having the number one priority, then we stand in jeopardy of losing a flight along with all the launch pad facilities. (p. 4)[10]

However, MTI management was not forthcoming with the resources necessary to solve the O-ring problem. As Boisjoly (p. 1) goes on to point out, "the MTI management style would not let anything compete or interfere with the production and shipping of boosters."

Thus, by 1985, the O-ring erosion problem had been well documented at Marshall and MTI; yet the management of both organizations ignored engineer concerns and labeled the problem an "acceptable risk" rather than suspending Shuttle missions until the problem was fixed. In addition, in that same year, NASA published a projection calling for 24 flights per year by 1990.

Arguably, NASA was under pressure throughout the early to mid-1980s to meet both customer commitments and Congressional approval—which meant not only launch a certain number of flights per year but launch them on time. Indeed, as the President's Commission (1986) concludes,

> From the inception of the Shuttle, NASA had been advertising a vehicle that would make space operations "routine and economical." The greater the annual number of flights, the greater the degree of routinization and economy, so heavy emphasis was placed on the schedule. (p. 164)

Within this context, Marshall managers responded to the O-ring problem not by canceling flights and fixing the problem (because delays were to be avoided) but by proceeding full speed ahead. As the President's Commission (1986) put it, in the face of "unrelenting pressure to meet the demands of an accelerating flight schedule," these managers considered the faulty seal "nonserious" and an "acceptable risk" (p. 152). The result was a pattern of risk-taking practices by Marshall managers.

While Marshall managers faced the imperative of a routine and economical flight schedule, MTI faced far-reaching contract negotiations with NASA and competition from other aerospace suppliers and manufacturers. As Malcolm McConnell (1987) argues, negotiations between NASA and MTI regarding the second phase of the lucrative Shuttle SRB contract were intensely troubling for MTI throughout much of 1985:

> In the 1970s contract, Thiokol was assigned the production of the first thirty-seven sets of boosters. Given the increased flight schedule, that number would be used by the end of 1986. Therefore, Thiokol was actively negotiating for the second-phase contract that would cover the next sixty sets of boosters, a procurement award worth a billion dollars. However, other aerospace companies had been lobbying Congress for at least 2 years to force NASA to break Morton Thiokol's monopoly on producing the SRB's. In the Fall of 1985 Thiokol's management was acutely aware of this lobbying effort that Congres-

sional staff members called a "full-court press," by Thiokol's competitors. (pp. 180-181)

Indeed, by winter of 1985 NASA initiated competitive bidding on the pending contract renewal—"thus seriously threatening for the first time Thiokol's 13-year monopoly" (p. 60). Consequently, MTI managers were not in the position to irritate their most prominent customer by suspending Shuttle flights until a new O-ring design was developed. So they, in the manner of their counterparts at Marshall, accepted escalating risk. In short, both Marshall and MTI management came to accept the O-ring problem as "unavoidable and an acceptable flight risk" (President's Commission, 1986, p. 148).

The Launch Decision

On January 27, 1986, NASA scrubbed the scheduled flight due to high crosswinds at the launch site and rescheduled *Challenger* for the following morning (President's Commission, 1986, p. 17). By the early afternoon of January 27, 1986, MTI engineers became increasingly concerned over the predicted low temperature of 29° F for the rescheduled launch time, especially in light of the near disaster one year earlier at 53° F. This concern led ultimately to a teleconference between Marshall and MTI officials on the issue of temperature. Data regarding the effect of low temperature on the O-rings and the joint seal were presented by MTI engineers, along with an opinion that launch should be delayed until the temperature was at least 53° F. Marshall requested that MTI prepare and telefax a more formal presentation to both Marshall and Kennedy Space Center officials (in Florida) for a full-fledged teleconference later that evening (p. 106).

At approximately 8:45 p.m. EST, the second teleconference commenced. The telefax presented a history of the O-ring erosion in the SRB joints of previous flights. Roger Boisjoly, the leading engineering specialist at MTI, expressed deep concern about launching at such a low temperature (President's Commission, 1986, p. 88). Boisjoly argued that the Shuttle should not be launched below a temperature of 53° F, because such temperature would result in the O-rings becoming less resilient and, therefore, incapable of sealing the joint before hot gases ignited to cause an explosion. As Boisjoly stated to the President's Commission (p. 89), it would be "like trying to shove a brick into a crack versus a sponge."

Indeed, by now both MTI management and engineers agreed that the Shuttle should not launch until temperatures reached at least 53° F. Notwithstanding, Marshall managers "were not pleased" with MTI's conclusions and recommendations (p. 90).

Marshall challenged MTI's data and conclusions primarily by accusing MTI of trying to establish new launch-commit criteria based on a 53° F standard. Eventually, Lawrence Mulloy, SRB manager at Kennedy, responded to MTI's concern about temperature by stating, "My God, Thiokol, when do you want me to launch, next April?" (President's Commission, 1986, p. 96). Mulloy (p. 1529) insisted that MTI's position was irrationally qualitative, based simply on experience rather than rational, quantifiable evidence. A further exchange between MTI and NASA representatives continued for quite sometime, MTI maintaining that launch should not occur outside the 53° F database. George Hardy, deputy director of science and engineering at Marshall, responded by stating, "I'm appalled at your recommendation" (p. 94).

Thus, MTI found itself on the defensive and experienced formidable coaxing to reverse their no-launch recommendation. MTI was placed in a social situation where they had to demonstrate convincingly it was not safe to launch, whereas in all previous preflight conferences, MTI was required to verify it was safe to launch. In other words, they had to prove the launch would fail![11]

Eventually the debate reached an impasse. Overwhelmed at having to prove that the joint would fail, MTI management sought a 5-minute, off-line recess to reevaluate the effect of temperature on the O-rings (President's Commission, 1986). The caucus (lasting at least 30 minutes) began with Jerry Mason, senior vice president at MTI, stating to the three managers around him, "We have to make a management decision" (p. 92). Assuming that management was about to consider reversing the earlier no-launch decision, the MTI engineers (especially Roger Boisjoly and Arnie Thompson) attempted a last-minute explanation of the effects of low temperature on O-ring resiliency. Boisjoly explained this attempt to the President's Commission:

> Arnie actually got up from his position which was down the table, and walked up the table and put a quarter pad down in front of the management folks, and tried to sketch out once again what his concern was with the joint, and when he realized he wasn't getting through, he just stopped.
>
> I tried one more time with the photos. I grabbed the photos, and I went up and discussed the photos once again and tried to make the point that it was

> my opinion from actual observations that temperature was indeed a discriminator and we should not ignore the physical evidence that we had observed. . . . I also stopped when it was apparent that I couldn't get anybody to listen. (pp. 92-93)

In short, these two engineers ardently tried to stop management from reversing their earlier unanimous no-launch decision.

During this exchange, it was clear that three of the four managers supported a launch but that Bob Lund, vice president of engineering, remained committed to the earlier no-launch decision (p. 108). After some further discussion of the data, with Lund remaining the sole holdout among the managers, Mason turned to Lund and instructed him "to take off his engineering hat and put on his management hat" (p. 93). The managers then agreed they had to make a management decision, as Mason states, "in order to conclude what we needed to conclude" (p. 1383). At this point, the engineers were excluded from the decision-making process and a final management review was conducted by the four managers only. The MTI managers, then, with Lund concurring, decided to reverse the decision of the engineers and approve the launch for the next morning. As the President's Commission put it,

> At approximately 11 p.m. EST, the Thiokol-NASA tele-conference resumed, the Thiokol management stating that they had reassessed the problem, that the temperature effects were a concern, but that the data were admittedly inconclusive. Kilminster read the rationale recommending launch and stated that that was Morton Thiokol's recommendation. (p. 96)

Managing to Kill

How can we begin to understand the fact that, in the face of a strong possibility of risk to human life, MTI engineers recognized this threat and argued against the launch, whereas, MTI managers yielded to Marshall pressure and voted unanimously to launch?[12] It is now well established in the sociological literature that gender is embedded in corporations, and that gender is accomplished through concrete corporate activities, resulting not only in gender divisions (e.g., gender divisions of labor, "male" and "female" jobs) but also in situationally specific gendered images, symbols, and practices (Acker, 1992). More specifically, corporations often are defined through metaphors of masculinity. As Joan Acker (1992) puts it,

> Today, organizations are lean, mean, aggressive, goal oriented, efficient, and competitive but rarely empathetic, supportive, kind and caring. Organizational participants actively create these images in their efforts to construct organizational cultures that contribute to competitive success. (p. 253)

The gendering of corporations involves a presentation of self as a gendered member of the corporation and, for the corporate manager, this means specific practices—such as rationality, instrumentalism, careerism, decisiveness, productivism, and risk taking—that help the corporation be successful (Kerfoot & Knights, 1993, p. 671). Indeed, as we have known for almost 20 years, corporate-managerial masculinity is measured by success in reaching corporate goals; accordingly, managerial gendered practices align themselves with corporate needs (Acker, 1990; Kanter, 1977; Tolson, 1977).

MTI managers, like other corporate managers, pursued such gendered practices to assist MTI in attaining its goals. Like other corporate managers, MTI managers consistently faced economic pressures that focused on the present and the near future: "the *next* milestone, the *next* contract, and the *next* stockholders' report are 'real' near-terms subjects that a manager must always address" (Dubinskas, 1988, p. 195). As indicated, the immediate situational goal of MTI was to preserve a lucrative government contract. Given the social situation of uncertainty in reaching this goal caused by the O-ring problem, rather than "hang tough" and continue to oppose the launch, MTI management engaged in risk-taking behavior to achieve their corporate objective. MTI managers rationalized giving greater weight to the advantage of risk-taking practices over halting Shuttle flights until the O-ring problem could be fixed. They chose the risk-taking path as more likely to advance both their individual masculine performance (gender) as well as corporate success (social class).[13]

When managers talk about "what is at stake" in their jobs, the answer invariably is "the growth of the organization" and, hence, their ultimate status (Dubinskas, 1988, p. 199). Interviews with corporate managers show that they regard a manager who fails to take risks as one who should not be in the business of managing, and risk taking is especially warranted when faced with possible failure to meet corporate goals (March & Shapira, 1987, pp. 1408-1409). To be sure, for managers faced with such uncertainty in meeting goals, "the desire to reach the target focuses attention in a way that leads generally to risk taking. In this case, the opportunities for gain receive attention, rather than the dangers" (p. 1413). Thus, we should not be surprised that the MTI managers reversed the decision of the engineers and approved the launch. Indeed, prestige accompanies the advocacy of such risk-taking and advocates of risk are perceived as especially capable managers, particularly when successful on the previous occasion (p. 1414).[14]

In this context, then, for MTI managers risk taking became the situational defining feature of managerial masculinity. Risk taking is widely documented as a masculine practice, where risk-ladened social situations are responded to more often by men or boys than women or girls as a challenge, an opportunity to "prove" one's worth and demonstrate prowess to others (Arch, 1993, p. 4).[15] The MTI managers were no different from many other men confronted with a risk-ladened situation; doing risk taking for them was, simultaneously, doing masculinity. What is different is that this risk-taking masculine practice was specific to the particular social situation of this corporation. Clearly, the unique social conditions surrounding *Challenger* flights—preserving a lucrative government contract—created a context for MTI managers to push the limits of SRB technology. Because these managers had to demonstrate that the SRBs could survive a rigorous flight schedule, rather than acknowledge design flaws, they demonstrated corporate-managerial competence by supporting the necessity for remaining on schedule. Thus, risk taking became an available resource for achieving corporate goals, because they "got away with it last time." As one member of the President's Commission (1986) observed,

> [The Shuttle] flies [with O-ring erosion] and nothing happens. Then it is suggested, therefore, that the risk is no longer so high for the next flights. We can lower our standards a little bit because we got away with it last time. (p. 148)

In other words, because flight after flight was "successful" (an explosion did not occur), this rationalized further risk taking. Having survived the challenge, MTI managers became increasingly comfortable continuing the risk-taking behavior; thus, risk taking became a practice not only for securing corporate goals but for solving the gender accountability problem at "the job." Doing risk taking was not solely a practice for demonstrating corporate loyalty but simultaneously for rendering such action accountable in terms of the normative conceptions and activities appropriate to the male sex category in this corporation. Because threats to profit making are concurrent threats to corporate-manager masculine accomplishment, risk taking is an acceptable means of resolving both problems: Risk taking is a resource in this particular setting for accomplishing profit (class) and masculinity (gender). Accordingly, risk taking was normalized among MTI management, permitting these men to draw on previously formed risk-taking behavior as a resource for doing masculinity. In short, managerial risk taking became an institutionalized practice, a masculine resolution to the spectacle of technological uncertainty.

Thus, MTI managers gave Marshall the green light to launch to, as the President's Commission (p. 104) stated, "accommodate a major customer." Indeed, throughout "the first 3 weeks of January 1986, NASA and Thiokol conducted negotiations over a one-billion-dollar contract," and extremely important contract discussions were scheduled for January 28—"the day after Thiokol managers made their recommendation to proceed with the launch, the day the *Challenger* was destroyed" (McConnell, 1987, p. 60). Given this milieu, agreeing to take the risk demonstrated not only loyalty to the corporation but, simultaneously, provided MTI managers with a resource for doing masculinity—and, simultaneously, corporate crime—in that specific social setting.

Moreover, the attraction to risk taking by these corporate-managers had as much to do with the social action itself as with what it produced in terms of corporate goals. The validation of manager effectiveness at MTI was one's proclivity to "go to the limit" in bringing a flight to "successful" fruition (President's Commission, 1986, p. 110). Each victorious challenge reconfirmed for others one's identity as an accomplished, proficient manager. Fervently effectuating risk-taking social practices provided these managers with the opportunity to exercise diligent control over the situation and bring it to a triumphant conclusion. This is consistent with other research on corporate-manager masculinity that indicates that such managers are ranked "in terms of their capacity to display attributes of control over the definition of the reality of events" and are "constantly preoccupied with purposive action in the drive to be 'in control' " (Kerfoot & Knights, 1993, pp. 671-672). Thus, every successful launch was taken as proof that one was "in control" and, therefore, possessed "the right stuff" to be a *man*(ager).[16] Indeed, the "enterprise of winning" by overcoming danger is for managers "life consuming" and results in "an inward turned competitiveness, focused on the self, creating, in fact, an instrumentality of the personal" (Donaldson, 1993, p. 665). As Kerfoot and

Knights (1993) argue, at the level of embodied experience, this corporate-manager masculinity results

> in the position whereby individuals feel "driven" for no discernible reason, other than as a part of what it means, and how it feels, to subscribe to an ideal of competence, and where the display of vulnerability is to threaten the image of that competence. (p. 672)

This translates into the denial or suppression of emotionality, fear, and uncertainty and, therefore, in the social situation of the off-line caucus, it should not be surprising to find MTI managers unanimously supporting launch; to do otherwise would mean exhibiting fear and uncertainty. These corporate-managers displayed, as Rosabeth Moss Kanter (1977) put it in her discussion of managerial masculinity, "a capacity to set aside personal, emotional considerations in the interests of task accomplishments" (p. 22). Indeed, MTI managers disregarded (at least publicly) during the entire teleconference and off-line caucus the fact that human beings were on *Challenger*. The task was to "get *Challenger* up," and all factors antagonistic to that goal—including human life—were deemed irrelevant.

This masculine discourse on the part of MTI managers is similar to the "technostrategic" discourse outlined by Carol Cohn (1987, 1995) in her important research on nuclear defense intellectuals. Cohn (1995) found that during professional meetings, these men systematically suppressed

> the emotional, the concrete, the particular, the human bodies and their vulnerability, human lives and their subjectivity—all of which are marked as feminine in the binary dichotomies of gender discourse. In other words, gender discourse informs and shapes nuclear and national security discourse. (pp. 134-135)

Similarly, MTI managers eschewed any discussion of human beings (the flight crew) and their vulnerability to the risky technology. And clearly, it was the masculine discourse that generated this *indifference* to the human consequences of managerial decisions. In short, being more attentive to the survival of their lucrative contract rather than the survival of human beings was a means of "doing masculinity" and, as a result, corporate crime.[17]

The decision to launch by MTI managers can be understood, then, in terms of its captivating and enticing masculine appeal—a social practice that had become normalized in MTI managerial relationships. And because masculinity is constantly renegotiated and "made," voting to launch (and, therefore, changing their earlier no-launch position) was an acceptable (that is, accountable) practice for its making in that particular social situation; a practice that "allowed" these managers to live up to a particular masculine ideal.

It is tempting to end the analysis here simply by reasoning that risk-taking masculinity "gave rise" to this corporate crime. Although this conclusion is attractive and not without substance, it disregards the diversity of masculinities actually constructed in corporations and, thus, their relation to corporate crime. Consequently, we must consider the varieties of masculinities at MTI, not just one type. Indeed, analyzing masculinities places us in a position to address why some men at MTI (engineers), despite the institutionalized and heavy emphasis on risk taking, ardently opposed the launch. It is to the engineers that we now turn.

Resisting Launch

"Of all the major professions," Judy Wajcman (1991) writes, "engineering contains the smallest proportion of females" and, like management, "projects a heavily masculine image" (p. 145). However, corporate managers validate masculinity by success at securing corporate economic goals, while engineers are concerned primarily with technical competence and achievements and tend to devalue economic goals (Cockburn & Ormrod, 1993, p. 161; Vaughan, 1989, p. 337). Indeed, managers and engineers "identify themselves as being in—and 'from'—different 'worlds' " (Dubinskas, 1988, p. 185). Consequently, both managers and engineers weave gendered distinctions into their everyday understanding of "the job," and thus construct masculinity differently.

The relationship between "technical competence" and the social construction of gender difference is well documented in the literature; as Cynthia Cockburn (1985) puts it, "femininity is incompatible with technological competence; to feel technically competent is to feel manly" (p. 12). Nevertheless, to argue that technical competence is "manly" is not to infer only one type of technical masculinity. Indeed, working-class and middle-class men construct masculinity differently, depending on their relation to technology in the workplace. For working-class men, the work environment of the shop floor is given significance by associating manual work with a physically strong and active type of masculinity. In other words, the masculinity of the shop floor stresses the presentation and celebration of physical prowess (Clatterbaugh, 1990; Cockburn, 1983, 1985; Willis, 1979).

Professional engineers, however, do not claim physical prowess but construct masculinity through their possession of abstruse and "expert" technical knowledge (Wajcman, 1991, p. 39). As Cockburn (1985) shows, for professional engineers, "intellectuality and analytical power are appropriated for masculinity" (p. 196). Wajcman (1991) further points out that this knowledge bestows masculine power on engineers "in relation to other men and women who lack this expertise, in terms of the material rewards this skill brings, and even in terms of their popular portrayal as 'heroes' at the frontiers of technological progress" (p. 144). Thus, technical competence is a key source of masculine power among men and "doing engineering" is simultaneously "doing" a particular type of technically competent masculinity. Indeed, being in control of the very latest technology (such as the Space Shuttle *Challenger*) "signifies being involved in directing the future" and so is a highly esteemed activity, whereas, mastery over other kinds of technology (such as machines on the shop floor) does not accord the same status or power (pp. 144-145). Professional engineering not only increases for engineers "their sense of the greatness of their sex," but in addition inculcates "a sense of being special" among the technically competent (Cockburn, 1985, p. 172).

Clearly, then, a major part of engineer masculinity is to be in command of the particular technology and, therefore, to know the limits of that technology. Consequently, engineers (relative to managers) place a very high priority on quality and safety (Starbuck & Milliken, 1988, p. 333). Indeed, Cockburn (1985) stresses the emotional investment engineers lodge in "their" technology:

> In the main these men identify themselves with technology and identify technology with masculinity. . . . Engineers identify so closely with the technology with which they are involved that many will choose their employment less by the salary it offers than by the complexity of the technology it opens up to them. (pp. 171, 172)

Anticipating Cockburn 20 years earlier, Samuel Florman (1976) emphasized the sensual pleasures secured from "doing engineering," and, most recently, Sally Hacker (1989) speaks of a "masculine eroticization of engineering," in which technological innovation is realized as exhilarating and a source of intense pleasure and arousal.

Given this emotional charge, engineers have a direct interest in the technology succeeding as planned and, concurrently, technological success delivers a virile status on engineers, thereby ensuring a claim to "engineer masculinity" (Wajcman, 1991). As a result, risk taking is *not* the appealing masculine practice to engineers that it is to managers. Indeed, for engineers, inasmuch as technical failure threatens their masculinity, it should not be surprising that MTI engineers would exhibit greater caution regarding O-ring capability and argue against launch. Thus, although managers see themselves as "realists" struggling with immediate economic crises that sometimes demand risk taking, engineers attempt to protect their work from myopic managers and are more inclined to disdain risk taking (Dubinskas, 1988, p. 201). Indeed, these strikingly different practices were accomplished situationally during the off-line caucus and brilliantly illustrate the relational character of masculinities. They demonstrate how the definition of masculinity is not only the collective work of a group of people—in this case, corporate managers and engineers—but is constructed differently through social interaction. Both groups exhibit the different ways in which masculinity is defined and sustained, and how this proprietary masculinity relates to their definition of work-related issues; managers and engineers actively confront the work situation and shape practices for solving problems. Yet they do this in distinctly different ways, and it is this contrasting social action that is central to the production of different masculinities. From essentially similar starting points—class, race, and gender privilege, as well as engagement in "mental labor"—two divergent masculinities are produced. Both groups of men pick up the theme of hegemonic masculinity regarding the importance of work in the paid labor market (and clearly both have benefited from the subordination of women), yet they rework that hegemonic theme in situationally specific ways.

In addition, the *relationship* between these masculinities is in part the basis of MTI organization. As with other male-dominated organizations (such as the military—general/soldier [Connell, 1995b]—and the police—office cop/street cop [Messerschmidt, 1993]), it is the relationship between engineer and manager masculinities—technically competent but subordinate to managerial authority on the one hand, dominating and economically competent on the other—that is, in part, the foundation of MTI organization. Yet as indicated, this relationship is far from one of simple complementarity but, rather, is embedded in a power hierarchy.[18]

At MTI, a difference in corporate masculinities was constructed in practice by the asymmetry of power between managers and engineers. "Decisions" were ultimately in the hands of management; yet as we have seen, the power to manage is not always easily exercised. Engineers can and do wield the weapon of "technical competence," at least to some degree, to make their collective voice heard. During the off-line caucus, two MTI engineers attempted to protect "their technology" by challenging managerial authority. There was a contest of masculinities, in which both managers and engineers were attempting to control the SRB technology. Nevertheless, there are limits to oppositional practices by the less powerful, as noted by the engineers themselves. For example, Boisjoly stated to the President's Commission, "I had my say, and I never take any management right to take the input of an engineer and then make a decision based upon that input, and I truly believe that" (p. 1421). Similarly, Brian Russell, another MTI engineer told the commission, "It was a management decision at the vice president's level, and they had heard all they could hear, and I felt there was nothing more to say" (p. 1487)[19]

What these statements reveal is that power is a relationship that structures social interaction between men in the corporation. By engaging in practices that reproduce the division of labor and power, managers and engineers are not only doing their job and, therefore, reproducing corporate organization, they are also constructing masculinities. Both managers and engineers are acknowledging through practice that the lopsided power relationships are indeed "fair."

In addition, the comment by Jerry Mason to Bob Lund during the off-line caucus—to take off his "engineering hat" and put on his "management hat"—is key to understanding the social construction of, and relationship between, masculinities. Lund was vice president of engineering, making him both an engineer and a manager. Initially, Lund put on his engineering hat and argued against launch. However, once he entered the social situation of the off-line caucus, Lund followed instructions, put on his management hat, and concurred with the other managers to approve launch.

What this reveals is that through the exchange of hats, Lund reestablished a corporate-manager masculinity that had been diminished by his earlier opposition to launch. The problem for Lund was to produce configurations of behavior that could be seen by others as normative. Yet as the social setting changed—from outside to inside the caucus—so did the conceptualization of what is normative masculine behavior. In short,

Lund formed different types of masculinity that could be assessed and approved in both social settings as normal.

The case of Lund demonstrates how we maintain different gender identities that may be emphasized or avoided, depending on the social setting. Men construct their gendered action in relation to how such actions might be interpreted by others (that is, their accountability) in the particular social context in which they occur. Given the power relation prevalent in the off-line caucus, Lund did masculinity differently, because the setting and the available resources changed.[20]

Overall, the disparate degree of power among men significantly affects the varieties of masculinities constructed and therefore support for, or rejection of, the launch as a resource for doing masculinity. Engineers were able to oppose the launch, because such a practice was—in this particular situation—a resource for doing gender; attempting to prevent the launch was an accountable practice for doing engineer masculinity. Thus, MTI managers (including Lund) advocated an unsafe launch, whereas engineers resisted such a launch, because of different masculine meanings attaching to the particular practice.

Conclusion

Gender is one of the most significant ways in which we make sense of our daily work environment, and work in the paid labor market is a crucial milieu for the construction of masculinities. Both managers and engineers construct masculinity at the workplace, but the way in which they do so reveals a fundamental difference. And this diversity is strikingly apparent in support for or rejection of the *Challenger* launch. Indeed, as David Morgan (1992) argues, the kind of work determines "the material out of which certain masculinities are shaped" (p. 86). The corporation sets limits for the type of masculinities that might be constructed and one's position in the corporate division of labor and power determines the resources available for masculine practices. The *Challenger* illustration reveals how the corporate division of labor and power is constituted by social action and, in turn, provides resources for doing masculinity. In this way, social structures both constrain and enable social action and, therefore, masculinities and corporate crime. In short, the data on the Space Shuttle *Challenger* explosion provides empirical support for structured action theory and, therefore, how in the same social situation, one type of masculinity (manager) was constructed through the commission of corporate crime, while contemporaneously another type of masculinity (engineer) was constructed through resisting that crime.

Thus, managers and engineers experience their corporate world from a specific position in the organization and, accordingly, construct masculinity in a uniquely appropriate way. Indeed, conceptualizing the *Challenger* explosion from a structured action perspective demonstrates that we are able now to explore sociologically which males commit which crimes in which social situations. In other words, why some men in corporations "manage to kill," whereas other men do not.

Notes

1. The report of the President's Commission provides the most thorough documentation of the events and decisions that led to the launch, and serves here as the primary data on the explosion.

2. I agree with Thorsten Sellin (1938), who long ago criticized criminologists for limiting their investigations to violations of the law. For Sellin, such a definition of crime disregards a fundamental criterion of science: "The scientist must have the freedom to define his[/her] own terms" (p. 23) In other words, criminologists should not be restricted in their research simply to violations of legal precedents. Consequently, although no one involved in the decision to launch *Challenger* were criminalized by the state, following Beirne and Messerschmidt (1995), I label this act "corporate crime," because it conforms to the following definition: "Corporate crime is any illegal and/or socially injurious act of intent or indifference, that occurs for the purpose of furthering corporate goals, and that physically and/or economically abuses individuals in the United States or abroad" (p. 22). As I show in this chapter, although the deaths of the seven crew members was not intentional, it clearly was a socially injurious act of indifference that occurred for the purpose of furthering corporate goals.

3. The content of this section is a summary of the perspective spelled out in Messerschmidt (1993, pp. 61-86).

4. This does not mean other social relations—such as class and race—are insignificant. Indeed, gender, class, and race relations perpetually constrain and enable social action and determine social position, and thus, we are always, to a certain extent, "doing" gender, class, and race. Nevertheless, the *salience* of each for influencing crime vary from one situation to another. That is, in one situation, gender and race may both be important for actuating crime, whereas in another, gender only may be relevant. As I show below, in the particular social setting of the *Challenger* launch decision, both gender and class (but not race) were highly salient to this behavior.

5. As McConnell (1987) states,

> They decided that the strap-on solid fuel boosters would be equipped with large parachutes to carry them to a soft water landing one hundred miles downrange from the launch site after their fuel was spent. The huge external tank would be sacrificed after use. But the orbiter would glide back to a shuttle landing field near its launch

site, be mated with a new fuel tank and refurbished solid rocket boosters, and be ready for flight again within two weeks. (p. 40)

6. A December 12, 1973, NASA selection board report stated (cited in President's Commission, 1986),

> Thiokol's cost advantages were substantial and consistent throughout all areas evaluated. . . . The Thiokol motor case joints utilized dual O-rings and test ports between seals, enabling a simple leak check without pressurizing the entire motor. This innovative design feature increased reliability and decreased operations at the launch site, indicating good attention to low cost (design, development, testing and engineering) and production. . . . Thiokol could do a more economical job than any of the other proposers in both the development and the production phases of the program. (p. 120)

7. MTI engineers based their SRB design on the Air Force's Titan III model. However, because the Titan had experienced occasional erosion of its single O-ring design, MTI engineers adopted a second, presumably redundant O-ring arrangement into each joint, to hypothetically make the *Challenger* safer.

8. Early tests performed between 1977 and 1980 showed that during the initial period of launch, pressure surge "joint rotation" occurred, causing the secondary O-ring to become completely disengaged from its sealing surface (President's Commission, 1986, pp. 122-123). Moreover, the orbital test flight series, which consisted of four flights from April 1981 to July 1982, repeatedly evinced O-ring erosion caused by "joint rotation." For example, after the third test flight, inspection revealed "that joint rotation caused the loss of the secondary O-ring as a backup seal" that could ultimately result in a "loss of mission vehicle and crew due to metal erosion, burn through, and probable case burst resulting in fire and deflagration" (pp. 125-126).

9. Vaughan (1994) provides an interesting discussion of how managers and engineers jointly defined the SRB joints an "acceptable risk." However, she fails to acknowledge and analyze the engineers changing position, especially the necessity of fixing the erosion problem prior to future flights. I examine this turnabout below.

10. The President's Commission (1986) would subsequently agree with Boisjoly, stating that the O-ring erosion history presented to MTI management by the engineers "was sufficiently detailed to require corrective action prior to the next flight" (p. 148).

11. As Bob Lund (1986), vice president of engineering at MTI, stated in testimony to the President's Commission, "We have dealt with Marshall for a long time and have always been in the position of defending our position that we were ready to fly . . . [now] we had to prove to them we *weren't* ready" (pp. 1456-1457). And as Roger Boisjoly put it, "This was a meeting where the determination was to launch, and it was up to us to prove beyond a shadow of a doubt that it was not safe to do so. This is in total reversal to what the position usually is in a pre-flight conversation" (p. 1421).

12. Due to space limitations, I concentrate my analysis in the remaining sections exclusively on the corporate (MTI) decision to launch.

13. Although all the major MTI managerial decision makers were Caucasian, the social construction of "whiteness" was not the salient feature to this situation as gender and class. In other words, class and gender were directly threatened by the O-ring problem

but not race. Moreover, this socially injurious act conforms to the definition of corporate crime outlined earlier (see Note #2), because the decision to launch helped further MTI's corporate goal of preserving a lucrative contract.

14. The importance of risk taking in the corporate-managerial world was recently highlighted in a book on women managers. According to Driscoll and Goldberg (1993), to gain entry to the masculine corporate-managerial "club," "women would do well to become risk-takers" because "risk-taking pays off . . . the greater the risk, the greater the reward" (p. 46)

15. The sociology-of-risk literature has shockingly ignored this important link with gender. See, for example, Short and Clarke (1992) and Luhman (1993).

16. It should therefore not be surprising to find that interview data of corporate managers shows that they "care about their reputations for risk taking and are eager to expound on their sentiments about the deficiencies of others" (March & Shapira, 1987, p. 1413).

17. Bob Lund, vice president of engineering at MTI, stated the following to the President's Commission (1986) when asked why he initially opposed launch: "You know this program has people on it, and so I am very concerned about that, and I want to make sure that if there is any hint of a problem, that we are not extending that" (p. 1459). However, though he is the only person to acknowledge such a concern to the Commission, there is no evidence that he announced this concern at any time during the launch decision process and, finally, he eventually voted—with the other managers—to launch *Challenger.* Thus, although MTI managers did not intend harm to the seven crew members, they clearly were indifferent to the human consequences of their actions and, therefore, committed corporate crime (see the definition of corporate crime in Note 2). Moreover, I must stress that it was the gendered interaction and discourse within the particular social situation of the teleconference and off-line caucus that generated this indifference.

18. Due to space limitations, I am able to consider only power relations at MTI. However, we also observe power relations between managers of the two organizations. MTI's reversal from a no-launch to a launch decision clearly must be understood in terms of its relatively powerless position vis-à-vis Marshall. That is, MTI must be responsive to its major customer or potentially suffer dire economic consequences. Marshall managers, by reason of their powerful position, had the resources to pressure MTI to prove that it was unsafe to launch. Consequently, a full understanding of the power dynamics involved in this event—something clearly beyond the scope of this chapter—must consider this relationship between the "men at Marshall" and the "men at MTI."

19. This comment by Brian Russell indicates that the two engineers—Roger Boisjoly and Arnie Thompson—who challenged the authority of management during the off-line caucus were acting as spokespersons for the other eight engineers.

20. Lund simply was not "jumping" from one masculinity to another. To "do" manager masculinity in this setting required Lund to actively demasculinize what had previously been an acceptable masculine practice for him (opposing the launch). When asked by the President's Commission (pp. 1568-1569) why he changed his mind when he changed his hat, Lund responded by supporting Mulloy's gendered dichotomy discussed above: irrational-qualitative (wimpish) versus rational-quantitative (masculine). In short, by supporting the launch, Lund was able to patently separate himself from what the particular situation of the caucus defined as "wimpish" and, therefore, be assessed as normatively masculine.

References

Acker, J. (1990). Hierarchies, jobs, bodies: A theory of gendered organizations. *Gender & Society, 4*(2), 139-158.

Acker, J. (1992). Gendering organizational theory. In A. J. Mills & P. Tancred (Eds.), *Gendering organizational analysis* (pp. 248-260). Newbury Park, CA: Sage.

Arch, E. C. (1993). Risk-taking: A motivational basis for sex differences. *Psychological Reports, 73,* 3-11.

Beirne, P., & Messerschmidt, J. W. (1995). *Criminology* (2nd ed.). San Diego, CA: Harcourt Brace.

Boisjoly, R. M. (1987, December). *Ethical decisions: Morton Thiokol and the Space Shuttle* Challenger *disaster.* Paper presented at the annual meeting of the American Society of Mechanical Engineers, Boston.

Clatterbaugh, K. (1990). *Contemporary perspectives on masculinity.* Boulder, CO: Westview.

Cockburn, C. (1983). *Brothers: Male dominance and technological change.* London: Pluto.

Cockburn, C. (1985). *Machinery of dominance: Women, men and technical knowhow.* London: Pluto.

Cockburn, C., & Ormrod, S. (1993). *Gender and technology in the making.* Newbury Park, CA: Sage.

Cohn, C. (1987). Sex and death in the rational world of defense intellectuals. *Signs, 12*(4), 687-718.

Cohn, C. (1995). Wars, wimps, and women: Talking gender and thinking war. In M. S. Kimmel and M. A. Messner (Eds.), *Men's lives* (pp. 131-143). Boston: Allyn & Bacon.

Connell, R. W. (1987). *Gender and power: Society, the person, and sexual politics.* Stanford, CA: Stanford University Press.

Connell, R. W. (1995a). *Masculinities.* Berkeley: University of California Press.

Connell, R. W. (1995b). Masculinity, violence, and war. In M. S. Kimmel & M. A. Messner (Eds.), *Men's lives* (pp. 125-130). Boston: Allyn & Bacon.

David, D. S., & Brannon, R. (1976). *The forty-nine percent majority: The male sex role.* Reading, MA: Addison-Wesley.

Donaldson, M. (1993). What is hegemonic masculinity? *Theory and Society, 22,* 643-657.

Driscoll, D. M., & Goldberg, C. R. (1993). *Members of the club: The coming of age of executive women.* New York: Free Press.

Dubinskas, F. A. (1988). Janus organizations: Scientists and managers in genetic engineering firms. In F. A. Dubinskas (Ed.), *Making time: Ethnographies of high technology organizations* (pp. 170-232). Philadelphia: Temple University Press.

Florman, S. C. (1976). *The existential pleasures of engineering.* New York: St. Martin's.

Giddens, A. (1989). A reply to my critics. In D. Held & J. B. Thompson (Eds.), *Social theory of modern societies: Anthony Giddens and his critics* (pp. 249-301). New York: Cambridge University Press.

Hacker, S. (1989). *Pleasure, power and technology: Some tales of gender, engineering, and the cooperative workplace.* Boston: Unwin Hyman.

Kanter, R. M. (1977). *Men and women of the corporation.* New York: Basic Books.

Kerfoot, D., & Knights, D. (1993). Management, masculinity, and manipulation: From paternalism to corporate strategy in financial services in Britain. *Journal of Management Studies, 30*(4), 659-677.

Kessler, S., & McKenna, W. (1978). *Gender: An ethnomethodological approach.* New York: John Wiley.

Kramer, R. C. (1992). The Space Shuttle *Challenger* explosion: A case study of state-corporate crime. In K. Schlegel & D. Weisburg (Eds.), *White-collar crime reconsidered* (pp. 214-243). Boston: Northeastern University Press.

Luhman, N. (1993). *Risk: A sociological theory.* New York: Aldine.

Maier, M. (1993). "Am I the only one who wants to launch?" Corporate masculinity and the Space Shuttle *Challenger* Disaster. *Masculinities, 1*(1-2), 34-45.

March, J. G., & Shapira, Z. (1987). Managerial perspectives on risk and risk-taking. *Management Science, 33*(11), 1404-1418.

McConnell, M. (1987). Challenger: *A major malfunction.* Garden City, NY: Doubleday.

Messerschmidt, J. W. (1993). *Masculinities and crime: Critique and reconceptualization of theory.* Lanham, MD: Rowman & Littlefield.

Morgan, D. H. J. (1992). *Discovering men.* New York: Routledge.

President's Commission. (1986). *Report of the Presidential Commission on the Space Shuttle* Challenger *accident.* Washington, DC: Government Printing Office.

Sellin, T. (1938). *Culture, conflict, and crime.* New York: Social Science Research Council.

Short, J. F., & Clarke, L. (Eds.). (1992). *Organizations, uncertainties, and risk.* Boulder, CO: Westview.

Starbuck, W. H., & Milliken, F. J. (1988). *Challenger:* Fine-tuning the odds until something breaks. *Journal of Management Studies, 25*(4), 319-340.

Thorne, B. (1993). *Gender play: Girls and boys in schools.* New Brunswick, NJ: Rutgers University Press.

Tolson, A. (1977). *The limits of masculinity.* New York: Harper & Row.

Vaughan, D. (1983). *Controlling unlawful organizational behavior: Social structure and corporate misconduct.* Chicago: University of Chicago Press.

Vaughan, D. (1989). Regulating risk: Implications of the *Challenger* accident. *Law and Policy, 11*(3), 330-349.

Vaughan, D. (1994, August). *Risk, work group culture, and the normalization of deviance: NASA and the Space Shuttle* Challenger. Paper presented at the annual meetings of the American Sociological Association, Los Angeles.

Wajcman, J. (1991). *Feminism confronts technology.* University Park, PA: Pennsylvania State University Press.

West, C., & Fenstermaker, S. (1993). Power, inequality and the accomplishment of gender: An ethnomethodological view. In P. England (Ed.), *Theory on gender/feminism on theory* (pp. 151-174). New York: Aldine.

West, C., & Zimmerman, D. H. (1987). Doing gender. *Gender & Society 1*(2), 125-151.

Willis, P. E. (1979). Shop floor culture, masculinity, and the wage form. In J. Clarke, C. Critcher, & R. Johnson (Eds.), *Working-class culture* (pp. 185-198). London: Hutchinson.

3

The Last Bastion of Masculinity

Gender Politics at The Citadel

JUDI ADDELSTON
MICHAEL STIRRATT

The Citadel, an all-male public college currently fighting litigation designed to admit women to the institution, illustrates the construction and fragility of hegemonic masculinity. This chapter will use the story of this litigation as a descriptive analysis of hegemonic masculinity. We are not testing an hypothesis; rather, we will use The Citadel as a case study to illuminate the construction of hegemonic masculinity. For more than 150 years, The Citadel has provided education and paramilitary training to male cadets with the aim of turning boys into "whole men." The public status of the institution has recently sparked a legal initiative to force the school to enroll women. Proponents of The Citadel have vigorously argued against the admittance of women, arguing that the presence of women would destroy the school's unique masculine character and mission, effectively collapsing both the walls of the institution and the boundaries of the whole man. The situation facing The Citadel was summarized by the words of a guidance counselor at the school who stated that members of the institution were in an "all-out fight to protect one of the last bastions of true masculinity left in the United States."[1]

This chapter is a qualitative study of an all-male institution currently involved in litigation to desegregate by sex. We will be viewing this institution through the two lenses of gender politics and institutional elitism. Although it is useful to identify these two strands of theory and research in analyzing this case, more often than not, the issues presented are so closely interwoven as to make separating them impossible. However, a detailed understanding of these two issues provides a comprehensive framework with which to view The Citadel. In this sense, we are viewing The Citadel as a "total institution" (Goffman, 1961).

Although writing about The Citadel as if it were an individual is grammatically awkward and ontologically misrepresentative, we will nevertheless portray The Citadel by the public voice it has used during these proceedings, as that is how the institution portrays itself. This voice encompasses the words of administrators, lawyers, public relations staff, cadets, expert witnesses, courtroom testimony, and media accounts. It is the collective opinions of this group of people that we invoke when we talk about The Citadel. We will also present the voices of individuals at The Citadel who do not echo this "party line"; there is a distinct difference between the collective voice and the individual voice at The Citadel.

We will not, however, present the story of Shannon Faulkner. Her fight to become a cadet has been well-documented in other publications (Applebome, 1995; Decker, 1995; Manegold, 1994; Peyser, 1995). Rather, we will use the ideological debates spurred by her court battle to investigate the dialectics of hegemonic masculinity. The possible entrance of a female into the male corp of cadets highlights the difference between sex and gender. Sex is a biological category based on anatomy; gender is the social interpretation of sex (Unger, 1979). Shannon Faulkner embodies The Citadel's anxieties about the conflation of these two concepts. If a *female* were to enter the corps, then becoming a "whole man"—the *performance* of hegemonic masculinity—is called into question. For if a woman can render the same performance as a man—achieve a Citadel degree—then there is little left to The Citadel's claims of the sexual dimorphism necessary to *create* "whole men" (Morgan, 1994).

The Citadel

The Citadel was founded in Charleston, South Carolina, in 1842. The school's defining characteristics are the all-male student population and the intensive program of paramilitary training that structures every aspect of life at the institution. The Citadel's all-male status is prescribed by its mission to mold student cadets into "whole men." The school handbook explains that the school aspires to

> develop and graduate "the whole man." The Citadel System is the completeness with which it matures, refines, trains and schools the totality of a young man's character. This finely balanced process is called the "whole man" concept. During four years, cadets will develop academically, physically, militarily and spiritually. (The Citadel, 1992-1993, p. 22)

Although The Citadel was originally founded to benefit "the poor but deserving boys of the state" (The Citadel, 1992, p. 32), the institution's long history in the South has elevated it to an elite status. Many Citadel "families" pass the privilege of attending the school from father to son, building an intergenerational tradition of fraternity surrounding the school.

For proponents of The Citadel, the key to turning boys into men is rigorous training and discipline in an exclusive homosocial environment. A rigid paramilitary hierarchy,[2] termed the Fourth Class System, teaches discipline to male cadets through a demanding code of conduct. In this system, the first-year cadets, called "knobs" due to the appearance of their shaved heads, have the lowest status at the school. Knob cadets must conform to special limitations on their behavior, while confronting harassment from upperclassmen and torturous initiation rites. Under the Fourth Class System at The Citadel, cadets gain greater status and privileges as they progress through their 4 years at the school, but they continue to be held to the institution's strict paramilitary rules and regulations.

The Citadel receives about 25% of its funding from South Carolina. The financial support of the state makes The Citadel and a similar school, The Virginia Military Institute, the only all-male, *publicly* funded colleges in the United States. Due to their status as publicly funded institutions that enroll only male students, these schools have been embroiled in litigation aimed at opening their doors to women.[3] In 1992, high school senior Shannon Faulkner was admitted to the school on the basis of her qualifications as detailed in an application that omitted any reference to her gender. On discovering her gender, The Citadel administration revoked her acceptance, and she then sued for access to the school. By order of the Supreme Court, Faulkner was admitted to the corps of cadets in the fall of 1995.[4]

Theories of Hegemonic Masculinity

Theories of hegemonic masculinity will provide a framework for interpreting the situation at The Citadel. Until recently, psychological research has typically conceptualized masculinity as a monolithic set of personality traits and behaviors, such as aggressiveness and inexpressiveness, that are present or absent in varying degrees within the individual (Morawski, 1985; Pleck, 1987). Social constructionist perspectives have produced the understanding that multiple forms of masculinity operate within society (Carrigan, Connell, & Lee, 1987; Connell, 1993). Feminist and postmodern critiques have underscored numerous limitations presented by defining masculinity as a unidimensional, bipolar trait. Such a conception of masculinity isolates the social phenomena of gender within the person and obscures the enactment of gender within social contexts and power relationships (Carrigan et al., 1987; West & Zimmerman, 1991). Recent conceptualizations of masculinities understand men's gender identity as a malleable construction, shaped by interpersonal, situational, and historical forces (Brod, 1987; Connell, 1993, 1995; Kimmel & Messner, 1992).

Hegemonic masculinity, as one prevalent form of masculinity, has supplanted traditional notions of the male sex role (Pleck, 1987). The term *hegemonic* is used to emphasize the dominance of this masculine paradigm within gender order among men. Hegemonic masculinity has been succinctly defined as "stark homophobia, misogyny, and domestic patriarchy" (Connell, 1993, p. 618). The nuances of hegemonic masculinity include

> the dread of and the flight from women. A culturally idealized form, it is both a personal and a collective project, and is the common sense about breadwinning and manhood. It is exclusive, anxiety-provoking, internally and hierarchically differentiated, brutal and violent. It is pseudo-natural, tough, contradictory, crisis-prone, rich, and socially sustained. Although centrally connected with the institutions of male dominance, not all men practice it, though most benefit from it. (Donaldson, 1993, pp. 645-646)

Two concepts related to hegemonic masculinity are hypermasculinity, defined as "exaggerated, extreme masculine behavior" (Pleck, 1987, p. 31), and protest masculinity, defined as the "instances of extreme sex-typed behavior on the part of some males . . . who are in conflict about or who are insecure about their identities as males" (Broude, 1990, p. 103). Both of these definitions are incorporated within the concept of hegemonic masculinity. By any name, this phenomenon involves behavior considered to be extremely masculine and an assertion of male entitlement.

It is our thesis that, although hegemonic masculinity invokes the power of male privilege, it is also a fragile construction due to its challenging prescriptions and its fundamental opposition to women and gay men. The social sciences and popular culture have often viewed the development of manhood as a treacherous path, fraught with the obstacles of overbearing mothers, absent fathers, feminized schools, homosexual influences, an increasingly bureaucratic workforce, and women's encroachment on traditional male spaces (Ehrenreich, 1983; Hantover, 1978; Herek, 1986; Kimmel, 1987; Pleck, 1987; Segal, 1990; Sexton, 1969). Moreover, hegemonic masculinity is narrowly defined by what it is drawn in opposition to: women, gay men, effeminacy, and so on. Without these borders to police and preserve the context of hegemonic masculinity, the construct begins to unravel. Donaldson (1993), therefore, summarizes the duality of hegemonic masculinity with the statement, "fragile it may be, but it constructs the most dangerous things we live with" (p. 646).

Method

A particularly rich understanding of the situation facing The Citadel emerges from background research that we conducted for the expert testimony of Dr. Michelle Fine. Dr. Fine is a social psychologist at the City University of New York Graduate Center who specializes in research on gender and education. She was asked by the American Civil Liberties Union (ACLU) to be an expert witness for the prosecution. In turn, she asked us, her research assistants, to investigate hegemonic masculinity at The Citadel. Not only was our area of academic research in gender and organizations, but our personal histories combined to afford us unique insights into this paramilitary fraternity—Judi had served in the Israeli army and Mike had been president of his fraternity in college.[5]

The research presented here, solicited by Dr. Fine and the ACLU, includes numerous sources of data that allow for a descriptive analysis of the gender dynamic surrounding The Citadel at this critical moment in its history. These data sources include court depositions and testimony (Faulkner, 1993; Rembert, 1993; Riesman, 1991; Snyder, 1993; Vergnolle, 1993), school documents and publications (The Citadel, 1992, 1992-1993), and media accounts and scholarly works regarding the situation at The Citadel (Applebome, 1995; Faludi, 1994; Mahan & Mahan, 1993; Smothers, 1994). Several days of observation, interviews, and focus groups with cadets, faculty, administrators, and staff during two site visits to the school in 1993 and 1994 were also provided for Dr. Fine's testimony

(Addelston, 1994; Addelston & Stirratt, 1993). The emergent themes from this research are recorded here.

Hegemonic Masculinity at The Citadel

The development and performance of hegemonic masculinity is a vital task for Citadel cadets. As delineated in The Citadel's mission statement, the explicit purpose of the school is to develop the "whole man." For The Citadel, the key ingredient of this process is the homosocial atmosphere, the immersion in an all-male culture. One cadet related a metaphor that Citadel instructors often use to explain the "whole man" philosophy to cadets:

> A whole man is like a table with four sturdy legs. The four legs of the table represent a solid grounding in the academic, military, physical, and spiritual realms, and the table top represents the attainment of the ideals of honor and loyalty. If one leg of the table is not well formed, then the entirety of the table—the whole man—is unsound.

Because the goal of becoming a whole man is held as the paramount aim for cadets at The Citadel, the elements of a whole man can be examined to illuminate the performance of masculinity at The Citadel. The following analysis will focus on the academic, military, and physical components of the "whole man."

Academically, many cadets stated that they attend The Citadel to experience the discipline of its academic program and to improve their grades. The school aims to promote study habits among cadets by reserving several hours of "study periods" each day during which cadets are to required to do homework. Many cadets felt that this programming and the austere environment at The Citadel helped them with their studies. Several cadets explained that their high school grades had suffered through involvement with partying, girlfriends, or alcohol and drug use, and that they have been able to reform their study habits at The Citadel. A sophomore cadet offered himself as evidence, stating, "Look, in high school I had a 2.3 GPA, but now I've got a solid 3.2."

The academic rigors of The Citadel are often undermined on several fronts, however. Although the cadets cited academics at The Citadel as one of its strengths, the school is ranked fourth out of five categories of academic competitiveness by *Barron's Profiles of American Colleges*

(Barron's Educational Series, 1992), earning the category "Less Competitive." Colleges in this category "admit students with averages below C who rank in the top 65% of the graduating class" and "usually admit 85% or more of their applicants" (p. 254). A female psychology professor confessed that the strenuous paramilitary training and hazing at the school meant that "invariably, there are two or three students who sleep through every class." One senior cadet explained that he believed the study periods were instituted to compensate for this problem, "so that we don't get overwhelmed with the military training." He also explained that cadets vary in the seriousness with which they use these hours; he preferred to spend them in the library, studying and talking with his girlfriend.[6]

The academic realm aids in the production of hegemonic masculinity through the social dynamics of the all-male classroom. Many cadets state that the absence of women in the classroom keeps them focused on their studies instead of interaction with women. One faculty member echoed this point, testifying that the "introduction [of] females in the classroom [would] distract the cadets because they are lusty" (Rembert, 1993, p. 87). The all-male classroom also shapes the relationship between students and faculty. A junior cadet, asked to explain who his favorite professors were, cited a male English teacher who, the cadet explained, was

> just cool . . . like, the first day of class, he will give this big speech about literature, and then he'll sit at his desk and say, "this semester, we're going to study the finer texts," and then he'll hold up a *Penthouse* that he has under his desk.

The cadet went on to say that his act inevitably produced a strong outburst of laughter among the student cadets. In this incident, the male faculty member used the homosocial context of the classroom to bond with the students through the pornographic ostracism of women. This "academic" exercise helps to establish women as the denigrated out-group.

Militarily, Citadel cadets hone their performance of hegemonic masculinity through the demands of the school's hierarchical Fourth Class System. This process begins on the first day when each cadet receives a short military haircut and the official uniform of The Citadel to be worn at all times. The cadets are organized into squads and receive military training to obey orders and act as a cohesive unit. Under the Fourth Class System, each cadet is subject to the authority of older upperclassmen and a specific code of conduct, and cadets gain status and privileges as they advance through the system. First-year knobs have the lowest status at the school and must conform to numerous restrictions placed on their conduct. Knobs are required to walk in the gutters and streets of the campus and never on the sidewalks or lawns, and during meals they are allowed to eat only after they have served the upperclassmen and have received permission to commence eating. Rooms in the barracks have no locks on the doors, allowing upper-class cadets to burst into knob rooms for inspections at any hour. The grueling nature of this system is reflected in the fact that approximately 15% of each knob class drops out of the school within the first month, and that the school publishes a handbook for parents to help them and their sons understand and adjust to the process (The Citadel, 1992).

The performance of hegemonic masculinity lies at the core of The Citadel's paramilitary training. Many cadets were aware of the rigorous demands of the Fourth Class System before they enrolled in The Citadel and cited this training as a reason they chose the school. A cadet in his junior year saw the paramilitary training as a test of his manhood, explaining, "I figured that if I could make it at The Citadel, I could make it anywhere." One Citadel administrator commented on his belief that the Fourth Class System had a transformative effect on cadets, stating that "lots of boys [who come here] are nerds and this place turns them around." The paramilitary structure of the institution not only provides cadets with a test of their masculinity, but it also unites them within a fraternal bond. One Citadel graduate explained, "I personally think the greatest experience I had at The Citadel was the experience I had learning how to become a team with my fellow classmates." Finally, the paramilitary training at The Citadel provides a context for cadets to display their masculinity before others. Every Friday afternoon, the cadets participate in a drill exercise and march before spectators who are usually composed of girlfriends, families, and school alumni. Taking the field in full-dress uniforms, rifles in hand, these cadets work to demonstrate their military precision and masculine prowess to themselves and to others.[7]

Physically, cadets at The Citadel prove their masculinity by engaging in sports, intensive training, and punishing hazing practices. Citadel athletes are pushed to great lengths to succeed in their sporting activities. The irony of being on a sports team at The Citadel is that athletes are expected to win every game (and often hazed if they do not). Also, they are not highly regarded by their peers, because they get out of many of the military exercises, replacing them with athletic practice (cf. Drescher, 1992).

Citadel cadets also endure a series of physically punishing institutionalized rituals and incidents of informal hazing. Near the end of the school year, knob cadets traditionally engage in the "stair-rushing ceremony." In this ritual, members of the knob class must successfully mount a flight of stairs in the barracks that is obstructed by senior class members. During a site visit to the school, this "ceremony" left one knob cadet hospitalized with a leg injury, and a senior cadet explained that several cadets invariably wind up in the infirmary after this ceremony. Another cadet described the birthday ceremony where a cadet's birthday is celebrated by stripping him of his clothes and tying him naked to a chair in the middle of the foyer of the barracks. One graduate explained the following:

> On one's birthday at The Citadel, if you are unlucky enough to have your birthday fall between September and June while you were in school, your classmates come and get you and they take all your clothes off. They take the black kind of dye that goes around the edges of your shoes and they paint your testicles. (Snyder, 1993, p. 34)

These types of rituals and hazing practices create a sense among the cadets that they have shared intimate experiences and have surmounted difficult tasks designed to test their masculinity. Snyder goes on to narrate the importance of this fraternal bond:

> I think everybody who ever meets a group or whoever has contact with The Citadel, will tell you its a special group. That they cannot believe that there is no [other] fraternity that has that closeness. . . . It's kind of like a brotherhood, or a fraternity of men that will stand by one another, that will fight for one another, that will do everything they can to help each other. (pp. 69, 71)

As in the homosocial bonding within fraternities, this creates a sense of in-group solidarity and superiority (Sanday, 1990).

Interpretations of Masculine Fortifications at The Citadel

As a "bastion of masculinity," certain objects at The Citadel act as "fortifications" that perpetuate masculine practices at the school and demark these practices from the outside world. These objects—the barracks, the uniforms, and The Ring—illustrate the meaning and practice of manhood at The Citadel. In each of these fortifications, we see the construction of The Citadel as a fragile institution, sheltering rites of manhood from the contaminating presence of women.

The confines of the barracks cloak a number of unofficial ceremonies at The Citadel that are predicated on nudity and hazing, such as the birthday ceremony.[8] Hazing, although forbidden, is practiced in the barracks away from the purview of the school's administrators. One such hazing practice is stringing up a cadet nude and threatening him with a sword near his testicles (Drescher, 1992). The barracks shelter these hazing rites that are designed to test the cadet's (hegemonic) masculinity and unofficially help to create the "whole man."

In the push to build the "whole man," the uniform is another essential ingredient necessary in ironing out difference and patching together manly solidarity. As Morgan (1994) states, "The uniform absorbs individualities into a generalized and timeless masculinity while also connoting a control of emotion and a subordination to a higher rationality" (p. 166). The homogenizing purpose behind the uniforms is most clear in the school's rhetoric around race that one administrator summarized by referencing the gray cadet uniforms: "I don't see black and white, just gray." However, one wonders how successful the uniform is at achieving such ends given the number of racist incidents of the school over the years.[9] Nonetheless, the uniforms intend to strip the cadets of their individual identities and foster a sense of solidarity and in-group equality.

The Ring is another material embodiment of masculinity at The Citadel. The goal for each Citadel cadet is to graduate from the school and receive "The Ring," a symbol for the completion of the school's demanding military regimen and the attainment of manhood. The attainment of The Ring is so important to some cadets that they initially tie it to their hand to ensure that it is not lost or stolen. The masculine symbolism of The Ring is evidenced by the unwillingness of cadets to have women touch or try on The Ring. When a female interviewer asked one cadet to show her his Ring, he adamantly stated that "you can't try it on though—that would bring bad luck." The Ring signifies attainment of manhood and membership in the exclusive fraternity of The Citadel. As such, one cadet mentioned a time when he was "nearly knocking over tables and chairs" in a restaurant to reach another man who was wearing The Ring. When the uniform comes off, and masculinity can no longer be contained by the gray, The Ring becomes the symbol of masculinity. In many ways, The Ring may be seen in the same light as a wedding ring; The Ring binds the cadet to The Citadel and all it embodies until death.

"Skirts," "Fags," and the Rhetoric of Difference

In providing an institutional context for the performance of hegemonic masculinity and the development of a male social identity, the all-male structure of The Citadel isolates women and gay men as critical out-groups that unite Citadel men into a collective masculine entity. Paramilitary trainers and peers constantly hold cadets to standards of hegemonic masculinity and chastise them through comparisons to women and gay men. One Citadel alumnus testified that at The Citadel, you could either be a

> "whole man" [or] a fag, a woman. Those are your choices. Get the ring or be a woman and that is the way it is presented to you every day. You spend your entire career . . . connoting women with negativism. When you screw up, you are a woman. I came out of The Citadel thinking that I was automatically fundamentally more superior than half of the human race. Every time I did anything wrong at The Citadel, someone made the point of telling me I was, with expletives, a woman, you're weak, why don't you go to a woman's school, you belong in a woman's school. What is the matter, are you having your period? Why can't you do the push ups? Are you a woman? Why don't we go get a skirt for you? (Vergnolle, 1993, pp. 80-84)

To explain this virulent misogyny, Riesman (1991) has testified that "boy's schools [are] permeated with boys values, and boys gain self-esteem and self-confidence by depreciation of girls and women" (p. 103). In this way, the construction of the "whole man" at The Citadel is predicated on denigrating women and gay men as out-groups.

The cadets speak very clearly and vehemently about their desire and need to exclude women from The Citadel. Many cadets said they passed over other coed schools and specifically came to The Citadel to avoid women's influence in their lives. In one focus group, all the cadets strongly agreed with the comment of one cadet who said that women in the classroom would "contaminate" the learning environment, because the male cadets would no longer feel able to speak or act freely in the classroom. The unity that the all-male environment provides them would be adversely affected by women who would contaminate their vehicle to becoming "whole men." For many cadets, the solution is to close the school and "just kill The Citadel" before admitting women; it would no longer be The Citadel if women were there. They see The Citadel as a haven, a place where the very structure and essence of the school protects them from outside forces that they see as obstacles on the road to manhood. Women embody those dangers through ideologies of oppositional difference; only in a woman-free space can they unite to truly become men (cf. Deaux, 1985).

To justify the exclusion of women from the corps of cadets, The Citadel relies on a rhetoric of gender differences (Fine & Addelston, 1996). These arguments outline differences between women and men physically, psychologically, and socially. In addition, they heighten concerns about male privilege and practical concerns regarding the admittance of women. One aspect of this discourse focuses on physical differences between men and women. Many of the cadets view women as physically weaker than themselves and, therefore, unable to meet the rigorous paramilitary style of The Citadel especially during the demanding "knob year." During a focus group, one cadet offered the example of a march where he had to carry an M-60, a heavy machine gun. He felt that a woman would not be able to carry this gun and, that if women were on that march, he and the other men would have to take extra duties to accommodate the women. The cadets felt that the paramilitary tasks and the physical hazing met by the cadets would need to be diluted for the women, and this, they claimed, would lower the standards at The Citadel and create resentment among the male cadets. In another example, all cadets have their heads shaved on entering The Citadel. Most cadets we spoke with said that they would want the women to shave their heads too, but they worried that this would not be required of the women, creating a difference that they found upsetting. The cadets claim the presence of "weak" women would depress them because of the supposed special treatment the women would require in the corps.

The second element of the gender difference rhetoric is psychological. Many cadets detailed the extreme physical and psychological stress induced by the grueling knob year and confessed their doubts that women could successfully complete such an emotionally demanding year. Two faculty members at The Citadel echoed this position by (mis)appropriating psychological research in a report justifying the exclusion of women from the school (Mahan & Mahan, 1993). They claim that the psychological research of Gilligan (1982) and Deaux (1985) demonstrates that women and men learn, interact, develop, and behave differently. This is cause for maintaining a woman-free environment for the cadets so they may develop "in freedom . . . away from the mother-dominant home . . . and safe from female reaction" (p. 3).

In arguing for the exclusion of women, The Citadel also underscores gender differences within the realm of social interaction. Many cadets felt that, if women were present, "good manners" would require them to pay greater attention to their personal appearance and demeanor. This relates to arguments that maintain that women in the classroom would be distracting, because women would divert the men from their scholarship by causing the cadets to think about sex. In this perspective, the construal of women shifts from that of a weak vessel unable to endure the rigors of The Citadel to a powerful threat of temptation to the cadets. However, women still remain delicate social entities in other ways. If women were admitted, the cadets also feel that they would no longer be able to use vulgar language because "ladies" are not supposed to hear such words. When a female interviewer asked several cadets to state the "bad" words that they used, they refused to speak them, claiming propriety. Ironically, women are thus construed to be at once weak and powerful agents that threaten The Citadel.

The Citadel further justifies the exclusion of women from the school through an assertion of male entitlement and privilege. Many cadets emphasize that they deliberately chose to attend The Citadel over other coed schools, because they wanted to immerse themselves in its all-male culture and participate in the attendant benefits of its fraternity. One cadet said that rather than enrolling in less expensive coed schools, he "paid good money" to experience The Citadel's all-male program. Many of the cadets further felt that admitting women to The Citadel would prompt a "lowering of standards" in the form of a weakened Fourth Class System and relaxed physical demands within the paramilitary training. Both in focus groups and individually, cadets claim that West Point and Annapolis had to lower their standards after women were admitted to these institutions, causing the schools to lose their respected, privileged status (Yoder, 1989).

Finally, The Citadel denies women access to the school due to practical concerns about the costs of integrating women into the corps of cadets. These arguments are based on the premise that women would require a separate barracks and new uniforms, and that there is no money to invest in these enterprises. If women were to be admitted, the school's preliminary plan would be to house them in the infirmary. Many people also feel that The Ring, as a potent symbol of the attainment of manhood, would need to be redesigned if women were admitted. Not only would smaller sizes be needed, but a new model should be designed to represent the fundamental change in the school. Concerns for The Ring and what it represents are so strong that one graduating cadet said that "if women come here, I'm not gonna wear my Ring."

Another key ingredient in making the "whole man" is the homosociality of The Citadel; homosociality defined by "social preferences for members of one's own gender but does not necessarily imply erotic attraction" (Britton, 1990, p. 423). There is much evidence of homophobia on campus; for example, when we asked the editor of the school newspaper about homosexuality on campus, he quickly replied it did not exist. Yet after a brief pause, he acknowledged that "about every three years, they catch two guys fooling around and throw them out." Citadel alumnus Vergnolle (1993) tells that one way to humiliate another cadet is to call him a "fag." The threat of being labeled a homosexual was used "jokingly" in one class we observed; the (male) professor chastised a cadet who was talking to a fellow student by saying, "Stop talking to your boyfriend."

Britton (1990) demonstrates that homophobia is an essential ingredient in the maintenance of patriarchal organizations and is even more virulent in same-sex institutions because "homophobia helps maintain the boundary between social and sexual interaction in a sex-segregated society" (p. 424). More pointedly,

> violations of prevailing norms threaten the collectivity. Homophobia's identity maintenance function [is the] fear of being labeled deviant [that] unites members. Men homosocial in outlook prefer other men's company and work to maintain all-male institutions. The relationship to homophobia lies in maintaining the boundary between social and sexual interaction in a homosocially stratified society. (p. 425)

Shilts (1993) also documents how homophobia is used as a tool to create a cohesive in-group in the armed forces. The Citadel is thus able to use homophobia as a tool to promote the homosocial bonding it requires to create the "whole man."

Collective and Individual Voices

"Just Say No . . . To Women At The Citadel"
—Bumper sticker on a cadet's car

"Death Before Dikes" (sic)
—Bumper sticker on a cadet's car

"Save the Males!"
—Button worn by cadets
at Citadel trial

The justifications for the exclusion of women described above permeate the collective voice of The Citadel cadets. In talking with groups in the classrooms, mess hall, or barracks, the cadets did not deviate from this "party line" while they were speaking in front of one another. Indeed, during a classroom focus group or at a mess hall lunch table, the cadets would often not only agree with one another, but they would even collectively advance an argument or describe a situation by building off of one another's sentences, creating a single coherent narrative from the voices of several individuals. The cadets' collective voice sheds insight into their notions of masculinity as they describe their attraction to The Citadel and the problems they have regarding the admission of women.

However, the collective voice the young men use when speaking in group situations often fractures within individual narratives. The contrast that may exist between collective and individual voices was illustrated by the case of one cadet. This cadet, when speaking before a group of his peers in a classroom focus group, was adamant about keeping women out of The Citadel, because he felt women would adversely affect his classroom studies. However, when we spoke with his professor after the group session, we found out that this cadet was taking classes at the (coed) College of Charleston and had privately told his professor how much he enjoyed having women in the classroom as there was more diversity and a wider range of opinions and ideas.[10]

Not every cadet feels that change at The Citadel is bad. Several of the seniors we spoke with alone feel that it is fine for women to be at The Citadel, but they are very glad to be leaving before that happens. They are happy that they were able to go through The Citadel the way it is now; they feel they benefited from their experiences, and feel sorry for the men in future classes because they will have to deal with the school as coed. Most of the African American and Hispanic cadets with whom we spoke agreed that if women want to come to The Citadel and are able to meet the physical requirements and survive the Fourth Class system, then they should be allowed to do so. They feel that no one should be excluded based on a social category but that anyone who can do the required work should be allowed to participate. One black cadet, who has publicly expressed his support for women entering The Citadel, used analogies of race to illustrate this point. He stated that when black cadets entered The Citadel, standards were kept the same but were altered slightly to accommodate the needs of the black cadets. He used the example of shaving. All cadets must be clean shaven at all times, yet this would create skin rashes for black cadets, who are thus allowed to shave every other day. And, he said, "The walls of The Citadel did not fall."

Almost all of the cadets we spoke with one-on-one said that although they are not happy about women coming to The Citadel, they see it as an inevitable event. Several cadets gave possible solutions to housing women cadets in this context. Some suggested that another barracks could be built, and one cadet said that they could use the existing barracks and alternate single-sex floors. This indicates that some cadets are thinking (albeit individually) of *how* and not *whether* women will be housed at The Citadel.

Another discrepancy between the collective and individual voice was heard in discussing academics. In group situations, especially in the classrooms, cadets claimed that the rigors of The Citadel helped them improve their academic standing. However, an alternative story was heard in talking individually with the cadets. Many cadets told us privately that their grades had slipped during the knob year due to the ordeal of paramilitary training. They stated that they did not have sufficient time or energy to put into their schoolwork, as the Fourth Class System took up most of their time. Several cadets said they would often fall asleep in class due to the fatigue of hazing and training. In addition, some seniors we spoke with said that their grades suffered in their last year due to excessive drinking and partying on weekends.

Many cadets said privately that if women are able to perform the physical tasks of The Citadel, they should be admitted. They could see women being admitted but were very clear that they did not want to see women get special treatment. The key for these cadets was that the system stay the same. The cadets did not want to see The Citadel's system of discipline and rigor changed.

We see, then, a tension between the official ideology of the organization and individual voices. Morgan (1994) claims this tension arises because of the conflicts in ideology between a military institution that focuses on a group identity and a liberal democracy that focuses on the rights of the individual. As The Citadel is a paramilitary organization, we can see that "there seems to be a possibility and indeed the requirement for the elaboration of a range of masculinities rather than a single hegemonic masculinity. Such a range is obviously not without bounds and some masculinities are more hegemonic than others. However, the military cannot be seen as straightforwardly a site for the construction of a single embodied masculinity" (p. 174).

Women at The Citadel

Despite all the claims The Citadel makes that women would be a distraction to the cadets and that the cadets need a male-only environment, there are women everywhere on The Citadel campus, both physically and symbolically. First, about 15% of the faculty are women.[11] The second category of women are on the staff: the secretaries, who are predominantly white, and the kitchen staff, who are black. The third category of women are the cadets' girlfriends. Although women are not allowed in the barracks, when the cadets are free to leave the campus, there are many young women hanging out outside the gates of each barrack. The fourth category of women are the night students and all the women who have access to the sports facilities and the library. We spoke with several women night students and they were uniform in their conviction that The Citadel should be coed, because they pay taxes that support the school. The fifth category of women, the mothers, are symbolically present as icons for the cadets to respect, yet distance from. The final category of women must also be imported. They are the icons of contempt used to insult and denigrate a cadet when he does not measure up to par.

Although women are present at The Citadel in many ways, the only category they are not present in is that of equal status peers. Research on the effects of equal status contact shows that it is an integral part of a comprehensive program to ameliorate prejudice (Katz & Taylor, 1988). The deleterious effects of lack of equal status contact between the male cadets and women is stated by a Citadel graduate: "[After graduation] I did not at the time know how to function around females who were my equals or superiors" (Vergnolle, 1993, p. 79). Another Citadel alumnus, who had joined the Army after graduation and was currently enrolled in the night program, told us that "these boys are in for a big shock when they join the real military because they will be operating with women as equals and superiors." This point is best narrated by a faculty member, also a Citadel graduate, who explained that "it's my belief that if the women are treated equally with the men, if regrettably they must attend The Citadel, *then it will cause the men to respect the women because there's not a double standard*" [italics added] (Rembert, 1993, p. 12). The importing of women as icons of contempt serves to police the borders of masculinity The Citadel strives to infuse into the cadets. These disdainful images of women remind the cadets to what depths they can fall if they do not measure up to The Citadel's standards of the "whole man." Deaux (1985) reports that these sex divisions serve to create oppositional categories; all that is "woman" is, therefore, "not man." This reinforces cadets' beliefs of differences between the sexes to maintain exclusionary practices and also serves to enhance in-group solidarity and boost self-esteem (Tajfel & Turner, 1979).

Conclusion

Each school has its own distinct "hidden curriculum" that is successfully absorbed by its students. The "hidden curriculum" within each school is the covert message that the school endorses and "teaches" to the students (Anyon, 1979). It is through this "hidden curriculum" that the fragility of hegemonic masculinity is best illustrated. Explicitly barring women from the corps, examples of *Penthouse* as great literature, being called a "skirt" or a "fag" in derision, and viewing women as contaminating agents are all examples of the "hidden curriculum." By giving the cadets women's backs to stand on, the cadets are psychologically elevated; by sacrificing the women to maintain their social order, the cadets reap social and economic benefits; denigration of homosexuals is used to bolster in-group cohesion. Ideological arguments for sameness and difference serve to camouflage possibilities for transformation and perpetuate institutional discriminatory practices. By making explicit what is illicit in hegemonic masculinity—power, hierarchy, and the denigration of out-groups—one is able to peel away the layers that hide the "hidden curriculum" of the institution. As a "total institution" (Goffman, 1961), The Citadel presents itself to the cadets as an all-encompassing monolith that holds total power over their lives. The uniform and hazing practices also serve to deindividuate the cadets and facilitate the degradation of the Self that The Citadel fosters to (re)build the "whole man" in its image.

Thus, the hidden curriculum at this total institution underscores how sex differences are used to justify exclusion, and how these differences illuminate the fragility of hegemonic masculinity. It is our thesis that hegemonic masculinity is inherently fragile, because it is built on the exclusion of the Other. Once members of the out-group become members of the in-group, what is left to bolster the "whole man?" The Citadel's mission is to create "whole men," a task they see as necessitating the exclusion of women and gay men; boys cannot become men unless they are in a (hetero) male-only environment and use women as a denigrated out-group to bolster their self-esteem as men. The subtext and "hidden curriculum" of the mission of The Citadel is that women and gay men are a bad influence on boys and must be kept out to promote boys' journey into manhood. If women and gay men, as out-groups, were to become part of the in-group, part of the corps, they would no longer be metaphorically available for the cadets to use as the denigrated Other. This construction of hegemonic masculinity is inherently fragile because its boundaries are precariously balanced on the exclusion of relevant out-groups. Should gay men and women penetrate this fortress of hegemonic masculinity, The Citadel believes its fortifications surrounding the "whole man" would collapse, and the institution would crumble.[12]

The Citadel's hidden curriculum has held men as distinct from and superior to women for more than 150 years. As The Citadel prepares for the landmark integration of women into its corps of cadets, the school will not only have to refine its mission, but the men of The Citadel will also need to redefine their version of masculinity. The presence of women as equal status peers will interrupt the homosociality of the organization and disable these men from propping their distinctive social identity on the crutch of an excluded and denigrated female out-group. Faulkner (1993, p. 19) herself has offered what is perhaps the best ideological suggestion for a gender integrated new Citadel, proposing that "it wouldn't be a brotherhood anymore, it would be a family."

Notes

1. The speaker of this quote is in essence stating that The Citadel is the last bastion of *hegemonic* masculinity.

2. Although The Citadel employs a paramilitary style, it is not formally connected to any of the branches of the Armed Services of America. Cadets wear uniforms and engage in the rudimentaries of a military-style basic training. ROTC exists on the campus, but only about 30% of the students enroll in it; the Fourth Class System and the paramilitary style of The Citadel are not connected to the ROTC program—rather—they *are* the essence of The Citadel.

3. The military service academies, such as West Point, opened their doors to women in 1976 (Yoder, 1989). It is ironic, then, that although The Citadel claims to emulate the military service academies, they are steadfast in their refusal to integrate by sex.

4. Shannon Faulkner dropped out of The Citadel after 1 week. She stated that the 2-year-long battle had taken its toll on her emotional health and she had become physically

ill during the first week in the corps. Her experience is not unlike that of the first African American children to attend white schools in Kansas; Shannon Faulkner was escorted at all times by Federal Marshals and had surveillance cameras placed outside her room. Apparently, the strength of hegemonic masculinity at The Citadel was powerful enough to push her out but not before she (an individual woman) terrorized an entire institution. Her legacy lies in all the women who are currently applying to The Citadel, about 200 in the last year, and with a female high school senior the courts have allowed to take Faulkner's place in the litigation.

5. Although we entered The Citadel with great trepidation and fears of being seen as "the enemy," we found an administration and a student body that was very willing to talk to us and present "their" side of the lawsuit. Both on and off the campus, cadets were eager to share with us their thoughts and feelings. We found a uniform story presented, regardless of whether Judi or Mike was asking questions. However, due to the sensitive nature of the legal proceedings, we were prohibited from taking names or identifying characteristics of respondents, including recording interviews and conversations, during our site visits to the school.

6. Although The Citadel is an all-male college, there are women everywhere on campus. The only place women are not allowed is in the barracks.

7. Each cadet is issued an M-14, with the firing pin removed. This illustrates what former Citadel president Vice-Admiral Stockdale called "playing soldier" (Drescher, 1993, p. 76). Faludi (1994) likens the impotence of the guns and other military hardware on the campus to "the over-all effect of a theme park for post-Cold War kids" (p. 64).

8. One cadet told us of the Senior Wool Burn that takes place at midnight on the quad. The seniors, just before they graduate, go to the quad wearing their winter wool uniforms, which are hated because they itch. They build a bonfire, strip, and throw their uniforms on the fire while dancing naked around it.

9. There have been several racist incidents over the years. The yearbooks from 1977 and 1982 portray cadets dressed as Klansmen (members of a white supremacy group) and in one photograph show the lynching of a black cadet. In 1987, a black student was awakened during the night by several other cadets in white hoods who left a burning paper cross in his room. Although he brought charges against them, they were not expelled but reprimanded, and he left the school a few days later. In 1992, a black cadet woke up to a noose dangling above his bed, allegedly placed there by white cadets after he refused to sing "Dixie" for them the previous day. One black cadet told us that he had problems during his first year of "a racial nature." He began lifting weights and transferred to a different company to escape his tormentors, employing an individual means of redress in the face of institutional denials of race problems.

10. The benefits of coeducational classrooms is an opinion shared by the majority of the faculty at The Citadel. In a survey of the faculty conducted in 1992 by the Faculty Council, 71% responded "yes" to the question "do you favor the admission of women to The Citadel Corps of Cadets." When asked to chose between making The Citadel a private college, establishing a separate military college for women in South Carolina, or admitting women to the corps of cadets, 80% of the faculty chose admitting women to the corps.

11. One woman professor we spoke with said that the cadets often call her a "feminazi," which she attributes to an effort to ridicule her and reduce her power over the cadets.

12. This construction of hegemonic masculinity is fragile not only because it may be breached by men's equal status contact with women but because "the traditional male role

is a self-denying and stoic-heroic combination of characteristics that takes its toll on men's physical and emotional health" (Levant, 1990). The fragility of men's health has been documented through multiple paradigms of psychological stressors (Eisler & Skidmore, 1987; O'Neil, Helms, Gable, David, & Wrightsman, 1986) and physical ailments (Doyle, 1995; Levant, 1995; Messner & Sabo, 1990).

References

Addelston, J. (1994). [Field notes.]

Addelston, J., & Stirratt, M. J. (1993). [Field notes.]

Anyon, J. (1978). Ideology and United States history textbooks. *Harvard Educational Review, 49,* 361-385.

Applebome, P. (1995, April 14). Appeals court opens way for female cadet at The Citadel. *New York Times,* p. 10.

Barron's Educational Series. (1992). *Barron's profiles of American colleges.* Hauppauge, NY: Author.

Britton, D. (1990). Homophobia and homosociality: An analysis of boundary maintenance. *The Sociological Quarterly, 31,* 423-439.

Brod, H. (Ed.). (1987). *The making of masculinities: The new men's studies.* New York: Routledge.

Broude, G. (1990). Protest masculinity: A further look at the causes and the concept. *Ethos, 18,* 103-122.

Carrigan, T., Connell, B., & Lee, J. (1985). Toward a new sociology of masculinity. *Theory and Society, 5,* 551-604.

Connell, R. W. (1993). The big picture: Masculinities in recent world history. *Theory and Society, 22,* 597-623.

Connell, R. W. (1995). *Masculinities.* Los Angeles: University of California Press.

Deaux, K. (1985). Sex and gender. *Annual Review of Psychology, 36,* 49-81.

Decker, T. (1995, August 13). She's a cadet. *New York Newsday,* p. A7.

Donaldson, M. (1993). What is hegemonic masculinity? *Theory and Society, 22,* 643-657.

Doyle, J. (1995). *The male experience.* Madison, WI: Brown & Benchmark.

Drescher, H. (1992). What is The Citadel? *Sports Illustrated, 77,* 71-79.

Ehrenreich, B. (1983). *The hearts of men: American dreams and the flight from commitment.* New York: Anchor.

Eisler, R., & Skidmore, J. (1987). Masculine gender role stress: Scale development and component factors in the appraisal of stressful situations. *Behavior Modification, 11,* 123-136.

Faludi, S. (1994). The naked Citadel. *The New Yorker, 70,* 62-81.

Faulkner, S. (1993). Deposition in *Johnson v. Jones.* U.S. District Court: Charleston Division.

Fine, M., & Addelston, J. (1996). On sameness and difference. In S. Wilkenson (Ed.), *Feminist Social Psychology II.* London: Sage.

Gilligan, C. (1982). *In a different voice.* Cambridge, MA: Harvard University Press.

Goffman, E. (1961). *Asylums: Essays on the social situation of mental patients and other inmates.* Garden City, NY: Anchor.

Hantover, J. (1978). The Boy Scouts and the validation of masculinity. *Journal of Social Issues, 34,* 184-195.

Herek, G. (1986). On heterosexual masculinity. *American Behavioral Scientist, 29,* 563-577.

Katz, P., & Taylor, D. (Eds.). (1988). *Eliminating racism: Profiles in controversy.* New York: Plenum.

Kimmel, M. (1987). The contemporary "crisis" of masculinity in historical perspective. In H. Brod (Ed.), *The making of masculinities: The new men's studies.* New York: Routledge.

Kimmel, M., & Messner, M. (Eds.). (1992). *Men's lives.* New York: Macmillan.

Levant, R. (1990). Psychological services designed for men: A psychoeducational approach. *Psychotherapy, 27,* 309-315.

Levant, R. (1995). *Masculinity reconstructed.* New York: E. P. Dutton.

Mahan, A., & Mahan, T. (1993). *The Citadel: The case for single gender education.* Unpublished manuscript submitted on behalf of the defendants in *Johnson v. Jones.* U.S. District Court: Charleston Division.

Manegold, C. (1994, September 11). The Citadel's lone wolf: Shannon Faulkner. *New York Times Magazine,* pp. 56-60.

Messner, M., & Sabo, D. (Eds.). (1990). *Sport, men, and the gender order.* Champaign, IL: Human Kinetics Books.

Morawski, J. (1985). The measurement of masculinity and femininity: Engendering categorical realities. In A. Stewart & M. B. Lykes (Eds.), *Gender and personality: Current perspectives of theory and research* (pp. 108-135). Durham: Duke University Press.

Morawski, J. (1990). Toward the unimagined: Feminism and epistemology in psychology. In R. Hare-Mustin & J. Marecek (Eds.), *Making a difference: Psychology and the construction of gender.* (pp. 150-183). New Haven, CT: Yale University Press.

Morgan, D. (1994). Theater of war: Combat, the military and masculinities. In H. Brod & M. Kaufman (Eds.), *Theorizing masculinities* (pp. 165-182). Thousand Oaks, CA: Sage.

O'Neil, J., Helms, B., Gable, R., David, L., & Wrightsman, L. (1986). Gender-role conflict scale: College men's fear of femininity. *Sex Roles, 14,* 335-350.

Peyser, M. (1995, August 28). Sounding retreat. *Newsweek,* pp. 38-40.

Pleck, J. (1987). The theory of male sex-role identity: Its rise and fall, 1936 to the present. In H. Brod (Ed.), *The making of masculinities: The new men's studies.* New York: Routledge.

Rembert, N. (1993). Deposition in *Johnson v. Jones.* U.S. District Court: Charleston Division.

Riesman, D. (1991). Deposition in *United States of America v. Commonwealth of Virginia et al.* U.S. District Court: Roanoke Division.

Sanday, P. R. (1990). *Fraternity gang rape: Sex, brotherhood, and privilege on campus.* New York: New York University Press.

Segal, L. (1990). *Slow motion: Changing masculinities, changing men.* New Brunswick, NJ: Rutgers University Press.

Sexton, P. (1969). *The feminized male.* New York: Random House.

Shilts, R. (1993). *Conduct unbecoming: Lesbians and gays in the U.S. military.* New York: St. Martin's.

Smothers, R. (1994, July 23). Citadel is ordered to admit a woman to its cadet corp. *New York Times,* p. 6.

Snyder, W. (1993). Deposition in *United States of America v. Jones.* U.S. District Court: Charleston Division.

Tajfel, H., & Turner, J. (1979). An integrative theory of intergroup conflict. In W. G. Austin & S. Worchel (Eds.), *Social psychology of intergroup relations* (pp. 33-47). Monterey, CA: Brooks/Cole.

The Citadel. (1992). *Parents guide.* Charleston, SC: Author.

The Citadel. (1992-1993). *The guidon.* Charleston, SC: Author.

Unger, R. (1979). Toward a redefinition of sex and gender. *American Psychologist, 34,* 1085-1094.

West, C., & Zimmerman, D. (1991). Doing gender. In J. Lorber & S. Farrell (Eds.), *The social construction of gender* (pp. 13-37). Newbury Park, CA: Sage.

Vergnolle, R. (1993). Deposition in *Johnson v. Jones.* U.S. District Court: Charleston Division.

Yoder, J. (1989). Women at West Point: Lessons for token women in male-dominated occupations. In J. Freeman (Ed.), *Women: A feminist perspective* (3rd ed.). Palo Alto, CA: Mayfield.

PART II

SEX SEGREGATION, HOMOSOCIALITY, AND HEGEMONIC MASCULINITY

4

The Occupational Masculinity of Computing

ROSEMARY WRIGHT

Is there an occupational masculinity in the computer profession? Just as the workplace has both organizational and occupational cultures (Trice, 1993; Trice & Beyer, 1993), there may well be occupational masculinities intersecting the organizational masculinities (Collinson & Hearn, 1994) described by others in this volume. The purpose of this chapter is to illustrate how an occupational culture of computing creates such an occupational masculinity, suggesting a reconciliation and combination of earlier research on why many women choose not to enter computer work and why, after suitable controls, more women than men choose to leave computer work.

Consider the following statistics: Although substantially more women than men in the U.S. labor force used computers at work in 1993—48% versus 35% (U.S. Bureau of the Census, 1993)—the data were significantly different when limited to computer professionals: In the same year, 2.5% of all men and 1% of all women in the labor force claimed an occupational title of computer programmer, computer systems analyst, or other computer specialist. Women constituted only 32% of the population holding these titles (U.S. Bureau of Labor Statistics, 1994). In computer work, as in many other fields, the workplace of the 1990s continues to reflect the disparities of gender segregation.

But what is the difference between computer users and professionals, now that many users program and many professionals are also users? Computer professionals or computer workers[1] are defined here, in accord with the Association for Computing Machinery (ACM) (Denning, 1991), as people whose work supports *other* people's usage of computer systems. The context of this volume notwithstanding, this is not the Management Information Systems (MIS) definition used by most researchers in the management literature.[2] For reviews of that literature, see Nash and Redwine (1988), as well as Ginzberg and Baroudi (1988).

Anecdotal evidence suggests to many casual observers that women have achieved or are close to achieving parity in the computer workplace. However, the situation is more complex, as shown in Figure 4.1, which shows that women *were* moving toward parity until the late 1980s, when they stopped doing so. Figure 4.1 shows two related trends: the change in the percentage that women make up of those employed in computer work, and the change in women's percentage of those receiving bachelor's degrees in computer and information sciences. These percentages are presented for the years between 1971 and 1994, using data from the U.S. Departments of Labor and Education.[3]

Women's representation in computer work has risen from 15% in 1971 to 36% in 1990, from which it has fallen back to 31% in 1994. Women's proportion of computer and information science degrees has followed a similar, but earlier, pattern. In 1971, women received 14% of these degrees. This figure rose to a high of 37% in 1984, but by 1993 had also fallen to 28%. The rise in women's participation in computer work is consistent with women's increasing participation in the general labor force during this period and is less interesting than its subsequent fall. The interesting question is not why are there fewer women in computer work than men, but why has the trend toward parity appeared to reverse in recent years? In other words, after decades of feminizing, why is the field remasculinizing?

Women's Choices Not to Enter and to Leave Computer Work

To answer these questions, we must consider women's decisions at two points in time—entry and exit. Women are choosing not to enter computer work, and women are also more likely than men to leave computer work, all other things being equal. Let us consider each separately.

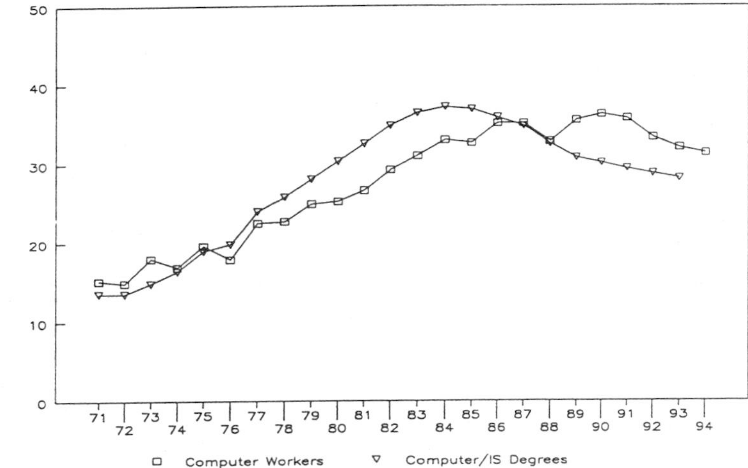

Figure 4.1. Women's Representation Among Computer Workers and Computer/IS Bachelor's Degree Recipients, 1971-1994

Regarding women's decisions not to enter, the degree data in Figure 4.1 provide only one set of evidence. The women who enter computer work do so from a host of different backgrounds, not just computer science degrees. Carey (1991/92) shows that 47% of all new entrants to computer work in 1986 were from other occupations within their employing organizations. Wright (1994) highlights the gender gap in these entrances by showing how women in the 1980s were significantly less likely than men to enter computer work from other scientific and technical fields.

The reasons most frequently cited for women choosing not to enter computer work are their socialization away from math and science; software being written mostly by and for men; the domination of computer training programs by boys, men, and male values; and a common perception that computer work is a field for men and antisocial individuals (Committee on Women, 1991; Decker, 1986; Hartman, Griffeth, Miller, & Kinicki, 1988; Newton, 1991; Steering Committee, 1993).

Factors put forward for the *falloff* in women's interest in computing include male backlash (Breene, 1993; Faludi, 1991) and women's attraction to alternative male-dominated fields such as business (Leveson, 1989). Factors suggested for the falloff in both men's *and* women's interest since the middle 1980s include an increasing misconception of the nature of the occupation (Cale, Mawhinney, & Callaghan, 1991); an increase in the number of students taking programming in high school; and the personal computer having demystified, as well as given greater access to, computers (Committee to Assess the Scope, 1992).

Regarding women's decision to leave, women are more likely than men to leave computer work, all other things being equal, as shown in a separate analysis of 6,200 members of the Survey of Natural and Social Scientists and Engineers from the 1980s. That analysis shows that after controlling for background, education, experience, period, specialty, and industry, women are more likely to leave computer work than are men (Wright & Jacobs, 1994).

How does that finding relate to earlier research about women's turnover from computer work? Earlier turnover studies have almost exclusively focused on computer workers in MIS; most intentionally excluded computer workers with engineering titles or responsibilities. To the extent that studies have drawn on job titles, they have missed a substantial number of people. When these studies have grouped people by organization, they have still frequently considered applications developers in MIS as representing all computer workers (Orlikowski, 1988), and they must be interpreted in that vein.

To review specific computer turnover studies, we must distinguish between occupational and organizational turnover. There appears to have been only one other gender study of occupational turnover, which found no significant gender difference in occupational tenure: Once in computer work, both men and women stayed an average of 12.8 years (Wagner & Benham, 1993). Assuming fewer women than men entered (see Figure 4.1), this means that translating backward, women's net rate was thus higher than men's.

Organizational turnover among computer workers has long been recognized as a management problem. Although the rate varies with the economy, the annual rate since the 1960s has ranged from 5% to 30% a year (Connolly, 1988; Gray, 1982; Willoughby, 1977), running about twice the rates for business managers and professionals (Lucas, 1989). With so many people constantly leaving, the time and cost of recruiting and training are enormous. The many management studies of the reasons for computer turnover have overwhelmingly emphasized individual and organizational differences, rarely distinguishing gender or asking questions related to home or family responsibilities. Heading the list of reasons in most studies are problems with salary, opportunity, and challenging work (see, e.g., Couger, 1990; Fidel & Garner, 1990). For a review of those studies, see Wright (1994).

While few in number, there have been at least three gender studies of organizational turnover of computer workers, all of which found little significant gender difference in either rates or reasons for turnover (Cournoyer, 1983; Freedland, 1987; Igbaria & Siegel, 1992). The rate data is consistent with larger studies of organizational turnover (e.g., Waite & Berryman, 1985), but the reason data should be regarded with suspicion: Although in many studies salary is the most frequently cited reason for computer turnover, it may not be the real reason, because articulating as a reason for a resignation a desire for higher salary is always more acceptable than admitting to supervisory problems or a lack of career advancement (Bradford & Cottrell, 1977). Even if sexual harassment or family responsibilities are included in the lists of possible reasons from which to choose, women and men may be reluctant to cite the former for fear of retribution (Siegel, 1992) and the latter for concern over perceived lack of professionalism (Schwartz, 1992).

These comments aside, the previous studies have examined limited numbers of organizations rather than the occupation as a whole, and have examined neither entry rates nor destinations. Wright (1994) shows from the National Science Foundation panel that even when men and women leave at the same rate, the net exit rate will be higher for women than for men, if women enter at a lower rate. And when men and women leave computer work, they leave for different occupations and receive different returns on their investment of time in the occupation.

Rather than challenge the lack of gender difference in uncontrolled turnover rates, the lenses of occupational culture and masculinity suggest a way to understand why there are differences after controls are introduced as in Wright and Jacobs (1994). And, rather than suggest that the proposed reasons for women's lack of attraction to the occupation are incorrect, viewing computer work through the lenses of occupational culture and masculinity suggests a way to unify seemingly disparate factors into a cohesive whole.

The Occupational Culture of Computing

To describe the occupational culture of computing, we must first define what we mean by occupational culture. Following Trice (1993), occupational cultures consist of ideologies (emotionally charged, taken-for-granted beliefs) and cultural forms (mechanisms for affirming and expressing these beliefs). Ideologies tell members what they ought to do.

Cultural forms include occupation-based stories, myths, ceremonies, symbols, legends, rituals, languages and gestures, physical artifacts, taboos, and rites. Occupational cultures are collective, inherently ambiguous, emergent over time, dynamic, intrinsically symbolic, and emotionally charged. They structure social relations, encourage ethnocentrism, and are dysfunctional as well as functional.

Computing's Cultural History. To understand the culture of computing, we must briefly review computing's history. Computers were first developed during World War II, when the first programmers of the Electronic Numerical Integrator and Computer (ENIAC) were women, called the "ENIAC girls." In the postwar years, computer work became a male preserve, viewed as requiring technical rather than mechanical skills (Kraft, 1979). During the 1950s and early 1960s, computer systems were built and programmed by electrical engineers, primarily for military purposes and secondarily for business use. Through the late 1960s and 1970s, computer use grew exponentially in the business sector. Large mainframes became legion throughout American corporations, joined by a host of minicomputers. Personal or microcomputers emerged in the 1980s. Accompanying the many hardware changes and reductions in size throughout these decades was a continual succession of operating systems, programming languages, and applications (Tarallo, 1987). By 1993, computers had become so widely deployed that almost half of all women and more than a third of all men in the labor force used them in some form at work (U.S. Bureau of the Census, 1993).

Supporting users and computers throughout this period has required a rapidly increasing population of computer professionals whose required knowledge has changed constantly (Steering Committee, 1993). Partly driven by the fluidity of the knowledge base, common interests and shared experiences have caused a distinct occupational culture to develop and evolve. The underpinnings of this culture were determined by the fact that electrical engineers built and maintained the first computers (Trice, 1993).

Physically constructed by electrical engineers, the first computers embodied engineering values and norms (Hughes, 1987). Electrical engineering—a strong, well-established occupation when electrical engineers developed computers—has dominated and controlled the work content of computer work, one of its subordinate occupations (Simpson, 1985). Because subordinate occupational cultures take on the ideologies and cultural forms of their dominant culture, the computer culture took on the occupational culture of electrical engineering (Trice, 1993). What may be surprising to readers is how much of that culture persists today. Trice and Beyer (1993) capture this historical tendency when they note that close examination of an occupational culture will "usually uncover residues of cultural ideas and practices that originated at earlier points in its history. . . . Even though these historical residues are buried under current preoccupations . . . they can still have powerful effects in guiding current behavior" (p. 6).

Putting the engineering focus aside for a moment, how can it be argued that there is only one occupational culture, when there is a large overlap between computer professionals and users? Turkle (1995) highlights a distinction between the two groups when she argues, based on cross-cultural interviews with and observation of 1000 informants of all ages and many occupations during the 1980s and 1990s, that since the middle 1980s, there have been two computer cultures—one of calculation and one of simulation, symbolized by the MS-DOS and Macintosh operating systems, respectively.

Like MS-DOS commands, the culture of calculation is rigorous and engineering in approach. It requires a "hard" programming style in which programming must be done in a mathematical, structured manner, following strict rules and top-down procedures (Turkle, 1995). The hard programming style is one with which more men than women are comfortable, as they find it consistent with hegemonic masculine values of power and discipline (Turkle, 1984). By contrast, like Macintosh icon manipulation, the culture of simulation supports a "soft" programming style in which programming can be done flexibly and nonhierarchically, by trial and error, jumping between large and small approaches to the problem at hand (Turkle, 1995). The soft style is one with which more women than men are comfortable, as they find it consistent with female values of negotiation and compromise (Turkle, 1984).

Which culture is dominant today? Both have strong adherents among both users and professionals. The culture of simulation is more predominant among users, but it is fighting an uphill battle among professionals (Turkle, 1995). Because the culture of calculation is still the dominant professional culture, though not the only one, it will be referred to in this chapter as "the" occupational culture of computing. It is a culture that Turkle (1995) has argued is antithetical to women and has turned many women off to computing.

Computing's Masculine Nature. Earlier studies of this culture suggest some of the reasons for many women's negative reactions. As Kiesler, Sproull, and Eccles (1985) described it in the 1980s, based on observations and interviews with users and support staff in video arcades, computer camps, high schools, and colleges, computer professionals consider computing "more than a set of skills. It is embedded in a social system consisting of shared values and norms, a special vocabulary and humor, status and prestige ordering, and differentiation of members from nonmembers" (p. 453). This system has a distinctly *masculine* culture, defined by the practices, norms, and values of its male practitioners, young and old:

> [The] adult world of computing is heavily dominated by males and transmitted to children by males. Primarily, it is men who design the video games, write the software, sell the machines, and teach the courses. . . . The culture of computing may be a reasonable explanation for the apparent difference in girls' and boys' attraction to computing. It is a world of electronic pool halls and sports fields, of circuits and machines, of street-corner society transmuted to a terminal room. This is hardly the kind of world girls find enticing (Kiesler et al., 1985, pp. 454-459).

In complementary ethnographic research with students and staff at Harvard University and the Massachusetts Institute of Technology, Turkle (1984, 1988) looked back to the computer itself to understand this masculine culture, arguing that the computer was *socially constructed* as a male domain—a symbol of what woman was not. As she described it, the computer was masculine by being associated with men, not women. As a symbol, it reflected both a general computer culture and a "hacker" subculture that dominated the larger culture, although actual hackers were few in number (Turkle, 1984).

Both cultures abounded with images of and jargon related to competition, sports, and violence—such as "killing" and "aborting jobs" (to stop them on the computer) and "sports death" (pushing body and mind beyond their limits). Hackers were the heroes of the larger culture, who took pride in being "nerds" (their term), being antisocial, and having no rules except mutual tolerance and respect for radical individualism, manipulation, and mastery of the computer. There were few, if any, women hackers, and men in the hacker culture saw it as incompatible with a life with women. Great hacks were mythologized, and overcoming small hacks (such as defeating the "cookie monster" who eats files) were rites of passage (Turkle, 1984).

The larger hacker-supporting culture lives on in what Turkle calls the culture of calculation. It is distinctly masculine, devoted to "mastery, individualism, nonsensuality. It values complexity and risk in relationships with things, and seeks simplicity and safety in relationships with people" (Turkle, 1984, p. 223). It is a culture that values technical over interpersonal skills, hardware over software, and engineering over business backgrounds (Turkle, 1984, 1988). Women in this culture are more likely to have soft programming styles, develop their interpersonal skills, work with software, and have business backgrounds; men are more likely to have hard programming styles, develop their technical skills, work with hardware, and have engineering backgrounds (Turkle, 1984; Weinberg, 1987).

Complementary research has shown repeatedly that women and men hold a number of stereotypes about computer professionals: Computing is seen as a "man's job" by both men and women in the workplace (Gutek & Bikson, 1985), in computer classes (Hess & Miura, 1985), in popular computer magazines (Ware & Stuck, 1985), by college students (Hartman et al., 1988), and by high school students (Newton, 1991). Furthermore, it is perceived as a job for the antisocial, who are low in social ease and frequency of social interaction (Decker, 1986). Computer workers are not held in high esteem and are rated significantly lower than both the computer itself and the future of computers (Silbey & Taggart, 1982). Although both men and women hold these stereotypes, women are more likely to endorse them than men, believing at the same time that they are personally unable to work effectively with computers (Collis, 1985).

Computing's Engineering Basis. Why does the occupational culture of computing appear alien to many women? First, we must note that it appears alien to many men, as well the first time they come in contact with it. Sproull, Kiesler, and Zubrow (1987) argue that computing is alien to college students who first encounter it because it differs in time and space, in reliability and controllability, in learning conventions, and in social context from other academic and work activities. People are socialized into the computer culture under conditions in which prior models and means for learning are neither appropriate nor useful. Their initial interactions produce reality shock, then confusion, then attempts to establish control, all while developing an image of the computer and the social organization surrounding it. If they manage control, they come to terms with the culture. If they don't manage control, they either become angry or withdraw from the culture.

Women are more likely than men to find this culture alien because of its masculine nature and to withdraw from it (Kiesler et al., 1985; Turkle, 1988, 1995). We can understand the reasons at a deeper level by returning to computer work's occupational roots in electrical engineering. Shaiken

(1984) was one of the first to argue that computer workers and engineers have similar occupational cultures. The similarities include servicing and being subordinate to management, working on projects in variously changing roles, and applying scientific management techniques to control and eliminate other workers in organizations. Implicit in Shaiken's list of shared attributes are some of the hegemonically masculine elements of this common culture. These elements become explicit by comparing Turkle's description to McIlwee and Robinson's (1992) depiction of the culture of engineering,[4] which draws on Hacker's (1990), Cockburn's (1988), and Bailyn's (1987) arguments that technical work is socially defined as masculine.

In interviews with 30 male and 52 female engineering graduates of two public universities in Southern California, McIlwee and Robinson (1992) find two major components in the culture—an ideology and an interactional style. The ideology emphasizes the dominance of technology, engineers (computer workers) as producers of this technology, and organizational power as the basis of engineering (computer) success. The interactional style requires looking, talking, and acting like an engineer (computer worker), which in most workplaces means looking, talking, and acting out a particular masculinity that McIlwee and Robinson generalize to the "male gender role." The culture emphasizes enactment of this masculinity, requiring aggressive displays of technical self-confidence and hands-on ability for success, defining professional competence in hegemonically masculine terms and devaluing the gender characteristics of women.

One of McIlwee and Robinson's interviewees, Ginger, illustrates some of the dilemmas faced by women in this culture. Ginger was a design engineer at one of the largest, best-known manufacturers of computer equipment in the United States. They describe one of her experiences in the laboratory:

> Competence in the lab was measured in no small part by hands-on skills. To be accepted as a good engineer, to compete and be taken seriously, it was not merely the higher engineering skills that were important, but basic mechanical abilities as well. Here Ginger had difficulty, beginning with her first day at work. She was working with an experienced male engineer, and he asked her to hand him a particular tool. She had no idea what he was talking about.
>
> "He just looked at me like, 'oh my god, here we go.'" . . . This kind of ignorance, of course, did not reflect on her ability as an engineer—she had not been exposed to tools, either as a child or in college, so there was no reason

> she should be familiar with them. But the experience was an assault on her sense of competence as an engineer, and it confirmed the stereotypes held by many of her co-workers. (McIlwee & Robinson, 1992, p. 122)

Women in this culture are particularly hurt by the obsession with technology and hands-on activities, because the gender socialization experienced by most women yields a distinct lack of experience in "tinkering" with electronics. Even when they acquire the necessary skills, women do not seem to become as comfortable or as obsessed as their male counterparts. They are also hurt by the criterion for success being aggressive presentation of competence. Technical proficiency must be individualistic, displayed aggressively and competitively, and concerned with physical technology rather than the social relationships that go with it. The display required is that of this masculinity, playing a role with which most women are uncomfortable, even when they're capable of its performance (McIlwee & Robinson, 1992). Combining McIlwee and Robinson's observations with Turkle's, hacking can be seen as an almost quintessential example of the interactional style described for engineers.

The evidence is strong that many computer workers in the 1990s still have an engineering-derived occupational culture, even with competition from the culture of simulation, the proliferation of MIS programs in business schools, computer programming courses in 2-year technical schools, and applications development for every conceivable business function. It is evident in the common practice of calling programmers software engineers (King, 1994), the curricula of academic departments of computer science having a strong engineering content and approach, even where they are not in engineering schools (ACM/IEEE-CS Joint Curriculum Task Force, 1991), and a recent call for practitioners to obtain computer science and engineering credentials (Steering Committee, 1993). Indeed, social scientists' descriptions of this culture notwithstanding, its engineering and masculine base is repeatedly cited and taken as given throughout a growing gender literature in computer science. See, for example, Martin and Murchie-Beyma (1992), Shade (1993), and Spertus (1991).

Even the nomenclature of corporate systems activity in the 1990s is drawn from engineering. Two cases in point are the "reengineering" of business operations and their computer systems, and the introduction of "Computer-Aided Software Engineering" (CASE) technologies into software development processes for all types of applications. Underway in varying degrees in many American corporations today, both reengineering and CASE introduction are "buzzwords" for programs to streamline work and reduce costs. Aside from the scientific management inherent in these programs, they are frequently based in or connected with MIS departments, whether the term "engineer" appears in any of those departments' job titles or not.

The Occupational Masculinity of Computing

Does having a masculine occupational culture indicate a separate occupational masculinity? As with occupational culture, we must first define occupational masculinity. Although the concept of masculinity is imprecise, Collinson and Hearn (1994) suggest material features (some combination of behavior, identities, experiences, relationships, practices, and appearances) and discursive features (language and relationship discourses) that are related more to men than to women. When these elements are relatively unique to and dominant in the culture of an occupation, as well as reinforcing of the male dominance of that occupation, it is surely appropriate to label the collection an occupational masculinity, much as Collinson and Hearn (1994) have identified multiple organizational/management masculinities.

Connell starts in that direction when he notes how "elements of sexual character are embedded in the distinctive sets of practices sometimes called 'occupational cultures' "(1987, p. 181). He uses engineering as one of his examples of the professions:

> Professionalism is a case in point. The combination of theoretical knowledge with technical expertise is central to a profession's claim to competence and to a monopoly of practice. This has been constructed historically as a form of masculinity: emotionally flat, centred on a specialized skill, insistent on professional esteem and technically-based dominance over other workers. . . . The masculine character of professionalism has been supported by the simplest possible mechanism, the exclusion of women. (Connell, 1987, p. 181)

Do physicians and computer professionals have the same masculinity, however? The occupational masculinity of computing described above must certainly be distinguished in some ways from that of physicians who, for example, do not feel the need for aggressive presentation of their technical knowledge. Rather, they take it for granted that their knowledge will be accepted (Bosk, 1979).

More difficult is distinguishing the computing masculinity from an engineering masculinity, because of the large overlap between the cultures. Although the computing culture closely overlaps that of engineering, an argument can be made that there will be some differences in experiences and relationships due to the requirements for professional certification that adhere to engineering but not to computer work. The greater similarities, however, suggest that it makes more sense to consider them so close as to have one and the same masculinity.

How can the occupational culture of computing, the hacker subculture, and the culture of simulation be reconciled in terms of masculinities? As we've seen, the hacker subculture is an extreme form, tolerated and admired but not emulated, by the men in organizational power in the larger computing culture (Turkle, 1984). The inconsistent practices of hackers and computer managers both contribute to the masculinity; a separate hacker masculinity is not warranted. The culture of simulation is a different case. Because its values are ones with which many women are comfortable, it doesn't warrant treatment as a masculinity.

Another way to distinguish an occupational masculinity is when an occupational culture's norms and values that are internally defined as masculine differ from those prized by hegemonic masculinity (Connell, 1987) or by one or more management masculinities (Collinson & Hearn, 1994). Reviewing the material above, one example stands out as meeting both of these criteria: The occupational culture of computing highly values hacking, even while it practices and supports management control. Hackers take pride in being "nerds" and being antisocial, not needing women in their lives. Contemporary hegemonic masculinity is certainly both social and heterosexual (Connell, 1987). Furthermore, hackers' individualistic values go against the values of cooperation, control, and career progression that are emphasized to different degrees in managerial masculinities (Collinson & Hearn, 1994). For these several reasons, we should view the engineering masculinity of computer work as a separate and subordinate occupational masculinity related to managerial function (Collinson & Hearn, 1994). The computing masculinity may, however, become the dominant organizational masculinity when, as in a computing-driven organization, the computing culture becomes the dominant organizational culture. Such a case is described in Kunda (1992).

Conclusion

We began this chapter by noting how women's representation among recipients of bachelor's degrees in computer science and among computer workers has fallen since the middle 1980s. We reviewed earlier research on why women choose not to enter computer work, and how women are more likely than men to leave computer work, all other things being equal. The factors put forward for women's choosing not to enter the field were girls' socialization away from math and science; software being written by and for men and boys; computer training programs being dominated by boys, men, and male values; and a common perception that computer work is a field for men and antisocial people. Factors suggested for the falloff in both women's and men's interest included a misconception of the occupation, an increase in students taking programming in high school, and the personal computer having demystified computers. Factors projected for the falloff in women's interest included male backlash and women's attraction to alternative male-dominated fields such as business.

Viewing computing as having a distinct occupational masculinity is a way to unify most of these themes. Math and science are at the core of the computing culture; proficiency in them is considered a masculine trait in much of our society. Software *is* written primarily by and for men (Huff & Cooper, 1987). Computer training programs *are* dominated by boys, men, and male values, although there are signs of improvement, especially in women's training on and use of the Internet (Shade, 1993). Women *continue* to perceive computer work as a field for men and antisocial people (Newton, 1991; Shade, 1993). All of these are compatible with computing having a distinct occupational masculinity.

As to the falloff in women's interest since the middle 1980s, more young women are indeed taking programming in high school, but they may merely be getting turned off *earlier* when they enter the male-dominated computer rooms and culture that many of them find alien (Sproull et al., 1987). Perhaps more women are misconceiving the nature of the occupation for the same reason—they're encountering the masculinity *before* they find the portions of the work that might attract them to the field. And what of the personal computer having demystified and given greater access to the field? Well, again, young women may find they don't like it before they enter it. In the past, they had to go into it to find out that they didn't feel comfortable.

Putting aside the issue of male backlash, which can't be proved one way or the other, there is a good case to be made for women choosing alternative destinations, although not necessarily to alternative male-dominated occupations. Jacobs (1995) has shown that the decline of women's entry into computer science is part of a general stabilization in women's entry into male-dominated majors. Turkle's culture of simulation suggests that the alternative destinations may well be *user* occupations in which women with soft programming styles may pursue their interest in computing without encountering the masculinity in the occupational culture of computing.

Turning to women being more likely than men to leave computer work, analyses presented elsewhere by the author show that although more men than women leave computer work on an absolute basis, the relationship reverses and women are more likely than men to leave after controlling for background, education, experience, specialty, and industry (Wright & Jacobs, 1994). In addition, more men than women in computer work are likely to be engineers. Consistent with the culture described above, being an engineer is a decided career advantage in this field, substantially increasing one's probability of moving to management (Wright, in press).

Once women enter computer work, they face a culture in which engineers are rewarded more than nonengineers. Women in computer work do not fit the cultural mold. They're not male and generally they're not engineers. These findings suggest that the occupational masculinity may be acting as a deterrent to women *after* they are in the field, as well as before they enter. Indeed, it may be telling them through the occupational culture that they're deviant, don't belong, and should avail themselves of what Jacobs (1989) has called the "revolving door" for women in male-dominated occupations.

Since the middle to late 1980s, computer downsizing and reengineering have required many, if by now not most, individuals in computer work to work with personal computers (Anthes, 1993; Horwitt, 1990). Supporting others on PCs requires more knowledge of and tinkering with hardware. In a sense, computer work is returning to the 1950s, when hardware knowledge was essential. The occupational culture of computing glorifies such knowledge (Hacker, 1990; McIlwee & Robinson, 1992), and some of women's departure from the field may be due to this requirement increasing with the rapid diffusion of PCs.

In sum, a good argument can be made that a major reason behind both women's declining interest and tenure in computer work is the occupational masculinity embodied in the occupational culture. With computer work the second fastest growing occupation in the United States in the 1990s (Silvestri & Lukasiewicz, 1992), the demand for computer workers is greatly outpacing the supply (Steering Committee, 1993), and computer workers in 1993 are already comprising one out of every 40 male and one out of every 100 female workers in the U. S. labor force (U.S. Bureau of Labor Statistics, 1994). Organizational analysts and others wishing to redress gender inequalities in the workplace would do well to recognize, as well as work to lessen, the gender exclusivity caused by this masculinity.

Notes

1. In this chapter, I use the terms "computer professional" and "computer worker" interchangeably. For varying arguments whether computer work is a profession by sociological definition, see Abbott (1988), Denning (1991), and Orlikowski and Baroudi (1989).

2. Most management researchers studying computer work have focused on computer programmers and systems analysts in MIS, excluding other computer workers such as systems engineers, database administrators, and operations managers (Orlikowski, 1988). Focusing on titles is problematic, in that it is especially difficult to distinguish between computer specialties and titles (Steering Committee, 1993). Even management analysts who recognize the title difficulty have excluded engineers in their definition of computer work (Orlikowski, 1988; Turner & Baroudi, 1986). The many close ties between computer science and engineering (Steering Committee, 1993) and the common practice in the 1990s of using the title software engineer for workers previously called programmer/analysts (King, 1994) lead me to include people with engineering titles as computer professionals.

3. The education data in Figure 4.1 are from Vetter (1992), supplemented by the U.S. Department of Education (1992-1993 and unpublished data for 1992-1993). Data are not presented on MIS majors, because they are not separately broken out of business majors in these data sources. The data are for academic years starting with 1970-71, marking each by the calendar year in which the academic year ends. The employment data in the figure are a combination of those for all computer categories used in different years by the U.S. Bureau of Labor Statistics (1976-1995 and unpublished data for 1971-1974). Details of the calculation are in Wright and Jacobs (1994).

4. McIlwee and Robinson (1992) draw extensively on research with electrical engineers to illustrate their general culture of engineering, arguing that the culture applies less well to their second case, mechanical engineers.

References

Abbott, A. (1988). *The system of professions: An essay on the division of expert labor.* Chicago: University of Chicago Press.

ACM/IEEE-CS Joint Curriculum Task Force. (1991). *Computing curricula 1991.* New York: ACM & IEEE Computer Society Press.

Anthes, G. H. (1993, December 6). Not made in the U.S.A. *Computerworld,* p. 123.

Bailyn, L. (1987). Experiencing technical work: A comparison of male and female engineers. *Human Relations, 40*(5), 299-312.

Bosk, C. L. (1979). *Forgive and remember: Managing medical failure.* Chicago: University of Chicago Press.

Bradford, P. A., & Cottrell, L. R. (1977, Autumn). Factors influencing business data processor turnover. *Computer Personnel, 7*(1-2), 3-6.

Breene, L. A. (1993). Women and computer science. *Initiatives, 55*(2), 39-44.

Cale, E. G., Jr., Mawhinney, C. H., & Callaghan, D. R. (1991). Student perceptions of information systems careers: Misconceptions and declining enrollments. *Journal of Research on Computing in Education, 23*(3), 434-443.

Carey, M. L. (1991/92, Winter). Occupational advancement from within. *Occupational Outlook Quarterly,* pp. 9-13.

Cockburn, C. (1988). *Machinery of dominance: Women, men, and technical know-how.* Boston: Northeastern University Press.

Collinson, D., & Hearn, J. (1994). Naming men as men: Implications for work, organization and management. *Gender, Work and Organization, 1*(1), 2-22.

Collis, B. (1985, May/June). Psychosocial implications of sex differences in attitudes toward computers: Results of a survey. *International Journal of Women's Studies, 8*(3), 207-213.

Committee on Women in Science and Engineering. (1991). *Women in science and engineering: Increasing their numbers in the 1990s.* Washington, DC: National Academy Press.

Committee to Assess the Scope and Direction of Computer Science and Technology. (1992). *Computing the future: A broader agenda for computer science and engineering.* Washington, DC: National Academy Press.

Connell, R. W. (1987). *Gender and power: Society, the person and sexual politics.* Stanford: Stanford University Press.

Connolly, J. (1988, August 8). Study: Crash hangover keeps turnover low. *Computerworld,* p. 57.

Couger, J. D. (1990, January 15). Motivating analysts and programmers. *Computerworld,* pp. 73-76

Cournoyer, P. E. (1983). *Mobility of information systems personnel: An analysis of a large computer firm's experience.* Unpublished doctoral dissertation, MIT.

Decker, W. H. (1986). Occupation and impressions: Stereotypes of males and females in three professions. *Social Behavior and Personality, 14*(1), 69-75.

Denning, P. (1991, October 10). The scope and directions of computer science: Computing, applications, and computational science. *Communications of the ACM, 34,* 129-131.

Faludi, S. (1991). *Backlash: The undeclared war against American women.* New York: Doubleday.

Fidel, K., & Garner, R. (1990, October 3). Computer workers: Career lines and professional identity. *Computers & Society, 20,* 118-123.

Freedland, M. (1987). *Computer/DP professional career survey.* New York: Deutsch, Shea & Evans.

Ginzberg, M. J., & Baroudi, J. J. (1988). MIS careers—A theoretical perspective. *Communications of the ACM, 31*(5), 586-594.

Gray, S. B. (1982). 1982 DP salary survey. *Datamation, 28*(11), 114-123.

Gutek, B. A., & Bikson, T. K. (1985). Differential experiences of men and women in computerized offices. *Sex Roles, 13*(3/4), 123-136.

Hacker. S. (1990). *"Doing it the hard way": Investigations of gender and technology.* Boston: Unwin Hyman.

Hartman, S. J., Griffeth, R. W., Miller, L., & Kinicki, A. J. (1988). The impact of occupation, performance, and sex on sex role stereotyping. *Journal of Social Psychology, 128*(4), 451-463.

Hess, R. D., & Miura, I. T. (1985). Gender differences in enrollment in computer camps and classes. *Sex Roles, 13*(3/4), 193-203.

Horwitt, E. (1990, March 5). Downsizing quandary for IS pros. *Computerworld,* p. 1.

Huff, C. W., & Cooper, J. (1987). Sex bias in educational software: The effect of designers' stereotypes on the software they design. *Journal of Applied Social Psychology, 17*(6), 519-532.

Hughes, T. P. (1987). The evolution of large technological systems. In W. E. Bijker, T. P. Hughes, & T. Pinch (Eds.), *The social construction of technological systems.* Cambridge: MIT Press.

Igbaria, M., & Siegel, S. R. (1992). The reasons for turnover of information systems personnel. *Information & Management, 23,* 321-330.

Jacobs, J. A. (1989). *Revolving doors: Sex segregation and women's careers.* Palo Alto: Stanford University Press.

Jacobs, J. A. (1995, April). Gender and academic specialties: Trends during the 1980s. *Sociology of Education, 68*(2).

Kiesler, S., Sproull, L., & Eccles, J. S. (1985). Pool halls, chips, and war games: Women in the culture of computing. *Psychology of Women Quarterly, 9,* 451-462.

King, J. (1994, May 30). Engineers to IS: Drop that title! *Computerworld,* p. 1.

Kraft, P. (1979). The routinizing of computer programming. *Sociology of Work and Occupations, 6*(2), 139-155.

Kunda, G. (1992). *Engineering culture: Control and commitment in a high-tech corporation.* Philadelphia: Temple University Press.

Leveson, N. (1989). *Women in computer science: A report for the NSF-CISE cross directorate activities committee.* Washington, DC: National Science Foundation.

Lucas, H.C., Jr. (1989). *Managing information services.* New York: Macmillan.

Martin, C. D., & Murchie-Beyma, E. (1992). *In search of gender free paradigms for computer science education.* Eugene, OR: International Society for Technology in Education.

McIlwee, J. S., & Robinson, J. G. (1992). *Women in engineering: Gender, power, and workplace culture.* Albany: SUNY.

Nash, S. H., & Redwine, S. T., Jr. (1988, January 3). People and organizations in software production: A review of the literature. *Computer Personnel, 11,* 10-21.

Newton, P. (1991). Computing: An ideal occupation for women? In J. Firth-Cozens & M. A. West (Eds.), *Women at Work: Psychological and Organizational Perspectives* (pp. 143-153). Philadelphia: Open University Press.

Orlikowski, W. J. (1988). The data processing occupation: Professionalization or proletarianization? *Research in the Sociology of Work, 4,* 95-124.

Orlikowski, W. J., & Baroudi, J. J. (1989). The information systems profession: Myth or reality? *Office: Technology & People, 4,* 13-30.

Schwartz, F. N. (1992). *Breaking with tradition: Women and work, the new facts of life.* New York: Warner Books.

Shade, L. R. (1993, August). *Gender issues in computer networking.* Paper presented at Community Networking: The International Free-Net Conference, Ottawa.

Shaiken, H. (1984). *Work transformed: Automation and labor in the computer age.* New York: Holt, Rinehart & Winston.

Siegel, D. L. (1992). *Sexual harassment: Research & resources.* New York: National Council for Research on Women.

Silbey, V., & Taggart, W. M. (1982). General user attitudes toward computers: A semantic differential perspective. *Proceedings of the 12th Annual Meeting of the Southeast American Institute for Decision Sciences,* 168-170.

Silvestri, G. T., & Lukasiewicz, J. M. (1992). Occupational employment projections. In *Outlook 1990-2005* (BLS Bulletin 2402, pp. 62-92). Washington, DC: Government Printing Office.

Simpson, R. L. (1985). Social control of occupations and work. *Annual Review of Sociology, 11,* 415-436.

Spertus, E. (1991). *Why are there so few female computer scientists?* (MIT Artificial Intelligence Laboratory Technical Report). Cambridge: MIT.

Sproull, L., Kiesler, S., & Zubrow, D. (1987). Encountering an alien culture. In S. Kiesler & L. Sproull (Eds.), *Computing and Change on Campus.* Cambridge, MA: Cambridge University Press.

Steering Committee on Human Resources in Computer Science and Technology. (1993). *Computing professionals: Changing needs for the 1990s.* Washington, DC: National Academy Press.

Tarallo, B. M. (1987). *The production of information: An examination of the employment relations of software engineers and computer programmers.* Unpublished doctoral dissertation, University of California at Davis.

Trice, H. M. (1993). *Occupational subcultures in the workplace.* Ithaca, NY: ILR Press.

Trice, H. M., & Beyer, J. M. (1993). *The cultures of work organizations.* Englewood Cliffs, NJ: Prentice Hall.

Turkle, S. (1984). *The second self: Computers and the human spirit.* New York: Simon & Schuster.

Turkle, S. (1988). Computational reticence: Why women fear the intimate machine. In C. Kramarae (Ed.), *Technology and women's voices: Keeping in touch* (pp. 41-61). New York: Routledge Kegan Paul.

Turkle, S. (1995). *Life on the screen: Identity in the age of the Internet.* New York: Simon & Schuster.

Turner, J. A., & Baroudi, J. J. (1986, December). The management of information systems occupations: A research agenda. *Computer Personnel, 10,* 2-11.

U.S. Bureau of Labor Statistics. (1976-1995). *Employment and Earnings,* January. Washington, DC: Government Printing Office.

U.S. Bureau of the Census. (1993). *Computer use in the United States: 1993* (Memorandum PPL-22). Washington, DC: Education and Social Stratification Branch, Population Division.

U.S. Department of Education. (1992-1993). *Digest of Educational Statistics.* Washington, DC: Government Printing Office.

Vetter, B. M. (1992). *Professional women and minorities: A manpower data resource service* (10th ed.). Washington, DC: Commission of Professionals in Science and Technology.

Wagner, J. L., & Benham, H. C. (1993, April). *Career paths in information systems: A longitudinal analysis.* Paper presented at the annual conference of the ACM Special Interest Group on Computer Personnel Research.

Waite, L. J., & Berryman, S. E. (1985). *Women in nontraditional occupations: Choice and turnover.* Santa Monica, CA: RAND.

Ware, M. C., & Stuck, M. F. (1985). Sex-role messages vis-à-vis microcomputer use: A look at the pictures. *Sex Roles, 13*(3/4), 205-214.

Weinberg, S. (1987). Expanding access to technology: Computer equity for women. In B. D. Wright, M. M. Ferree, G. O. Mellow, L. H. Lewis, M. D. Samper, R. Asher, & K. Claspell (Eds.), *Women, work and technology: Transformations.* Ann Arbor: University of Michigan Press.

Willoughby, T. C. (Autumn, 1977). Computing personnel turnover: A review of the literature. *Computer Personnel, 7*(1-2), 11-13.

Wright, R. (1994). *Women in computer work: Controlled progress in a male occupation.* Unpublished doctoral dissertation, University of Pennsylvania.

Wright, R. (in press). Women in computer work: Controlled progress in a technical occupation. In J. Tang & E. Smith (Eds.), *Minorities and Women in American Professions.* Albany: SUNY.

Wright, R., & Jacobs, J. A. (1994, June). Male flight from computer work: A new look at occupational resegregation and ghettoization. *American Sociological Review, 59,* 511-536.

5

Stand by Your Man

Homosociality, Work Groups, and Men's Perceptions of Difference

AMY WHARTON
SHARON BIRD

The increasing demographic heterogeneity of the United States workforce is a well-documented trend (Johnston & Packer, 1987). The implications of this trend are clear: "More and more individuals are likely to work with people who are demographically different from them in terms of age, gender, race, and ethnicity" (Tsui, Egan, & O'Reilly, 1992, p. 549). Ironically, although this transformation has inspired numerous studies of the experiences of workers from numerically underrepresented groups, it may be workers from the numerically dominant racial and gender categories who react most dramatically to these changes. As portrayals of the "angry, white male" suggest, these men may perceive themselves with most to lose from changes in the status quo and, thus, may be more sensitive to changing workplace demographics than other groups.

The research described here grows out of Wharton and Baron's (1987) previous study of male workers' attitudinal responses to the gender composition of their work setting. This previous research, analyzing data from a disproportionately white male sample, suggested that men's views of work and overall work-related well-being are shaped in part by the gender demographics of their jobs. In particular, the research showed that men reported more negative reactions in gender-heterogeneous work settings than in those where they were either a majority or a small minority. Furthermore, later research by Wharton and Baron (1991) and other authors (Tsui et al., 1992) indicates that male workers' levels of commitment and attachment are more sensitive to gender composition than are women's responses. These patterns have been explained by a number of factors, ranging from men's patriarchal interests in preserving dominance over women to theories of social identity. Underlying all these explanations is an assumption of male homosociality, expressed in intergroup relations as a preference for interacting with similar others.

Although most invoke men's similarity to other men as the mechanism that explains their apparent preference for predominantly male work groups, two issues remain unresolved. First, findings from previous studies have associated *being different* (e.g., being male vs. being female) with *perceiving difference.* Men's perceptions of similarity and difference have not been examined directly. Hence, it remains unclear whether male workers are more likely to perceive themselves as similar to other men than to women, and it is unclear what role these perceptions of similarity and difference play in shaping men's more general reactions to their jobs. A second issue concerns the diverse types of *work groups* that have generated the findings on workers' reactions to gender composition. Given this diversity, Martin (1991) suggests a number of unanswered questions regarding the links between group dynamics and gender, such as, "Which groups should students of gender inequality study and why and how? . . . Are the gendering dynamics of some groups more consequential than others?" (p. 222). Not only are the effects of gender composition likely to vary, depending on what type of group is examined, but the theoretical mechanisms that explain these consequences should also operate differently in different contexts.

This chapter examines these two issues through an exploratory analysis of data on men's work group relations in one organization. Like most other researchers on these topics, we examine data collected primarily from white, heterosexual males. The central theoretical premise of this research is the claim that these men's responses to work are shaped not only by men's own characteristics (such as their gender) but also by the distribution of status characteristics among other relevant organizational members (Tolbert & Bacharach, 1992). Consistent with prior research, we show that the gender composition of men's work groups does influence how men view their coworkers, themselves, and their jobs.

Gender, Work Groups, and Homosociality

A Social Relational View of the Workplace

This research is guided by Baron and Pfeffer's (1994) social relational view of the workplace. Two assumptions of this perspective are especially relevant for our analysis. First, Baron and Pfeffer argue that "social relations at work represent a major source of satisfaction and are an important reward and preoccupation for individuals in the workplace" (p. 192). In contrast to economistic approaches that treat the workplace as a set of macroeconomic variables and view workers as atomistic "social morons" (DiMaggio, 1990; Sen, 1977, p. 336), a social relational view calls attention to the multiplicity of relations that permeate workers' organizational lives. Although social interaction in the workplace—particularly that which involves coworker intimacy and self-disclosure—has been relatively neglected by scholars (Marks, 1994), many have come to share Baron and Pfeffer's (1994) belief that the social relations of work are an important vehicle through which social inequality is reproduced. For instance, Martin (1991) argues that the "mechanisms through which organizations gender their members and activities involve interaction" (pp. 220-221); thus, she claims that "interpersonal interaction contributes to gender inequality at work." Along the same lines, Marks (1994) observes, "With the help of coworkers, ethnic statuses may get reaffirmed and enlivened, and age and gender identities may be consolidated, celebrated, reorganized, and even transformed" (p. 855).

Following from the presumed importance of workplace social relations is a second assumption. Here, Baron and Pfeffer (1994, p. 192) invoke the well-documented social psychological principle that "similarity is an important basis of interpersonal attraction and consequently of social integration and cohesion." As noted earlier, this principle serves as the theoretical foundation for much current research on the consequences of work group gender composition (e.g., Ely, 1994; O'Reilly, Caldwell, & Barnett, 1989; Tsui et al., 1992; Wagner, Pfeffer, & O'Reilly, 1984). The similarity-attraction principle "maintains that similarity in attitudes is a major source of attraction between individuals" and that "high interpersonal attraction may include frequent communication, high social integration, and a desire to maintain group affiliation, that may result in low turnover" (Tsui et al., 1992, p. 551). Within organizations, similarity attracts not only because this preference enhances self-esteem (e.g., a preference for similar others implies a preference for self), but similarity is also presumed to affect task performance (Kanter, 1977). As Ibarra (1992) observes, "Social homogeneity in the workplace makes communication easier, behavior more predictable and fosters relationships of trust and reciprocity, thus also enhancing instrumental relationships" (p. 423).

Although these assumptions offer general theoretical guidelines for examining men's work group relations, they say little about gender as a specific type of social category and basis of social relations. Gender is seen as one of many potential traits that may shape workplace interactions and from which similarity may be inferred. Under these circumstances, it becomes important to consider how and why gender—and the dominant masculinity in particular—may operate as a basis for group identification.

Masculinity, Homosociality, and Work

Some argue that gender is a "primitive category" that is always, at some level, activated in social life (Deaux & Major, 1987; Messick & Mackie, 1989). This does not imply that gender distinctions are "real" in a primordial sense but, rather, that social arrangements, such as the gender division of labor, continually reinforce gender boundaries. Inside the workplace, high levels of gender segregation serve as pervasive and entrenched markers of gender difference. As a result, gender comes to play an important role in workers' classifications of self and others. Men and women perceive themselves as belonging to different social categories and, thus, define themselves as members of different psychological groups.

Although gender may be an omnirelevant social category in certain respects, its relative salience may be highly variable across individuals, groups, and situations (Thorne, 1993). "Salience," in this context, represents "a person's awareness of a dimension in defining and describing the self at a given time" (Cota & Dion, 1986, p. 71). Although organizational research identifying the conditions under which social categories become salient to individuals is sparse (Wharton, 1992), there is some evidence that gender may be differentially salient to women and men.

As many have noted, because males—and especially white, heterosexual males—benefit from the persistence of workplace gender distinctions, this group may be most actively involved in maintaining gender boundaries (Wharton & Baron, 1987). Arguing from a psychoanalytic perspective, Williams (1989) claims that gender distinctions benefit men psychically, as well as economically. Hence, in her view, men have a stronger stake in the maintenance of gender than women and thus have more incentives to use it as basis of categorization. Tsui et al. (1992) provide an indirect test of this hypothesis, as they explore the relative effects of several types of demographic heterogeneity on organizational attachment. They found that the negative effects of "being different" were greater for members of the dominant gender and racial group—namely, white males—than for other categories. In other words, this group expressed the strongest preference for a homogeneous work unit. In earlier research, Wharton and Baron (1987, 1991) revealed a similar pattern: Male workers' psychological well-being was more dramatically affected than women's by the gender composition of their work settings. Moreover, consistent with Tsui et al. (1992), Wharton and Baron (1987, 1991) found that men in all-male work settings reported the highest rate of job-related well-being. Other research continues to show that the demographics of work groups affect different social categories in different ways (e.g., Tolbert, Simons, Andrews, & Rhee, 1995).

Where Do We Go From Here?

Although this research is useful, a number of issues remain unresolved. This chapter initiates discussion of two such topics. First, as noted earlier, previous research tends to associate *being* different with *perceiving* difference. For example, Tsui et al. (1992) assume that "perceptions of the similarity or dissimilarity of others" can be "indexed by demographic attributes" (p. 553). That is, these researchers assume that demographic differences are perceived as such by individuals. Although this may be a reasonable assumption, it remains an empirical question as to whether male workers do perceive themselves as more like men than women. Because perceptions of similarity and difference are the conceptual link between demographic homogeneity and the various psychological and behavioral outcomes of interest to researchers (e.g., satisfaction, commitment, turnover), it seems important to explore perceptions directly and to examine their effects on these factors.

A second unresolved issue concerns the type of work group used as the basis for the analyses. As noted earlier, previous findings have been derived from several different types of work groups. For example, research on the effects of gender composition has defined groups as single organizations (Ely, 1994), occupational locations by industry (Wharton & Baron, 1987, 1991), academic departments (Tolbert et al., 1995), work units (Tsui et al., 1992), and self-defined work groups (South, Bonjean,

Markham, & Corder, 1982, 1987). There has been little discussion of the entities to which men's preferences for homogeneity and similarity may or may not apply (see also Martin, 1991, for a discussion of this issue). For example, do men prefer an all-male workplace to one that also employs women? Or are men indifferent to the gender composition of the workplace but do prefer an all-male work group?

These are difficult questions, and we do not propose to resolve them here. However, for the purposes of this chapter, we use self-defined work groups as the focus of our analyses. This approach seems most consistent with the theoretical perspective outlined earlier that assumes that similarity attracts, in part because it facilitates communication and trust. For these reasons, we created respondents' work groups by asking them to identify "those people with whom you most frequently interact in the course of performing your job." By using amount of work-related interaction with a person as the operational definition of a work group member, we thus ensured that there was at least some direct contact between the respondent and other group members. In addition, this strategy avoids the dubious assumption that departmental boundaries necessarily coincide with workers' interactions on the job. (In some cases, work group members were from the same department, but this was not true in every instance.) Although it may be true that other types of groups are also psychologically salient to workers (an issue we are exploring in our ongoing analyses), it seems very *unlikely* that workers would be unaffected by the characteristics of those with whom they must frequently interact on the job. Indeed, we will show that male workers are affected by these characteristics.

Some Exploratory Hypotheses

Previous research suggests that white males may have greater incentives than other groups to be responsive to the gender demographics of their work situation. The similarity-attraction hypothesis, thus, may be particularly applicable in this instance. If males and especially white males prefer interacting with other males, then this should be reflected in higher job satisfaction among men who work with other men than among men whose work groups contain more women.

More important, however, studies imply that men's perceptions of attitudinal similarity to coworkers should also vary according to the gender composition of their work group. Men whose work groups are disproportionately male should perceive greater similarity to coworkers than men in work groups with fewer males. Moreover, this logic implies that the relations between perceived similarity and men's levels of satisfaction should vary according to the gender composition of men's work groups. In particular, similarity should have a positive effect on this outcome among men in predominantly male work groups, whereas it should have a negative effect on satisfaction among men in disproportionately female work groups. If men identify with the social category of gender, they should perceive themselves as better off to the extent that they differ from female members of the work group.

The Data: Men's Work Group Relations

The Sample

The data for this study consist of responses to a survey distributed to the staff employees of a medium-sized Northwest university. The sampling frame consisted of departments employing at least 10 classified or exempt (i.e., nonfaculty) personnel. Units with fewer than 10 employees were eliminated from the study due to concerns that work group data would be more difficult to obtain from smaller units. In this organization, a department is defined as "a sub-division of [the university] that represents a group of employees and their supervisor who together have a defined responsibility for conduct of some portion of the organization." After eliminating the smaller units, 78 departments containing 1,815 employees remained.

Survey responses were obtained from all but one of the 78 departments and the overall response rate was 44.4%. Respondents' demographic characteristics approximate those of the larger pool of classified and exempt employees from which the sample was drawn. For example, at the time of the research, 56.6% of the staff were female and 43.4% were male, compared to 60.2% female ($N = 472$) and 39.4% male ($N = 309$) among survey respondents providing their gender identification. The sample's racial composition also approximates that of the organization's overall racial distribution of classified and exempt employees. The sample was disproportionately white (92.2%), while 89.2% of classified and exempt employees overall claim this racial identity. Represented here are 364 job titles and 77 departments. This chapter analyzes data collected from the

248 men who work with at least one other person and who had nonmissing data on the work groups portion of the survey.

The Measures

We collected data on many facets of employment but were particularly interested in work group relations and workers' views of their coworkers. Hence, the survey was designed explicitly to explore those aspects of organizational demography described above. Our data were unique in certain respects, however, and improved on earlier research on gender composition. Most important, these data asked workers to identify members of their work groups (defined as "those people with whom you most frequently interact in the course of performing your job"), rather than assuming that work group boundaries coincide with department boundaries. With this information, we were able to construct measures of work group gender composition that more accurately reflect people's day-to-day work-related interactions.

After asking respondents to identify members of their work group, we asked several questions designed to assess their perceptions of work group members. These items all addressed respondents' perceived similarity to this set of coworkers. We asked two questions that directly tapped respondents' perceived similarity to work group members. The first asked respondents whether they participated in *similar nonwork activities* as their workmates. Responses to this variable ranged from 1 (*most of our interests are the same*) to 4 (*none of our interests are the same*). A second question asked about similarity with respect to beliefs, attitudes, and personal characteristics. Responses to this variable ranged from 1 (*we are alike in most ways*) to 4 (*we are different in most ways*). Three additional questions also tapped respondents' feelings of closeness to coworkers. For example, we asked the following:

1. "How many people you presently work with would you consider close friends?" Responses to this variable ranged from 1 (*none of the people I work with now are close friends*) to 5 (*four or more of the people I work with now are close friends*).
2. "To what extent would you say you are able to really be yourself with other members of your work group?" This was coded as a dummy variable (1 = *I am always able to be myself*).

3. "How often do you spend a social evening with any or all of the members of your work group?" Responses ranged from 1 (*almost every day*) to 7 (*never*).

Four other questions tapped respondents' perceptions of the cohesiveness of their work group. Respondents were asked to identify their level of agreement with these statements:

1. The members of my work group, including myself, all get along well together on the job.
2. Members of my work group and I don't usually help each other on the job.
3. The members of my work group all stick together on the job.
4. The members of my work group, including myself, are always ready to defend each other from outside criticism. Responses to these items ranged from 1 (*strongly disagree*) to 4 (*strongly agree*).

Finally, we included several measures of job satisfaction. Workers responded to six items, indicating their degree of satisfaction with various facets of employment (i.e., relations with supervisor, relations with co-workers, opportunities for promotion, pay, and nature of work) and their overall job satisfaction, taking everything into consideration. Responses to each item ranged from 1 (*strongly disagree*) to 4 (*strongly agree*).

Results: Men's Work Groups

The means for selected descriptive variables are presented in Table 5.1. Results in the first column of this table show that the average male respondent is 44 years old, a college graduate, and earns an annual gross income of approximately $33,700. The majority (82%) are married or cohabiting with female partners; only 2% of men with partners reported having a male partner. Represented in the male sample are 164 job titles, ranging alphabetically from Accountant to Warehouse Worker II (not shown in the table).

With respect to the theoretically relevant variables, Table 5.1 reveals that, of those whose jobs require some interaction with others, the average work group has 4.4 members, only 1.4 of whom are female. Men's work groups in this sample are, on average, 31% female. Approximately 34% of men are employed in work groups containing no women, whereas slightly over 20% work mostly with women. (Roughly 4% of men work

TABLE 5.1 Means for Selected Variables by Gender Composition of Men's Work Groups

	Gender Composition of Work Groups				
Variables	*Total Sample (N = 248)*	*All-Male (N = 85)*	*Mostly Male (N = 59)*	*Gender Integrated (N = 53)*	*Mostly Female (N = 51)*
Age	44.2*	46.2	43.6	43.8	42.0
High school graduate	.07**	.13	.02	.04	.06
Some college	.29	.31	.36	.21	.25
College graduate	.39	.35	.41	.43	.39
Advanced degree	.24	.19	.22	.30	.29
Married or cohabiting	.82	.86	.86	.79	.74
Annual earnings	$33,724	$34,091	$35,334	$31,871	$33,052
Size of work group	4.54***	4.00	5.34	4.77	4.29
Perceptions of Similarity					
Similarity of nonwork activities	3.20	3.21	3.05	3.24	3.29
Similarity of attitudes	2.63**	2.69	2.40	2.81	2.62
Be myself at work	.44*	.53	.47	.36	.34
Number of close friends at work	2.14	2.34	2.16	2.04	1.90
Spend social evening with coworkers	5.44	5.55	5.12	5.40	5.65

$*p < .10$; $**p < .05$; $***p < .01$.

in all-female work groups.) All-male work groups are slightly smaller than others, whereas work groups that are predominantly male are slightly larger than the average work group. These data are not surprising, as they suggest that most men—even those employed in an organization whose staff is disproportionately female—interact primarily with other men on the job.

Perceptions of the Work Group

Are men who work with other men more likely than those in more gender-integrated work groups to perceive their coworkers as similar to themselves? We examined this issue several ways, using alternative measures of both work group gender composition and perceptions of similarity. First, we explored bivariate associations between the percentage of women in men's work groups and men's responses to the two most direct measures of similarity (i.e., similarity of nonwork activities and similarity of attitudes). Neither result was statistically significant, and both correlations were in the opposite direction than predicted. Bivariate analyses for other measures of similarity yielded findings more consistent with expectations, however. For example, there was a negative, statistically significant correlation between the percentage of women in the work group and men's perceived ability to "be themselves" with their coworkers ($r = -.14$, $p < .04$). Along similar lines, men in work groups having more males reported having more close friends in the work group than men whose work groups contained higher numbers of women ($r = .12$, $p < .06$). There was no association between the percentage of women in the work group and the number of social evenings spent with work group members.

A continuous measure of the percentage of women in the work group may obscure nonlinear associations between gender composition and the various measures of similarity. Therefore, we constructed a categorical measure of gender composition and used analysis of variance to explore the issues described above. As noted above, all male work groups, containing no female members, employed approximately 34% of the sample. Another 24% of men were in predominantly male work groups that ranged from 1% to 39% female. The next category, labeled gender-integrated, contained work groups that were between 40% and 59% female. This category employed 21% of the sample. Finally, predominantly female work groups were defined as those that were at least 60% female. Approximately 20% of men worked in these groups. These categories are shown in columns 2 through 4 of Table 5.1.

Table 5.1 describes differences in perceptions of similarity among men in all-male, predominantly male, gender-integrated, and predominantly female work groups. Columns 2 through 4 of this table show two significant differences between these four groups of men. First, the analysis reveals that men employed in predominantly male work groups are most likely to perceive attitudinal similarity among their coworkers, whereas those in gender-integrated work groups are the least likely to perceive coworkers as having similar attitudes. In contrast, men in all-male and predominantly female work groups offer roughly the same assessment of their similarity to coworkers: Men in both groups view themselves as "somewhat different" from their coworkers.

Though further research is needed to unravel this finding, we can speculate as to what this pattern may imply. It may be that gender is more likely to be used as a basis for inferring similarity in heterogeneous groups than in those more gender homogeneous. This would explain why men in work groups containing only some women (i.e., between 1% and 39% female) perceived themselves as most similar to their coworkers, whereas men in work groups where the proportions of women and men were roughly equal or men were a small minority (i.e., between 40% and 59% female) perceived themselves as most different. Perhaps men in the two more gender-homogeneous categories (i.e., all male and predominantly female) relied on traits other than gender to infer their degree of attitudinal similarity to coworkers.

The results for men's perceived ability to "be themselves" at work are also significant and in the expected direction. For instance, although 53% of men in all-male work groups report that they are "always themselves" at work, only 34% of men in predominantly female work groups give this response. Although this difference cannot be fully explained without further analyses, these results suggest that gender is a salient social category for these men that shapes their feelings of interpersonal comfort and self-consciousness in the workplace. As Table 5.1 shows, however, there are no other significant differences between work groups and men's perceptions of similarity.

In sum, these findings offer equivocal support for the claim that men in predominantly male work groups are not only more similar to their coworkers in demographic terms, but they also perceive themselves as more similar than do men in more gender-integrated work groups. Most consistent with this notion are the findings relating to men's ability to be themselves on the job. Although most men feel at least somewhat able to "be themselves" on the job, this tendency is significantly greater in all-male work groups. It remains to be seen whether these men's higher levels of interpersonal comfort with coworkers translate into higher levels of job satisfaction and commitment. However, these findings provide at least some evidence that men derive interpersonal rewards from homosocial work groups and, accordingly, may perceive some psychological costs in working directly with women.

In addition, there is some evidence that the number of close friendships men form in their work groups is higher when there are fewer women in the group. Men in all-male work groups are close friends with more than two members, while men in predominantly female groups are close friends with less than one member. Although these relations are weak, they are consistent with the claim that demographic dominance translates into perceived benefits for men. In our ongoing analyses, we are continuing to explore these patterns.

Not all indicators of similarity performed as expected, however. The percentage of women in men's work groups was not related to how often men spent a social evening with coworkers or with their perceived similarity in leisure pursuits. These findings underscore the complexity of the issues under investigation. Although the gender composition of men's work groups is related to their perceptions of attitudinal similarity to coworkers, this relationship is not straightforward.

Gender Composition, Similarity, and Satisfaction

Do men in all-male work groups view their work groups as more cohesive than men in work groups containing more women? What role do perceptions of similarity play in men's overall assessment of their jobs? Our preliminary attempts to answer these questions yield some surprising results. As described earlier, four survey items tapped respondents' assessments of work group cohesiveness. We averaged the responses to these four items to create an overall measure of work group cohesiveness. The results show statistically significant differences in cohesiveness among the four work group categories. As the percentage of women in the work group rises, perceived cohesiveness also increases ($r = .19$, $p < .004$). In particular, men in all-male work groups report the lowest levels of cohesiveness, whereas men in predominantly female work groups report the highest levels of this variable (F prob. $< .004$). This pattern persists even when age and education are entered into the model as covariates.

Though this result seems counterintuitive, it may be that our measures of cohesiveness tapped behaviors more likely to be characteristic of women than men. As Tannen (1994) argues, men's characteristic style of interaction involves competition with one another and contests for status. These tendencies may be especially prevalent in all-male (as well as white and heterosexual) work groups. In contrast, women tend to interact in ways that emphasize supportiveness and consideration for others (Tannen, 1994), behaviors that may be more directly evoked by our survey items than those more typical of men's interaction patterns.

The final set of issues that we examined pertained to the relations between the gender composition of men's work groups, their perceived similarities to coworkers, and their overall levels of satisfaction. First, we examined the bivariate associations between the various indicators of similarity to work group members and men's overall levels of job satisfaction. These results were unambiguous: All indicators of similarity except one (i.e., perceived similarity in nonwork activities) were positively correlated with job satisfaction. This underscores the earlier theoretical claim that workplace social relations play an important role in workers' overall assessments of their jobs. In particular, these findings suggest that men's interpersonal comfort may represent a job reward that is most available in all-male work groups.

Do these patterns hold for men in all types of work groups? In particular, we were interested in whether perceived similarity to work group members had the same effects on job satisfaction among men in predominantly female work groups as men in work groups containing more males. Our preliminary explorations of this issue suggest a negative answer to this question. We regressed men's overall level of job satisfaction on men's perceived attitudinal similarities to work group members and three types of work groups: predominantly male, gender-integrated, and predominantly female (all-male work groups represented the reference category). In the next step, we interacted the predominantly female category with perceived attitudinal similarity. These results indicate that perceived attitudinal similarity to work group members is positively related to men's overall levels of job satisfaction. In addition, they reveal that men in predominantly male and gender-integrated work groups report significantly higher levels of job satisfaction than men in work groups only containing men. The satisfaction of men in predominantly female work groups is not significantly different from men in all-male work groups, however. Although these findings diverge from previous studies showing a positive effect of demographic homogeneity on men's levels of job satisfaction, it is important to remember that our model did not include controls for other job and individual characteristics.

Of particular interest, however, are the results for the interaction between predominantly female work groups and perceived attitudinal similarity. This interaction term is statistically significant, suggesting that similarity to coworkers has a different effect on men in predominantly female work groups than those in work groups containing more males. As hypothesized, similarity has a negative effect on the job satisfaction of men in predominantly female work groups, whereas this independent variable has positive effects on satisfaction for other groups of men. This can be seen more clearly by comparing the mean levels of job satisfaction for each group of men. Among men in predominantly female work groups, those who perceive themselves and their coworkers as "alike in most ways" report slightly lower levels of job satisfaction (mean = 2.91) than men who perceive themselves and their coworkers as "mostly different" (mean = 3.0). By contrast, among men in work groups containing only men, those who describe themselves and their coworkers as "alike in most ways" report higher levels of job satisfaction (mean = 3.33) than those who describe themselves as "mostly different" from their work group (mean = 2.67).

These results help refine our understanding of the similarity-attraction hypothesis, as they suggest that the benefits of similarity for men may be outweighed in some circumstances by the advantages of perceiving oneself as different from women. As Williams (1989) notes in her study of male nurses, men in predominantly female settings have an incentive to differentiate themselves from their female counterparts. This strategy may provide economic benefits by enabling men to reap the rewards associated with the assumed possession of more highly regarded masculine traits (e.g., ambitious, career oriented, etc.) and avoid the penalties associated with negative female stereotypes. Moreover, Williams (1989) argues that men in predominantly female settings may be psychologically motivated to see themselves as separate from their female coworkers.

The findings reported here are especially consistent with this latter argument, as they suggest that men in work groups containing more women are less likely to feel they can "really be [themselves]" at work than are men in all-male groups. There could be many factors that prevent men in gender-heterogeneous work groups from being themselves on the job. Though research suggests that women in gender-integrated groups conform more to men's styles of interaction than men in these groups conform to women's (Tannen, 1994), working with women may force men to at least somewhat alter their interaction patterns and behaviors. This would explain why men in predominantly female work groups are those least likely to report that they are always able to be themselves in their work group. In addition, gender may be more salient to men when they work with women than when they interact in all-male work groups. Men—especially those who are white and heterosexual—may feel more self-conscious about their displays of masculinity in groups containing women than in those where women are absent. As noted, being perceived as appropriately masculine in these circumstances has advantages that may not be as available or as recognized in all-male groups. Recognition of these advantages might encourage men who work with women to behave in ways different from how they would behave when their gender was less of a resource. However, although men who work with women may derive benefits from being normatively masculine, they also incur the costs of not being able to be themselves at work. As Connell (1995) notes, "not many men actually meet the normative standards" (p. 79) of the culturally dominant (or what he calls hegemonic) masculinity. To the extent that men who work closely with women perceive advantages to enacting forms of masculinity they may not necessarily fully embrace or possess, we might expect these men to be more self-conscious and less themselves on the job than men in all-male work groups. On a more fundamental level, this finding may reflect Williams' (1989) assertion that being male in American culture means not being female. Hence, men can feel really themselves only when they are apart from women.

Concluding Comments: A Research Agenda

Research on organizational demography and workplace social relations has begun to provide useful accounts of processes too often left unexamined in early attempts to understand the workings of gender in organizations. These research traditions acknowledge that workers are embedded in social relations and organizational contexts that play powerful roles in shaping their identities, perceptions, and behaviors. This approach has allowed us to move beyond a one-sided emphasis on economistic, structural accounts toward more nuanced conceptions of the interplay between individuals' perceptions and behavior, and the larger contexts within which these are embedded (Baron & Pfeffer, 1994).

The findings reported here both draw on and seek to extend this agenda. By examining an important, yet unexplored, conceptual link in the process through which demographic composition is said to shape workers' views and behavior, we show both support and qualification for current theoretical positions. The similarity-attraction hypothesis has been a staple in much current research on the effects of demographic composition, but few have explored whether demographic differences along gender lines are reflected in workers' perceptions of their coworkers. Analyzing data from a sample of disproportionately white, heterosexual males, we showed that perceptions of similarity are dependent on the gender demographics of men's work groups in certain respects, although these findings were not always consistent. Perhaps the most interesting findings in this research concerned the relations between perceived similarity, gender composition, and job satisfaction. Consistent with other research, we found that perceived similarity to coworkers was associated with higher job satisfaction. Our analyses qualify this relationship in one important respect, however: Perceived similarity to coworkers decreased the satisfaction levels of men in predominantly female work groups. This finding is precisely what would be expected, given the advantages men who work with women accrue from adhering to normative masculinity.

We have stressed throughout that these findings should be regarded as preliminary in some respects. As we continue to examine other variables and expand our models of various outcomes, our conclusions may have to be refined and revised. At the same time, we feel confident that the research agenda initiated in this chapter will yield useful insights regarding how men and women, working apart and together, come to understand and relate to one another. Like Martin (1991), we believe that it is at least partly through such interactions that gender distinctions are produced in the workplace, and gender inequalities are maintained. Although this makes it important to study the dominant gender and racial groups as we have done here, it is also imperative to examine other social categories and to explore the ways that these categories are activated in organizational settings. As our research progresses, we hope to shed light on these important issues.

References

Baron, J. N., & Pfeffer, J. (1994). The social psychology of organizations and inequality. *Social Psychology Quarterly, 57,* 190-209.

Connell, R. W. (1995). *Masculinities.* Berkeley: University of California.

Cota, A. A., & Dion, K. L. (1986). Salience of gender and sex composition of ad hoc groups: An experimental test of distinctiveness theory. *Journal of Personality and Social Psychology, 50,* 770-776.

Deaux, K., & Major, B. (1987). Putting gender into context: An interactive model of gender-related behavior. *Psychological Review, 94,* 369-389.

DiMaggio, P. (1990). Cultural aspects of economic action and organization. In R. Friedland & A. F. Robertson (Eds.), *Beyond the marketplace* (pp. 113-136). New York: Aldine de Gruyter.

Ely, R. (1994). The effects of organizational demographics and social identity on relationships among professional women. *Administrative Science Quarterly, 39,* 203-238.

Ibarra, H. (1992). Homophily and differential returns: Sex differences in network structure and access in an advertising firm. *Administrative Science Quarterly, 37,* 363-399.

Johnston, W. B., & Packer, A. H. (1987). *Workforce 2000: Work and workers for the 21st century.* Indianapolis, IN: Hudson Institute.

Kanter, R. M. (1977). *Men and women of the corporation.* New York: Basic Books.

Marks, S. R. (1994). Intimacy in the public realm: The case of co-workers. *Social Forces, 72,* 843-858.

Martin, P. Y. (1991). Gender, interaction, and inequality in organizations. In C. L. Ridgeway (Ed.), *Gender, interaction, and inequality* (pp. 208-231). New York: Springer-Verlag.

Messick, D. M., & Mackie, D. M. (1989). Intergroup relations. *Annual Review of Psychology, 40,* 45-81.

O'Reilly, C., III, Caldwell, D. F., & Barnett, W. P. (1989). Work group demography, social integration and turnover. *Administrative Science Quarterly, 34,* 21-37.

Sen, A. K. (1977). Rational fools: A critique of the behavioral foundations of economic theory. *Philosophy and Public Affairs, 6,* 317-344.

South, S. J., Bonjean, C. M., Markham, W. T., & Corder, J. (1982). Social structure and intergroup interaction: Men and women of the federal bureaucracy. *American Sociological Review, 47,* 587-599.

South, S. J., Bonjean, C. M., Markham, W. T., & Corder, J. (1987). Sex differences in support for organizational advancement. *Work and Occupations, 14,* 261-285.

Tannen, D. (1994). *Talking from 9 to 5.* New York: William Morrow.

Thorne, B. (1993). *Gender play: Girls and boys in school.* New Brunswick, NJ: Rutgers University Press.

Tolbert, P. S., & Bacharach, S. B. (Eds.). (1992). Introduction. *Research in the Sociology of Organizations, 10,* 3-220.

Tolbert, P. S., Simons, T., Andrews, A., & Rhee, J. (1995). The effects of gender composition in academic departments on faculty turnover. *Industrial and Labor Relations Review, 48,* 562-579.

Tsui, A. S., Egan, T. D., & O'Reilly, C., III. (1992). Being different: Relational demography and organizational attachment. *Administrative Science Quarterly, 37,* 549-579.

Wagner, W. G. Pfeffer, J., & O'Reilly, C., III. (1984). Organizational demography and turnover in top-management groups. *Administrative Science Quarterly, 29,* 74-92.

Wharton, A. S. (1992). The social construction of gender and race in organizations: A social identity and group mobilization perspective. *Research in the Sociology of Organizations, 10,* 55-84.

Wharton, A. S., & Baron, J. N. (1987). So happy together? The impact of gender segregation on men at work. *American Sociological Review, 52,* 574-587.

Wharton, A. S., & Baron, J. N. (1991). Satisfaction? The psychological impact of gender segregation on women at work. *Sociological Quarterly, 32,* 365-388.

Williams, C. L. (1989). *Gender differences at work.* Berkeley: University of California.

6

Hegemonic Masculinity Among the Elite

Power, Identity, and Homophily in Social Networks

MARTIN KILDUFF
AJAY MEHRA

What does it mean to be a man? For many people, manliness may connote aggressiveness, strength, power, and authority, as well as a facility with technology (Wright, this volume) and a rejection of anything feminine. The stereotypical male is in charge, has muscles, and can fix the car. To the extent that people define being a man in these terms, they endorse what has come to be known as *hegemonic masculinity,* a sharply defined male identity popularized by Hollywood and other important contributors to Western cultural norms, including schools and universities (Connell, 1987). Male fantasy figures, such as Rambo, demonstrate the widespread appeal of male hegemonic identity. This male identity subordinates both other males as well as women to lower status. Other identities available to males or females are much less well-defined with the result that, for example, "there is no femininity that holds among women the position held by hegemonic masculinity among men" (Connell, 1987, p. 187).

One of the arenas where male hegemony appears to hold sway is male professional sports (Messner, 1992). For example, a recent *Sports Illustrated* story detailed how many male professional athletes identify ardently with the TV soap opera character Victor Newman, who "relies on

AUTHORS' NOTE: We thank Dan Brass, Cliff Cheng, and Kelly Mollica for helpful comments on an earlier draft of this chapter.

intimidation, manipulation" and who "runs his business with the ruthlessness of a Chinese warlord and sheds his redundant wives as easily as he does his tuxedo" (Lidz, 1995, p. 6). A previous issue of *Sports Illustrated* (July 31, 1995) presented evidence of the widespread violence toward wives and girlfriends on the part of male professional athletes.

The impact of sports training and sports watching on male identity can hardly be exaggerated as far as Western countries are concerned. As Connell (1995) says, "In historically recent times, sport has come to be the leading definer of masculinity in male culture" (p. 54). Through sports watching and playing, males are taught the importance of strength, skill, and overcoming pain to compete against others. Despite efforts to promote athletics for women in the United States, for example, there are no female equivalents to the NFL, the NBA, or championship boxing in terms of presenting vivid and recurrent images of gendered identity. Furthermore, male identification with athletic heroes starts early and develops through the stardom accorded athletes in schools and universities.

But does male hegemony characterize the world of business? There are reasons to suspect that it does. The business world, like the world of professional sports, tends to admire aggressiveness and power. Sports metaphors abound in discussions of business success and failure, and successful sports figures, such as basketball coach Pat Riley, earn large sums as motivational speakers at business gatherings (Katz, 1995). Successful sports stars appear on the cover of the leading business publications (e.g., Michael Jordan featured on the cover of *Fortune,* January 15, 1996). Business leaders, such as Rupert Murdoch, are routinely described as "arrogant" and "utterly ruthless" (Donaldson, 1993, p. 655). To the extent that hegemonic masculinity is "naturalized in the form of the hero and presented through . . . sagas, ballads, westerns, thrillers" in books, films, and television (p. 646), a natural exemplar of such masculinity is the business hero. People such as Jack Welch of GE and Ted Turner of Turner Broadcasting are constantly depicted as heroes of business wars on the covers of news magazines and on television. Biographies and autobiographies of businessmen, such as Lee Iacocca, sell in the millions, and sometimes the success of such idolizing prompts political ambitions (witness the presidential bid by Ross Perot in the United States).

Male hegemony is not just about a certain type of male identity, it is also about "the winning and holding of power" (Donaldson, 1993, p. 644) in organizations and society. As developed by Gramsci (1971) in his prison notebooks, *hegemony* refers to the process by which the ruling class exerts control over society while representing this in terms of universal social advancement. One of the key arenas for the understanding of hegemony is the educational system, particularly the parts of the system that train business leaders and, therefore, function as the portals to the ruling elites in capitalist societies. Despite the importance of education for producing and reproducing male hegemony, there has been "surprisingly little discussion of the role of education in the transformation of masculinity" (Connell, 1995, p. 238; but see Addleston & Stirratt, this volume).

A good place to begin to understand the effects of hegemonic masculinity on the ruling elite in capitalist societies, therefore, is in the social relations among students at elite business schools. The current research examines the extent to which male hegemonic identity appears to play a role in the career transitions of elite business students in the United States.

The need for systematic examination of the male hegemonic thesis is quite evident. Despite an outpouring of theory and informed speculation (see the reviews by Connell, 1987, and Donaldson, 1993), there has been such an absence of focused empirical work that Donaldson (1993), for example, declares, "A sociology of ruling class men is long overdue" (p. 655). Previous research on men's friendships has tended to focus on working-class males (e.g., Wellman, 1992) or specific demographic categories of males (e.g., Franklin, 1992) and has neglected males of high socioeconomic status. In the present chapter, we attempt to formalize some aspects of the male hegemonic thesis and examine its importance for aspirants to the ruling class of American executives. We take as our sample one year's graduating class of master's of business administration (MBA) students at one of the elite business schools in the United States. This particular business school emphasized the study of finance and prided itself on placing many of its graduates in the cutthroat competitive arena of Wall Street deal making. Competition and aggressiveness appeared to be prominent elements in the culture of the school.

The first prediction is that both males and females will tend to identify within sex rather than across sex. In an elite MBA program, identities are being reconstructed as students prepare themselves for entry into the American ruling class. These students are in transition between their previous careers as engineers, waitpersons, students, and so on and their new careers as executives. They spend 2 years constructing new identities for themselves through continuous socialization by peers, drawing on the culture of the business school (Van Maanen, 1983). According to social comparison theory, people learn about themselves by comparing themselves to similar others (Festinger, 1954). One of the principal bases of similarity is sex. Males are likely to look to other males for evidence of how to behave, given the prevailing emphasis on male hegemonic values in the culture of the business school.

What about women in such programs? In a male hegemonic organization, female identity becomes problematic. One possibility is for women to identify with male hegemony and become surrogate males, internalizing the values of ruthless competition and domination that feature so strongly in the annals of business success. In male hegemonic organizations, ambitious women "act pretty much like men" (female respondent in Ely, 1994, p. 221). But the overwhelming cultural emphasis on the masculinity inherent in the male hegemonic identity makes this option relatively unattractive for many women. As one female respondent in a recent study of partners in U.S. law firms explained, "I don't like the idea of being partners with these [men]. They're all so different from me, and it's such a powerhouse type of mentality. I just don't think that's really for me" (Ely, 1995, p. 621).

The images associated with male hegemonic identity (Humphrey Bogart, John Wayne, Sylvester Stallone; see Connell, 1987, p. 185) leave little room for a negotiated female presence. One of the major forms of femininity that appears in reaction to male hegemony is what Connell (1987, p. 183) calls emphasized femininity, one that is oriented to accommodating the interests and desires of men. As one of Ely's (1995) respondents explained, "Every once in a while [when you're dealing with men], if you want to get something done, you get into your little-girl-cutesy-flirtsy mode" (p. 620). Other possible female identities involve complex interactions of compliance, resistance, and cooperation. To the extent that women attempt to construct and maintain identities separate from the male hegemonic identity that we can assume is dominant in the elite business school culture, women should identify themselves with other women rather than with other men. To summarize, therefore, both men and women are predicted to identify within sex from a male hegemony perspective.

> Hypothesis 1: Both men and women in elite MBA programs are likely to identify with members of their own sex.

The question remains: For which group, men or women, will the pressure to conserve a gendered identity be greater? In the particular arena covered by the present chapter, we are assuming that male hegemonic identity is nonproblematic. Men, therefore, should be reasonably relaxed in their gendered selves (especially during the second year of the MBA program), as they discover the day-to-day emphasis within the MBA program on male hegemonic values of competition, ruthlessness, and dominance. Men, from this perspective, can allow themselves to identify to some extent with women whose characters they admire, because masculine identity is not threatened.

Women, on the other hand, are likely to be uneasy with the promotion of male hegemonic values to the extent that it crowds out the possibility of constructing and maintaining femininity. An elite MBA program may contain many threats to the gendered identity of women. From this perspective, women may feel relatively unable to identify with males, because female identities are under daily attack in the elite business school environment. Therefore, we are likely to find that women, more than men, identify within sex.

Hypothesis 2: Women in elite MBA programs will show a greater tendency to identify within sex than will men.

Power is an important factor in business success, and in an elite MBA program, power takes the form of social connections; such programs are arenas for building networks that will create and sustain opportunities for career advancement. Networking has become the route to good jobs and swift advancement (Baker, 1994). Power, therefore, involves being central in the friendship network. There are many ways to define centrality in social networks (Freeman, 1979). Bonacich (1987) has argued that centrality depends not just on having lots of friends but in having the right friends. Thus, power can be increased by having connections to friends who themselves have lots of friends. Because both strong relations to personal friends and weak relations to friends of friends are important for discovering opportunities and capitalizing on them (Granovetter, 1974), we measure individuals' power as including both direct and indirect ties to others with ties to central others weighted more heavily than ties to peripheral others.

The theory of male hegemony suggests that power and dominance is more important to male identity than it is to female identity. As Connell (1987) suggests, "All forms of femininity in this society are constructed in the context of the overall subordination of women to men" (pp. 186-187). This suggests that, on average, female power (in the social network) should be less than male power in the context of an elite MBA program.

Hypothesis 3: In elite MBA programs, men will be more powerful than women.

The theory of male hegemony also suggests that power within the social world of the elite business school is distributed not randomly but according to the logic of male dominance. Thus, those who achieve power in this arena will tend to be people who ally themselves with males rather than with females. Given the choice of a connection to a male or a female, someone interested in building a power base that will help promote career advancement will tend to invest time in making male friends (cf. Brass, 1985). From the perspective of male hegemony, this is true for both men and women: Powerful people of either sex will prefer male friends, because males dominate the business world and are therefore more useful as allies in the competition to get ahead. The surprising conclusion, therefore, from this perspective is that powerful males will be more likely to make friendships within sex compared to powerful females. From the perspective of male hegemony theory, friendship relations in an elite MBA program are another arena for competition to gain entrance to the networks that determine success and failure in the world of work.

Hypothesis 4: In elite MBA programs, powerful men, relative to powerful women, will be more likely to make friendships within sex.

For men, therefore, there will tend to be consistency between attitudes and behavior: Those men who tend to identify with other males will also be free to make friends with other males. For women, though, there may be a disparity between the tendency to identify with other women and the necessity in this male hegemonic world for women who want power to make strategic friendships with males. Thus, we predict that for men more than for women, those who identify within sex will also make friends within sex.

Hypothesis 5: In elite MBA programs, the tendency for those who identify within sex to make friendships within sex will be stronger for men than for women.

But dominance is not just a behavioral phenomenon, it is an important aspect of male hegemonic identity that is relatively absent from emphasized femininity or other kinds of feminine identity. As Connell (1987) suggests, the "note of domination that is so important in relations between kinds of masculinity is muted" (p. 187) with respect to femininity. In other words, men who achieve social dominance or power in a context that emphasizes male hegemony are likely to be admired as fulfilling expectations concerning male identity. Women who achieve social dominance in this context, however, are less likely to be admired, because social dominance is more difficult to reconcile with feminine identity.

Hypothesis 6: In elite MBA programs, powerful men are likely to be more admired than powerful women.

Methods

Respondents

The research population consisted of one year's graduating class of 209 people from a nationally ranked (top 5 to top 20, depending on the poll) MBA program. Nonresidents of the United States were excluded, because they were ineligible to work in the United States and were therefore unlikely to participate in the competition for power and admiration that we have linked conceptually to the search for good jobs. The average age of respondents was 27, and 70% were male. Of the 209 graduates, 181 (87%) completed mailed copies of the social network questionnaire prior to graduation. Missing data reduced the sample to 159 people (105 men and 54 women), 76% of the original population.

Measures

Network Measures. Two networks were assessed: The identity network and the friendship network. To measure which others a particular individual identified with, we asked (on the questionnaire) each respondent to look carefully down a list of second-year MBAs and place checks against the names of people he or she considered to be especially similar to himself or herself. The bases of similarity were not specified, so each individual was free to choose to identify with anyone else based on criteria that were individually important rather than on the basis of researcher-imposed constructs (cf. Kelly, 1955).

Similarly, friendship was measured by asking respondents to look carefully down a list of second-year MBAs and place checks next to the names of people they considered to be personal friends. The friendship and identity data were arranged into matrices of size 159 × 159 with cell entries of 0 or 1. For example, a 1 in a cell formed by the intersection of Row 110 and Column 83 in the friendship matrix meant that Person 110 had nominated Person 83 as a personal friend.

Identity and Friendship Homophily. We measured homophily to take into account not only the proportion of cites to people of a different sex for each person but also the availability of people of each sex. Because there were over twice as many men as women in the sample, it was numerically easier for women to cite men than for men to cite women. For each person, therefore, we computed the two homophily indices to correct for availability bias (see the review by Gower & Legendre, 1986, and the empirical example in Ibarra, 1992). For each person we counted (a) the number of cites to people of the same sex, (b) the number of cites to people of different sex, (c) the number of people of the same sex the respondent could have cited but omitted, and (d) the number of people of different sex whom the respondent could have cited but omitted. For each person, an identity homophily index and a friendship homophily index were then calculated, using the following formula:

$$H = \frac{ad - bc}{\sqrt{(a+c)(b+d)(a+b)(c+d)}} .$$

The homophily index ranges from –1 to +1: Negative values indicate a tendency to cite members of the other sex, controlling for availability, whereas positive values indicate a tendency to cite members of the same sex, controlling for availability.

Admiration and Power. We used the identity matrix to measure admiration, given that people are likely to chose to identify with others they admire rather than with those they are indifferent or negative toward. Given our emphasis on the importance of network ties in the MBA program for job search and advancement, we studied power in terms of the friendship network in the MBA program. We were interested in taking into account not only direct ties between people but also indirect ties. Bonacich (1987) has argued that individuals' centrality is boosted by being connected to others who are central: Not all connections are equally valuable. Thus, in the current data set, being connected to someone who has many friends can be an important boost to reputation and social capital. Admiration and power indices, therefore, were computed for each individual i as *Bonacich Power* applied to the relevant adjacency matrix (A), using the following formula to compute the centrality of vertex i, c_i:

$$\sum_j (\alpha + \beta c_j) A_{ij},$$

where alpha and beta are parameters. Alpha is used to normalize the measure, and is automatically selected "so that the sum of the squares of the vertex centralities is the size of the network" (Borgatti, Everett, & Freeman, 1992, p. 82). We selected a positive value of beta, to give weight to being connected to central actors, and kept its value less than the absolute value of the reciprocal of the largest eigenvalue of the adjacency matrix (Borgatti, Everett, & Freeman, 1992, p. 83). The calculation of Power followed exactly the same logic as that of Admiration, except that the formula was applied to the friendship matrix instead of the identity matrix. The program used to calculate the Bonacich power indices automatically symmetrized the friendship and identity matrices by taking the underlying graph (Borgatti, Everett, & Freeman, 1992).

Analyses and Results

Our underlying assumption in this chapter has been that the elite MBA program in the United States is an arena in which people prepare themselves for elite positions in U.S. corporations. Only if this assumption is valid is there any reason to suppose that MBA students compete to forge bonds with elite members of the MBA class—with people they expect to move into increasingly important corporate positions.

The placement record of the class of 1987 surveyed in this research suggests they were indeed headed for elite positions in American business: Each student averaged 16 on-campus interviews with major corporations, resulting in a mean of three job offers each. Their mean starting salary in 1987 dollars was $43,698 (ranging from $27,500 to $65,000).

The first prediction from the perspective of a theory of male hegemony was that both men and women in elite MBA programs were likely to identify with members of their own sex. The first line of Table 6.1 shows this that was the case: The identity homophily indices for men and women were both positive, showing that, controlling for availability, both men and women tended to identify with members of their own sex. The second

TABLE 6.1 Homophily and Power in Men's and Women's Networks

Variable	*Men (n = 105[a])* *Mean (SD)*	*Women (n = 54)* *Mean (SD)*	*t*
1. Identity homophily	.037 (.080)	.085 (.079)	–3.590*
2. Friendship homophily	.028 (.144)	.058 (.106)	–1.487
3. Power	38.381 (26.782)	31.995 (24.221)	1.470
4. Admiration	6.449 (6.209)	5.420 (4.391)	1.210

a. n = 104 for Identity Homophily and Friendship Homophily due to missing data.
* $p < .001$.

line of Table 6.1 also shows that men and women tended to form friendships within sex: Again, the homophily indices were positive.

The second prediction was that the tendency of elite MBAs to identify within sex was likely to be more pronounced for women than for men, given the male hegemonic culture of the business school. Again, this hypothesis was supported. As the first line of Table 6.1 shows, women were significantly more likely to identify within sex than were men ($t = -3.59$, $p < .001$). Furthermore, the trend of the data in the second line of Table 6.1 shows that males, relative to females, tended to make less friendships within sex, although this difference did not reach statistical significance.

Table 6.1 gives only slight support to the third prediction that men in the MBA program would be more powerful than women. The third line of Table 6.1 shows no significant difference between the average power of men and women, although the mean value of power for men was higher than that for women. The fourth line in Table 6.1 shows that men and women also did not differ in terms of how much they were admired by others. In summary, there were no significant social capital differences between men and women: The average female received approximately the same amount of power and admiration as the average male.

Table 6.2 shows Pearson correlations between variables broken down for men and women. In Hypothesis 4, we predicted that powerful men, relative to powerful women, would be more likely to make friendships within sex. In other words, we expected powerful people to tend to ally themselves with males rather than with females. This hypothesis was supported: Both prestigious men and prestigious women tended to form male friendships. As the fourth line in Table 6.2 shows, prestigious men

TABLE 6.2 Correlations Between Variables for Men's and Women's Networks

Variables	*Men* $n = 105^a$	*Women* $n = 54$	*Fisher's z*
1. Identity homophily/ friendship homophily	$.36^{**}$	.19	.99
2. Identity homophily/power	.10	.15	–.29
3. Identity homophily/admiration	$.17^{+}$	.29*	–.75
4. Friendship homophily/power	$.21^{*}$	–.11	1.86^{*}
5. Friendship homophily/ admiration	.01	.12	–.65
6. Power/Admiration	$.45^{**}$	$.33^{*}$	.85

a. $n = 104$ for identity homophily and friendship homophily due to missing data.
$+p < .10$; $*p < .05$; $**p < .001$.

tended to form within sex friendships ($r = 21, p < .05$), whereas prestigious women tended to form cross-sex friendships ($r = -.11$, *ns*), and this difference between correlations was significant (Fisher's $z = 1.86$, $p < .05$).

We also expected to find greater consistency between attitudes and behavior for men compared to women so that for men, more than for women, there would be a correlation between identifying within sex and actually forming friendships within sex. As the first line in Table 6.2 shows, there was some support for Hypothesis 5. Men who identified with other men did tend to form male friendships ($r = 36$, $p < .001$), whereas there was no significant tendency for women who identified with women to form female friendships ($r = .19$, *ns*). However, the difference in correlations between men and women was not significant (Fisher's $z = .99$, *ns*).

The third prediction concerning Table 6.2 was that males who were powerful in the social world, relative to females who were powerful, would tend to be more admired by others (Hypothesis 6). Power, it was predicted, would be more important to male identity than to female identity. The trend of the correlations in the sixth row of Table 6.2 supported this hypothesis, but the difference in correlations for men ($r = .45$, $p < .001$) and women ($r = .33$, $p < .05$) did not reach statistical significance (Fisher's $z = .85$).

Finally, there is some evidence in Table 6.2 that those who identified with members of their own sex tended to be admired. For women, this tendency was significant ($r = .29$, $p < .05$) but for men only barely so ($r = .17$, $p < .10$).

Discussion

In summary, the results demonstrate the subtle influence of male hegemonic identity on the social worlds of elite MBA students, both male and female. Men tended to identify within sex, but not as much as women in this male hegemonic environment. Furthermore, although both men and women achieved similar levels of social capital in terms of power and admiration in social networks, the powerful actors of either sex tended to ally themselves with males rather than females; and there is some evidence that, for men more than for women, social dominance was admired.

The overall picture is one in which male identity is less problematic than female identity in the context of an elite MBA program in which male hegemonic values are extolled. Men who identified within sex tended to make friends within sex, unlike women who, if they sought to be powerful, had to make cross-sex connections. One of the chief paradoxes these data reveal is that there appears to be significantly less pressure on males to protect their gendered identity in the elite business school environment where male hegemonic values are reinforced. Women's identities appear to be under siege, with high levels of within-sex identification and friendship combined with the necessity for cross-sex friendship alliances for those who aspired to power.

The predictions from male hegemony theory tend to differ somewhat from those that emphasize the importance of demography. Thus, for example, Ibarra (1993, p. 67) predicted that women would tend to have less homophily in their social networks than men, whereas the evidence in the current chapter shows quite the opposite. Ely (1995) found support for the hypothesis that women in sex-integrated contexts were free to enact male or female identities as they saw fit, whereas in the current study, the high degree of sex integration (in the demographic sense discussed by Ely) did not appear to allow women to identify across gender lines. Although 30% of the MBA class in the current study was female (well above the 15% criterion established by Ely as indicative of sex integration), women were less likely than men to identify across sex lines.

In taking into account male hegemony, then, we are going beyond the mere demographic exercise of counting the percentage of men and women present in a social setting. More important, perhaps, than demography is the cultural context of interaction. The researcher must ask, to what extent is this setting one in which male hegemonic values are extolled and encouraged? Places where male hegemonic values of aggressive competition and power are emphasized and reproduced are likely to be quite different from sites where other values are espoused.

Schneider (1987) has suggested that the people make the place: Arenas of competition and struggle attract people who already accept these values. Thus, both men and women who are accepted into elite business schools are likely to also accept the inevitability of male hegemonic values in society. For men, this means tailoring their identities to a widely accepted cultural norm for males. For women, though, the acceptance of male hegemonic identity is inevitably disruptive of female identity, because male hegemony is premised on the subordination of femininity.

Women who graduate from elite MBA programs, therefore, and pursue executive careers are likely to find themselves increasingly dissatisfied with the demands of identity repair that the corporate life demands. Indeed, the phenomenon of high-flying corporate women changing careers in midstream is attracting attention: "Many [executive women] have simply wearied of the male-dominated game and seek to do business more on their own terms. They change not only their jobs but their ideas of success as well" (Morris, 1995, p. 62). Such highly successful women are reevaluating the price they must pay to succeed in the hegemonic male corporation for which they were trained in business school.

An emphasis on male hegemony, therefore, redirects research attention to several aspects of organizations that have been neglected. First, to what extent do organizations systematically promote values and images that reinforce aggressiveness, competition, and power? A prediction from male hegemonic theory is that in male hegemonic contexts, homophobia, racism, and sexism will tend to be rife. Recent revelations concerning military and police organizations in the United States provide anecdotal evidence of the connection between male hegemonic organizations and a culture of subordination of minorities.

Second, organizations that promote male hegemonic values are likely to mute the leadership potential of women. Recent evidence from the Israeli military show that only men can produce self-fulfilling prophecy effects in female recruits in this particular context (Dvir, Eden, & Banjo, 1995). The authors' conclusion that women in general cannot produce the

Pygmalion effect ignores the possibility that the military context itself undermines the leadership identity of women.

Third, research could profitably investigate how individual personality is shaped by the striking availability of gendered identities for men and women. Is it the case that certain personality types (such as high self-monitors—see Kilduff & Day, 1994) tend to adapt themselves to clearly defined and available identities, such as male hegemony? What are the consequences for career success of such personality malleability?

The focus on power, social interaction, leadership, and personality suggested by the male hegemonic perspective opens many new arenas for research on organizations. In analyzing what it means to be a man in contemporary society, such research may also provide insight on enduring problems of racism and sexism in organizations.

References

Baker, W. E. (1994). *Networking smart: How to build relationships for personal and organizational success.* New York: McGraw-Hill.

Bonacich, P. (1987). Power and centrality: A family of measures. *American Journal of Sociology, 5,* 1170-1182.

Borgatti, S., Everett, M. G., & Freeman, L. C. (1992). *UCINET IV version 1.0 reference manual.* Columbia, SC: Analytic Technologies.

Brass, D. J. (1985). Men's and women's networks: A study of interaction patterns and influence in an organization. *Academy of Management Journal, 28,* 327-343.

Connell, R. W. (1987). *Gender and power: Society, the person and sexual politics.* Stanford, CA: Stanford University Press.

Connell, R. W. (1995). *Masculinities.* Berkeley, CA: University of California Press.

Donaldson, M. (1993). What is hegemonic masculinity? *Theory and Society, 22,* 643-657.

Dvir, T., Eden, D., & Banjo, M. L. (1995). Self-fulfilling prophecy and gender: Can women be Pygmalion and Galatea? *Journal of Applied Psychology, 80,* 253-270.

Ely, R. J. (1994). The effects of organizational demographics and social identity on relationships among professional women. *Administrative Science Quarterly, 39,* 203-238.

Ely, R. J. (1995). The power in demography: Women's social construction of gender identity at work. *Academy of Management Journal, 38,* 589-634.

Festinger, L. (1954). A theory of social comparison processes. *Human Relations, 7,* 117-140.

Franklin, C. W. (1992). "Hey, home—Yo, Bro": Friendship among black men. In P. M. Nardi (Ed.), *Men's friendships,* (pp. 201-214). Newbury Park, CA: Sage.

Freeman, L. C. (1979). Centrality in social networks: Conceptual clarification. *Social Networks, 1,* 215-239.

Gower, J. C., & Legendre, P. (1986). Metric and Euclidean properties of dissimilarity coefficients. *Journal of Classification, 3,* 5-48.

processes. The notion that individuals try to influence what others think of them has been argued conceptually (Swann, 1984, 1987, 1990) and observed in the field (e.g., McNulty & Swann, 1994). It seems that people employ at least three separate strategies to develop a social environment that supports their self-concepts. They may signal who they are to others, strategically choose interaction partners who confirm their self-concepts, and adopt interaction strategies (for instance, use interpersonal prompts) that elicit confirmatory reactions from others, even when information received is negative. Using these strategies, individuals will attempt to help others figure out and respond to who they are and, thus, verify their masculinities. For instance, a Hindu male may wear the *rakhi* (a colorful woven thread worn like a bracelet) that his sister tied to his wrist on Rakshabandhan (a Hindu festival symbolizing love and affection between brothers and sisters where the brothers vow to protect and take care of their sisters for life). Someone who defines himself in terms of a gay masculinity may keep a photograph of his loved one on his desk. In this way, each signals the identity he wishes others to respect. Alternatively, during lunch breaks, men may seek the company of others who confirm their masculine identities. In addition to developing a compatible social structure, people are likely to process information so as to support their self-views. They will selectively attend, encode, retrieve, and interpret information to ensure that their self-concepts survive. A more detailed account of verification strategies and of empirical evidence appears in Swann (1983, 1990, in press).

The fact that individuals actively seek negative self-verifying feedback from others (e.g., Swann, Pelham, & Krull, 1989) and prefer to verify rather than enhance identities (e.g., Swann, de la Ronde, & Hixon, 1994) attests to the strength of self-verification processes.[3] Arguably, most people would agree that individuals seek to verify their positive identities. The notion that people also seek to verify negative or less desirable identities may be more surprising. This tendency is important when one thinks in terms of verifying subordinated or marginalized masculinities. Some may believe that a person who defines himself according to a subordinated identity (e.g., an African American man) may prefer to blend into an organization or to adjust his self-concept to accommodate the dominant hegemony. In fact, one could argue that such beliefs are part of an ethnocentric hegemonic folklore that sustains a system of dominance. Yet, evidence suggests that those who define themselves through alternative masculinities will attempt to verify these "lesser" identities. This will happen to the extent that a person is certain of the identity (Swann, 1984), values the identity across situations (i.e., the identity is a core identity), or considers the identity to be salient in a particular situation (cf. Brewer, 1991; Markus & Kunda, 1986).

This chapter does not explore the specific content and nature of masculinities, beyond suggesting its conceptualization as pluralistic and briefly describing some of the characteristics often associated with the current dominant masculinity. As elements of an individual's self-concept, masculinities may be either attribute based or group based. The latter social identities (e.g., Asian man) result from individuals categorizing themselves as members of groups and internalizing these social categories or memberships (Tajfel, 1982; Tajfel & Turner, 1985). The former (e.g., gentle man) results from individuals categorizing themselves in terms of characteristics. Self-verification arguments apply, regardless of content specifics. And, as Connell (1987) points out, it is not necessary to clearly define masculinities other than hegemonic masculinity to discuss them. Achieving hegemony may, in fact, involve preventing the cultural definition and recognition of alternatives. Instead, what is important is to recognize that the dominant masculinity does not describe all male masculinities, and men are likely to seek validation for alternatives that are important to them. To this end, they will engage in identity negotiation.

Organizations Negotiate Masculinities With Their Members

An individual's masculinity will be verified within an organization to the extent that other organization members validate and sustain it.

> Identities are socially bestowed. They must also be socially sustained and fairly steadily so. One cannot be human all by oneself and, apparently, one cannot hold on to any particular identity all by oneself. (Berger, 1963, p. 85)

When a masculinity is verified, the individual who holds it feels that he can enact this masculinity and that others are aware of it and will support it. Thus, he experiences order and coherence in his mental and social worlds and can turn his attention to other business.

The extent to which verification occurs depends on an identity negotiation process or dance, if you will, within which all interaction partners attempt to lead. Organization members come to the dance and enter interactions with independent and at times conflicting self-concepts.

These multiple self-concepts, including assorted masculinities, are sources of uncertainty that need to be worked out within relationships. People need to attain the collective equivalent of the mental and social coherence that we spoke about earlier at the individual level of analysis. Workmates need to be reliable, predictable interaction partners, and identity negotiation proceeds as they resolve interpersonal ambiguities between them, establishing who is who so as to create fluid collective movement or, at least, to avoid stepping on each other's toes. Thus, through a process of identity negotiation, people sort out identities (e.g., masculinities) that they are to assume during their interactions with each other (Goffman, 1959; Swann, 1987).

Identity negotiation is a sense-making process; that is, it is a process through which people make their situations accountable to themselves and others (cf. Morgan, Frost, & Pondy, 1983) by individually and collectively trying to create order and interpret them (cf. Berger & Luckmann, 1967; Mead, 1934). The process is at once social, psychological, and cultural. Just as Mead and followers emphasized that self-views grow out of a series of transactions between society and individuals, the masculinities of organization members grow out of interpersonal transactions between them.

Thinking of each individual as both a target and a perceiver, each participates in negotiating his own identity and those identities that others are to assume. Specifically, as targets, men attempt to verify their own masculinities. Simultaneously, as perceivers, they strive to form accurate impressions of and hypotheses about others and to validate their own expectancies. When people bring others to see them as they see themselves, verification effects occur. This describes the situation where a man achieves having workmates confirm his self-defined masculinity. It would occur, for instance, in the situation where, on noticing the *rakhi* of a Hindu man, a Westerner inquires about extended family members, including women whom the Westerner would label as cousins but whom the Hindu would call sisters and, thus, watch out for as part of his Hindu masculinity. In contrast, when men who define themselves through alternative masculinities accommodate social cues indicating that others expect hegemonic masculinity, appraisal effects occur. These effects refer to the situation in which a gay man attempts to behave like a hegemonic man in response to the expectancies of others or in which the Hindu man takes off his *rakhi* at work in response to coworker disapproval. Such appraisal effects may be moderated by what individuals think that others think of them, that is, by reflected appraisal effects. To the extent that a gay man believes that others accept his alternative masculinity (regardless of whether, in fact, they do), he may enact it over hegemonic masculinity. Thus, identity negotiation unfolds through self-verification, appraisal, and reflected appraisal effects.

And organization culture provides the context and often the medium for this sorting-out process. Interpersonal identity negotiations may be affected by both an organization's ideology and by concrete manifestations of that ideology. Ideologies are "shared, relatively coherently interrelated sets of emotionally charged beliefs, values, and norms that bind some people together and help them to make sense of their worlds" (Trice & Beyer, 1993, p. 33). Concrete manifestations of this ideology or cultural forms are "observable entities through which members of a culture express, affirm, and communicate cultural substance to one another" (Trice & Beyer, 1993, p. 77). These observable entities may be symbols, language, narratives, practices, or a combination of these.

Inasmuch as an organization's ideology and cultural forms support hegemonic masculinity, alternative masculinities—masculinities critical to some of its members' self-concepts—may not be verified within the organization. As stated earlier, subordination of some masculine identities is inevitable within a hegemonic system. Subordination occurs as a dominant masculinity assumes an ideological character and, thus, becomes taken for granted and socially desired, as cultural forms within the system support the hegemony, and as social interaction reflects these.

People assign meanings to gender differences and relate to each other on the basis of these meanings (Rubin, 1975). As long as hegemonic masculinity is taken for granted, it may be interpreted as natural and, hence, inevitable and universal. Individuals within the social system (in this case, an organization) come to expect each other to practice hegemonic masculinity, and they use cultural forms and interpersonal strategies to send out cues, informing others about their expectations. Thus, the dominant masculinity becomes the standard for appraisal effects. Males may respond to the accompanying cues and enact the dominant masculinity, in which case appraisal effects occur. Or, they may think about the standards implicated by organization action and respond to what they believe others think, thereby exhibiting reflected appraisal effects.[4] Thus, those who define themselves through the dominant masculinity come to have the power of culture behind their expectancies and social behaviors. In these environments, hegemonically masculine men are more likely than others to have their masculinity verified. Those who seek to verify alternative masculinities have to do so against the grain of the social structure that confronts them.[5]

Organizations and the people within them purposefully or inadvertently accept or reject and marginalize or subordinate identities all the time. Often, this occurs in ways that mirror verification attempts and involve cultural forms. For example, organizations signal acceptance of gay masculinities by extending medical benefits to same-sex spouses, that is, by sending an identity cue through the medium of the cultural form *organization practice.* People within organizations may also either socially welcome or ostracize Asian men who openly value and enact, rather than withdraw from, their unique masculinity. They may, for instance, use language to highlight "unacceptable" differences or tell stories about Asian males who failed to "measure up," because they could not "go for the throat" in negotiation or otherwise display the aggression needed to succeed. In these and other ways, organizations encourage employees to support the dominant masculinity, as they extend "real men don't cry" standards into industrial life.

Pluralistic or Hegemonic Agreements Result

To recapitulate, so as to foster understanding of themselves, men will attempt to signal masculinities that are important to them. Their interaction partners will enact parallel efforts to bring others to see them as they see themselves. And both parties will attempt to get others to enact the masculinities that each personally expects. Through a culturally framed identity negotiation process, members of an organization will arrive at an implicit agreement regarding the identities that each will assume at work. As events unfold, men will seek confirmation of their own masculinities from others but also may adjust their masculinities to those of others. Each will internally resolve competing demands that may arise from multiple self-definitions.

Adjustment may occur through chronic clashes, adaptation, assimilation, or a combination of these (Trice, 1993). Sometimes, differences in the identities within and between individuals will conflict. At other times, they will be compatible. This may depend on the degree to which sources of conflict (e.g., values or behaviors associated with identities) are mutually exclusive, central to those involved, or both. Related issues may be critical to some individuals and irrelevant to others. In general, however, conflicts that implicate selves can be expected to be particularly central to the selves who are implicated.

Theoretically, it seems that the optimal solution would be an identity agreement that verifies the core and most important situational identities of all members, while not jeopardizing the ability of the organization to meet its goals. Inasmuch as both conditions are met, workable identity agreements may include mutual tolerance and accommodation, egalitarian relations, or a combination of these.[6] Such integrative bargaining solutions run counter to hegemonic masculinity. In hegemonic environments, assimilation labels often mask varying degrees of the domination of one identity over others. Inasmuch as the hegemony represents a taken-for-granted ideology, it becomes invisible—often being neither overtly advanced nor consciously recognized. It just becomes part of "the way it is" and people cease to question "it." Yet, despite the silence, or maybe particularly because of it, it is important to contemplate outcomes associated with hegemony. What happens in settings in which non-hegemonic males attempt to verify their self-concepts? And why should organizations care about this? The next section explores these "what happens" and "so what" issues, by considering one particular organization outcome—the extent to which one who defines oneself in terms of an alternative masculinity cooperates with others at work.

Verifying Masculinities May Promote Cooperation

Few would argue with the statement that many business problems require the collective attention and cooperation of people with varying skills and orientations—assets that often come attached to a range of identities—including masculinities. These people, with their varying identities, cooperate when they work together toward a common goal.

Cooperation is a behavior that varies in form, depending on the extent to which people further their own interests, those of others, or both, and the extent to which they a priori expect their actions to be reciprocated. As depicted in Figure 7.1, depending on these factors, cooperative behavior may be mutual, helping, or altruistic. In all cases, the interests of another are or have the potential to be advanced. One of the requirements of cooperation is the willingness of people to further the well-being of others (Deutsch, 1993; Kohn, 1992). In the process of being cooperative,

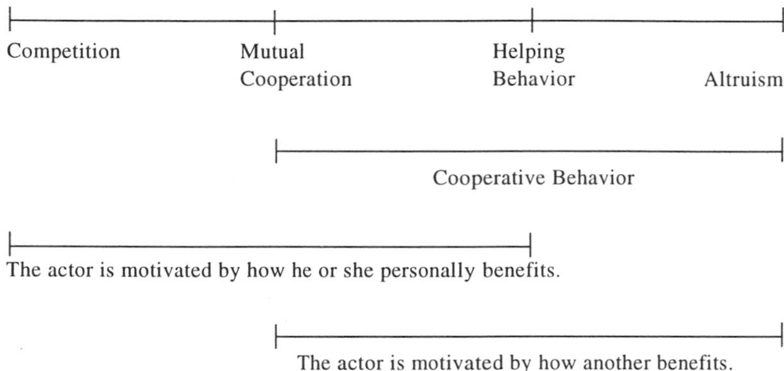

Figure 7.1. Cooperative Behavior as a Function of Whose Interests Are Believed to Be Served

sometimes individuals gain personally and sometimes they do not.[7] Often, external rewards—that have received so much attention in previous work (Argyle, 1991)—are involved, but this is not necessarily the case. When people act on their own to exclusively meet their own needs, they engage in individual behavior. If they act with others to pursue compatible goals, enjoy a joint activity, or further the relationship between them (Argyle, 1991) and a priori expect reciprocity equal to their contribution, they engage in mutual cooperation. When individuals do not expect reciprocation equal to their contributions or at all but act both to assist others and to personally benefit, they engage in helping behavior. When empathy for others, rather than self-interest, drives actions, individuals engage in altruism (Batson, 1991), the third form of cooperation. Actors may benefit post hoc, for instance, by feeling personally satisfied. However, because anticipation of this satisfaction did not drive their behaviors initially, this eventual benefit does not change the altruistic nature of the actions.

Thus, it is not the behavior that prompts the label—it is the motive behind the behavior. Furthermore, the motive may vary among people. I argue, however, that organization members will be more cooperative in situations or relationships in which their masculinities are verified than in those in which they are not. They will also be more likely to engage in less self-serving forms of cooperation (namely, helping and altruistic behavior). As discussed, when working together, people negotiate the identities that they are to assume during their interactions. Often, the assumption seems to be that if people can be "helped" to identify with subgroups or companies, then they will assimilate their identities and cooperate, or alternatively, if they can be induced to behave cooperatively, then the issue of multiple identities need not be addressed. But this is a dangerous assumption. Although these strategies may work in some situations, they arguably suffer from an inadequate understanding of self-verification and, hence, are fallible for at least two reasons.

First, assimilation or "higher" identity solutions often assume that people can and will change their identities. Neither may be true. Assimilation is sometimes framed in terms of transcending individual identities, as one becomes attached to a larger whole. Conceived of in this way, the extent to which people "give up" who they are may be construed as an indication of their commitment to a larger entity (e.g., a work group or firm). Sacrificing identities assumes a moral overtone, and the difference between behavioral integration (in a social system in which various identities compatibly coexist) and assimilation (where one identity dominates) is often lost. Similarly, difficulties inherent in changing identities are overlooked. As discussed, people tend to behave in ways that are consistent with their self-concepts, including masculinities, and they structure their lives to support these conceptions. The opportunity structures that result can be difficult to change, and people may want to alter neither their identities nor the structures that support them. To deny a valued masculinity by behaving as a hegemonically masculine person or by going underground is tantamount to rejecting oneself. This denial may be fraught with hazards.

Studies have shown that there are reasons why it may not be wise to expect individuals to sacrifice identities they value. Adjusting to new groups can be anxiety producing, and it seems that a strong self-concept helps people to deal with the ambiguity of new cultures (Hoffman, 1990). It may also help them to cope with organizational change. In addition, hampering a person's ability to maintain consistent recognizable identities may result in self-shock as the individual experiences inconsistent, conflicting self-images. Self-shock emerges when unshared meanings for behaviors simultaneously increase one's need to confirm identities and decrease one's ability to do so (Zaharna, 1989). When in self-shock, people cannot maintain a consistent sense of self as they face the challenge of changing behaviors that sustain their self-concepts, and they cannot read the reactions of others accurately. This may lead to a loss of self-confidence, feelings of self-doubt, discomfort, confusion, and anxiety (Zaharna, 1989). These and other effects may lessen their ability to contribute to organizations and productively cooperate with others.

Second, assimilation assumes that people will cooperate in situations where salient identities are not verified. This may not occur when men who are certain of their masculinities expect to have these verified in situations in which they are not. In these situations, men can be expected to cooperate more with others who validate their masculinities than with those who do not. This will happen as a byproduct, when men purposefully or inadvertently construct their social environments to support their masculinities. Specifically, it will occur as men choose some interaction partners over others, become committed to relationships within which their masculinities are validated, and distort perceptions of social reality to support their masculinities. The connection between each of these verification strategies and cooperation is now explored.[8] In the process, empirical evidence from social psychology is sampled and extended to illustrate connections between cooperation and men trying to validate and sustain their masculinities. Links to other organizational outcomes are suggested in the following section. Evidence that supports the tendency of people to gravitate toward interaction partners who confirm their sense of self is first highlighted.

In a laboratory experiment, Swann, Wenzlaff, Krull, and Pelham (1992) tested the hypothesis that people seek self-verifying partners. They told individuals who appraised themselves either positively or negatively that they had been evaluated by two persons and would soon select one with whom to interact. They then showed participants comments alleged to have been written by each of the two evaluators. One set of comments was favorable, and one set was negative. People with positive self-views preferred to interact with the favorable evaluator, whereas those with negative self-views preferred the unfavorable one. In the experiment, people with negative self-views preferred interacting with evaluators who appraised them negatively over participating in another experiment. In a later field study, Swann et al. (1994) found that marriage partners were more likely to spend time with and be otherwise intimate with partners when the partner's appraisal of them was similar to rather than different from their own self-views.

Just as people prefer interaction partners who confirm self-attribute and skill evaluations, so may men prefer to interact with people who verify their masculinities over those who do not. By definition, cooperation is a social behavior; it must involve the interests or actions or both of two or more people. Thus, cooperation will inevitably be affected by people's choices of interaction partners. Think, for instance, of a man who defines himself through an Asian masculinity. This man may elect to work overtime on a project with colleagues in a unit other than his own, because they value his collective orientation. In contrast, he may not do so with colleagues in his own unit who religiously ascribe to a dominant, competitive, hypermasculine ideal type. These people may value his business contacts and, therefore, "put up with" his "strange, effeminate, nerdish" ways. He may read the signature of their disapproval in his interactions with them and, thus, seek support for his valued masculinity elsewhere (see Cheng, in this volume, for a discussion of Asian and Asian American identities and stereotypes). Choices regarding workmates may reflect not only a preference to work with self-verifying others but a lack of commitment to those who do not verify valued, situationally active masculinities. This connection between commitment and cooperation lies at the heart of the second piece of evidence linking self-verification strategies to cooperation.

In their field study, Swann et al. (1994) found that efforts to self-verify influence people's preferences for relationship partners outside of the lab, and that self-verification is reflected in commitment to relationships. Specifically, they found that people were committed to marriage relationships to the extent that their spouses evaluated them in the same way as they viewed themselves. Those with positive self-views displayed more commitment when spouses evaluated them favorably, whereas those with negative self-views showed more commitment when spouses appraised them unfavorably. Even people with positive self-views were less committed to spouses who were overly positive. Hence, self-verification rather than self-enhancement seemed to be the critical process.

The connection between commitment to an organization and prosocial behavior (one form of cooperation) has been empirically established. O'Reilly and Chatman (1986) found two forms of commitment (identification and internalization) to be related to prosocial behavior. Although both were operationalized in terms of the psychological attachment a person feels toward an organization, identification maps particularly well onto Swann et al.'s (1994) work. These researchers operationalized commitment in terms of a person's desire and plans to stay in a relationship, whereas O'Reilly and Chatman defined identification as involvement based on a desire for affiliation. Thus, inasmuch as verification is associated with commitment to relationships and collectives, it seems reasonable to expect that it will also predict cooperation within these. Arguably, men will be more committed to and, thus, cooperative with people and organizations that verify their masculinities than to those that do not.

As previewed, a third link between verification strategies and cooperation stems from individuals' tendencies to selectively perceive social reality to support their self-concepts. Evidence shows that people are especially attentive to, preferentially encode and recall, and endorse feedback that fits with their self-conceptions (see Swann, 1987, for a review). In the process of perceptually buffering themselves, people often seek support from others. Given a preference for interacting with others who verify their self-concepts, individuals gravitate toward relationships that confirm their sense of self both inside and outside of organizations. This is important in that intimates who support an individual's self-concept tend to buffer that person from discrepant feedback, that is, from feedback that does not support the individual's self-concept (see Swann & Predmore, 1985, for empirical evidence). Thus, these intimates may insulate a man from organizational attempts to change or discredit valued masculinities. As part of an individual's support network, they may help sustain individuals who distance themselves mentally or physically from organizations after their mental and social coherence has been jeopardized by the organization's failure to verify masculinities. In this and other ways, not verifying masculinities may lead to distancing and, thus, to reduced cooperation between organization members. Any event that causes people to question who they are, for instance, having a key masculinity criticized, may intensify a person's efforts to self-verify (cf. Shibutani, 1961). The tendency for feedback that diverges from an individual's self-concept (i.e., self-discrepant feedback) to focus attention on elements of the self-concept that seem to be challenged has been shown by Swann and Hill (1986)[9] and recognized elsewhere (cf. Zaharna, 1989). To the extent that self-discrepant feedback primes masculinities, it should increase the probability that these identities guide subsequent behavior. Primes may, in fact, trigger or intensify in- and out-group categorizations and thereby enhance in-group bias and affect cooperation between groups or individuals in organizations (cf. Brewer, 1979; Hamilton & Trolier, 1986; Kramer, 1991).

On a more positive note, if masculinities are supported within organizations, the interests of organizations may become aligned to the interests of members. In these situations, deeper (i.e., less self-serving) forms of cooperation, such as helping behavior and altruism, become consistent with maintaining one's self-concept. Individuals may extend their self-definitions to include the organization involved; that is, they may internalize an organization identity as an element of the self that is consistent with rather than discrepant from valued masculinities. As individuals consciously or subconsciously behave consistently with the image they have of themselves, they tend to cooperate in organizations that preserve their self-concepts (Dutton, Dukerich, & Harquail, 1994). In the process, they may become more attracted to members of their organizations, making cooperation more likely (Abrams & Hogg, 1988).

There is a large and growing literature, arguing that people manage their lives to maintain congruent roles, occupations, and even organizations. O'Reilly, Chatman, and Caldwell (1991) found that person-organization fit predicted organization commitment. Tom (1971) found that the greater the similarity between an individual's self-concept and his image of the organization, the more he preferred that organization. Extending this observation, it is reasonable to expect that the greater the similarity between an individual's masculinities and those an organization either represents or verifies, the more he may prefer that organization over another. As he verifies his masculinity, this preference may be reflected in increased contact with or commitment to the organization or both and, thus, it may predict his cooperation within or with the organization. Preference or attraction may eventually be reflected in identification with the organization, and this identification may drive cooperation. Either way, verification serves as an important antecedent and sustaining feature of cooperation; in one case, it precedes attraction, and in the other, it precedes identification.

Verification Is Reflected in Other Organization Outcomes

In this chapter, I opted to explore in depth one organization outcome, cooperation, as an example of how self-verification affects organizations. Strategies that individuals use to verify their masculinities may also explain other organization phenomena. For example, preferences for interacting with people who verify masculinities and perceptual distortion to support one's self-concept may be reflected in social integration and in coalitions within organizations. Both social integration (Katz & Kahn, 1978; O'Reilly, Caldwell, & Barnett, 1989) and coalitions are influenced by the extent to which people socialize with, are mutually attracted to, and are satisfied with each other. Coalitions may affect organizations through informal networks and internal politics. Higher degrees of social integration may be associated with higher satisfaction and morale and more efficient task coordination (McGrath, 1984; O'Reilly et al., 1989). As a potential antecedent to organization commitment, verification may be related to a host of other outcomes. Organization commitment has been associated with job satisfaction and turnover (Meyer, Allen, & Smith, 1993; O'Reilly et al., 1991), voluntary absenteeism (Meyer et al., 1993), job performance (Angle & Perry, 1981; Meyer & Allen, 1991), and innovativeness (Katz & Kahn, 1978).

When organizations prime individual differences by not verifying masculinities, they may also stimulate stereotype threat. In this case, knowing that others expect him to behave in a certain way, because he is a member of a negatively stereotyped group, a person may become apprehensive and act as expected (Steele & Aronson, 1995), withdrawing from the situation to protect his self-esteem. Steele and Aronson (1995) and Spencer and Steele (1994) found race and gender stereotype threat to be associated with performance differences between black and white and between female and male students and with those in the negatively stereotyped categories (i.e., black and female), performing lower and confirming stereotypes as a consequence of withdrawing effort from a task (e.g., writing a math exam). In a similar fashion, men who define themselves through marginalized or subordinated masculinities may withdraw effort and confirm stereotypes when they feel threatened. Situations where their masculinities are not verified may prime such feelings of threat, and organizations may be affected as men fulfill stereotyped expectations. In situations where men receive little or no validation for core masculinities, disintegration, anxiety, and accompanying stress may escalate and interfere with work. Effects may be especially noticeable when performance depends on self-verification, for example, in situations where a firm sense of identity predicts success. This may include situations in which an employee represents his company abroad (cf. Hawes & Kealey, 1981) and situations in which the employee or the company is experiencing a transition (cf. Bennett, 1977).

When individuals are unable to verify masculinities that are important to them, they may also spend more time and energy trying to negotiate these than they otherwise would. This diverted energy may detract from productivity. Identity negotiation concerns recess, and people focus on other goals only after they have sorted out their identities. Identity agreements become reflected in the behavioral norms that characterize relationships. Harmony prevails to the extent that all live up to their negotiated identities. If someone fails to honor an identity, for example, if a gay man openly declares himself to be homosexual, confusion, conflict, or both may result. In this case, the pursuit of organization goals may be interrupted, as those who interact with the now self-declared homosexual man revisit previously taken-for-granted identity agreements. Inasmuch as identity agreements override or mask masculinities that people value, these agreements can be expected to break down, and those involved will spend more time and energy renegotiating than will those whose agreements reflect who people really are.

Sustaining false identities may prove difficult in the long run. Men will likely honor masculinities they actually define themselves through more easily than those they do not.[10] Thus, when men enact their authentic identities, they may be more predictable interaction partners. When men fake masculinities, identity leakage may occur, as their masks slip, and they emit clues as to their real masculinities. Consequently, identity agreements may breakdown and have to be renegotiated. Men may also become alienated from their workplaces, if being there involves continually faking masculinities. Marx argued that people become alienated when separated from the products of their physical labor. Hochschild (1983) extended Marx's reasoning to speak of emotional labor or labor that "requires one to induce or suppress feeling in order to sustain the outward countenance that produces the proper state of mind in others" (p. 7). In the spirit of this discussion, I suggest that the "identity labor" or labor that requires one to enact and believe in identities to be accepted by and work within one's organization may be equally or more alienating. Rafaeli and Sutton (1987) describe the state of emotional harmony as a state that exists to the extent that the emotions that individuals feel match the emotions that they display to meet the expectations of others. Borrowing from Rafaeli and Sutton's work, one could say that "identity harmony" prevails to the extent that one enacts "real" rather than "feigned" identities, and these identities are validated by interaction partners. Those who ascribe to a dominant identity may always have the advantage of such harmony, whereas those who do not may continually experience gradations of turmoil that are reflected in their personal and work worlds. If deep acting, or acting beyond surface display, is required to put forth and feel a false emotional face, then subterranean acting may be needed to maintain and believe in false identities.

Boundary Conditions of the Verification Argument

A framework that illustrates connections between verifying gender identities and organizational consequences that have been explored in this chapter appears in Figure 7.2. Consistent with an open systems perspective, this framework is intended to serve as a foundation for speculation about how verifying gender identities may affect organizations. As a heuristic framework, it does not attempt to reflect all the complex and multiple causal linkages among constructs.

It is important to realize, however, that relationships between verifying alternative masculinities and positive organizational outcomes are unlikely to be linear. There may be a threshold above which things are good and below which they are not. Several conditions may attenuate relationships. For example, men will vary in how much they wish to validate their masculinities at work. As discussed, verification needs will be stronger for those who are certain of the masculinities they ascribe to, and who consider these to be situationally salient or core personal identities or both. Verification at work may also be more of a concern for individuals who define themselves primarily through their work lives.

Factors other than self-verification will also affect each of the outcomes discussed. For instance, structure, by way of work settings (Browning, Beyer, & Shelter, 1995) or rewards (cf. Axelrod, 1984; Eccles & White, 1988; Miller & Hamblin, 1963) may predict cooperation. Individual dispositions (Chatman & Barsade, 1995) and objective levels of interdependence between people (Kramer, 1991) may also be important. I am not arguing that verifying masculinities and other self-concept elements is all that affects cooperation and other organization outcomes but, rather, that it may an important, perhaps pivotal, contributor that deserves much more attention than it has received.

There is also likely an upper limit on the extent to which organizations can support idiosyncratic identities and on the extent to which organization members would desire this. The concept of integrative bargaining within identity negotiation bespeaks give and take, and living within a collective requires adjustment to support community needs. Hence, the notion of a threshold level of verification becomes important. It is unlikely that organization members will cooperate to the extent that all can enact each of their identities, however deviant. There are both identity and structural reasons for this. In some cases, verifying someone's identity, for example, as an aggressive hypercompetitive person may violate

Moderating Conditions

Organizational Ideology

Cultural Forms

Social Interaction That Supports Hegemony

Interpersonal and Task Interdependence

Verification Strategies	*Intrapersonal Mediators*	*Consequences for Organizations at Varying Levels of Analysis*		
		Individual	*Interpersonal (dyads, groups)*	*Organization*
Develop an opportunity structure that supports gender identities • Display signs and symbols • Selectively interact with others who verify identities • Use interaction strategies that elicit validating reactions	Certainty about the gender identity	Self-confidence	Mutual attraction	Behavioral and social integration • Satisfaction and morale • Efficient task coordination
	Whether the gender is a core identity	Disintegration anxiety and stress	Mutual commitment	
	Situational salience of the gender identity	In- and out-group categorizations	Behavioral and social integration	Intraorganizational cooperation
		Stereotype threat	Cooperation (mutual, helping, and altruistic)	Intraorganizational coalitions • Informal networks • Organizational politics
		Time and energy task	Mutual social support	
Selective perception to confirm identities • Attending • Encoding • Retrieving • Interpreting		Ability to cope with ambiguity and change		Success of organizational change efforts
		Alienation from self, others, and workplace		Performance and productivity

Predictable behavior

Attachment to/distancing from the organization

Attraction to the organization

Contact with the organization

Organizational commitment

- Prosocial behavior
- Voluntary absenteeism
- Job satisfaction
- Turnover
- Performance
- Innovativeness

Organizational identification

NOTE: As a heuristic framework to be used for speculation, this figure does not attempt to reflect all the multiple and complex causal linkages among constructs.

Figure 7.2. Framework for Studying the Organizational Consequences of Verifying Gender Identities

one's own identity. In other cases, identities (e.g., a gang member or an aggressive person) may not be compatible with the interests of the collective. Compromises that would be needed to resolve situations such as these may not always be possible. As discussed earlier, a perfect agreement would be one that verifies the core and most important masculinities of all members and also supports the goals of the organization. The identity mix involved must be acceptable to all, and it must work. Trade-offs will be needed and difficult choices faced. This will likely mean different forms of resolution for different groups (cf. Trice 1993), but it need not imply a homogenized identity that assimilates alternative masculinities into a hegemonic order.

Connections Between Verification and Symbolic Interaction Perspectives

Most ideas discussed in this chapter are compatible with symbolic interactionism. As Franklin (1988) explains, symbolic interactionism emphasizes group living or negotiations between people, shared meanings, and the social construction of behavior. This chapter argues that people within organizations socially construct their identities through negotiation processes that occur within a social system of shared meaning. The process is subjective and includes both conscious and subconscious elements. Males are argued to "become men," as they take on meaning within a social system. These meanings affect how people relate to each other. Thus, masculinities arise and are sustained through social interaction, a perspective consistent with symbolic interactionism (cf. Blumer, 1969; Mead, 1934). Given its emphasis on reflected appraisal, symbolic interactionists appear to assume that people are conscious of the processes involved. A verification perspective does not. The latter argues that people are not conscious of at least some of the processes. The main difference between the verification perspective relayed in this chapter and a purely symbolic interactionist one is, however, essentially one of emphasis.

A symbolic interactionist would likely assign a greater, perhaps critical, role to social context as constraining identity negotiation (cf. Stryker & Gottlieb, 1981) and would assert more strongly that an individual's masculinity is a reflection of his perceptions of how he appears to others (cf. Shrauger & Schoeneman, 1979). Symbolic interactionism and verification theory make the same identity and behavioral predictions in situations where men and their interaction partners agree on and share masculinities. Variance becomes obvious, however, when predicting identity and behavioral adjustment in situations where there is dissonance or tension between the two. In these cases, target tendencies to verify their self-concepts may compete with tendencies for them to behave in ways that confirm others' expectancies. Symbolic interactionism implies that individuals resolve such discrepancies by changing their self-concepts or behaviors. Identities are seen to originate socially in reflected appraisals or "looking glass selves" (cf. Cooley, 1902); hence, individuals experience themselves indirectly through others rather than directly (cf. Mead, 1934). On the other hand, verification theory suggests that people have reasonably clear and stable self-concepts that may not readily conform to the discrepant appraisal of others. It also provides a motive for this lack of individual adjustment; notably, individuals seek coherent mental and social lives. Hence, in a discrepant situation they are expected to try to bring others to see them as they see themselves, that is, to confirm and support their masculinities (cf. Shrauger & Schoeneman, 1979).

This chapter extends a verification perspective within a framework that is compatible with symbolic interactionism to examine consequences of failing to verify masculinities that are important to men's self-concepts. From a verification point of view, assimilation beyond a certain point may endanger the integrity of a social system; it sets up a system of acting rather than of being. A healthy social system is arguably one in which the identities of members (identities that may exist independent of the views of others) are verified at least to some collectively acceptable threshold.

Conclusions and Implications

There are both theoretical and empirical reasons to expect organization outcomes and verifying alternative masculinities to become aligned through identity negotiation processes. Ultimately, people gravitate toward and become committed to relationships and environments that confirm their self-concepts. When a masculinity is a core or situationally salient element of a man's self-concept, he will, like others, seek to validate his sense of self. In the process, he may coalesce with those in an organization who verify his masculinity and become his support network. If verification is not forthcoming, he may physically or psychologically distance himself from a hegemonic organization as he reverts to a bunker or seeks validation elsewhere. In the military, bunkers are fortified, partly underground shelters that are used as hideouts. They may become secure places for communication and planning, or they may be just places to tremble in the dark waiting for the shelling to cease. In days of old, bunkers were the coal bins on ships—places where marginalized or subordinated crew members toiled—members whose role was critical to the ship moving forward but who would rarely be invited to play major "on deck" roles. In both cases, as selves revert to bunkers, those within the shelters may bond, or, alternatively, they may tremble or perhaps just steel themselves against interpersonal connection in an effort to protect who they are. In each instance, all that selves in bunkers could achieve beyond their hideouts becomes lost to the organizations that employ them and the societies that support these organizations.

This chapter extends our understanding of how organizations are affected by the needs of individuals to validate their self-concepts—in this case—masculinities. In particular, by focusing on one specific process through which cooperation arises, it provides additional insight into why individuals cooperate in some settings over others. The main contributions of the chapter are its extension of the self-verification literature to masculinities, its merger of self-verification and social construction of the self theories with organization outcomes, and its use of the latter merged literature to challenge arguments that favor assimilation of identities within organizations. The chapter clearly recognizes that people behave as they do because of who they are. Understanding this "who" paves the way for predicting how people will behave both in situations in which action is consciously motivated and in those in which it is nonvolitional.

A fourth contribution of the chapter is that it clearly articulates a critical role for organization culture in identity negotiation processes and suggests research into the role of hegemonic ideology and the use of cultural forms to sustain hegemonic identities. In addition, the chapter leads to research concerning factors that cause specific identity negotiations to be relatively target- or perceiver-driven[11] and also furthers research that focuses on the effects of overlapping and multiple social relationships on business. These relationships are resident in groups that individuals identify with and gravitate toward. Granovetter (1985) noted that social networks penetrate economic activities irregularly and in different degrees, and Scott (1992) pointed out the importance of determining how other involvements affect business. By examining how men's needs to validate their masculinities may affect social and business networks, we should better understand factors that affect penetration of external concerns and the processes through which this occurs.

Throughout this chapter, I have used examples to describe various masculinities and thereby illustrate points being made. For instance, I spoke of an African American man, an Asian man, a gay man, and a Hindu man. In closing, it is important to caution that within each of these social categories, men may ascribe to a variety of masculinities because of differences between them, for example, differences in social roles, social class, religions, and subcultures (cf. Gilmore, 1990). An individual's self-concept resides within himself. The masculinity that a man ascribes to is the one that he applies to his self-definition, however idiosyncratic this may be.[12]

From a philosophic point of view, cooperation and other behaviors at work may be viewed as surface behaviors that reflect the multidimensional and layered identities of individuals enacted on a collective level. All aspects of a person, not only those that organizations create, are represented in these identities. Arguments that favor identity assimilation often do not recognize the complex pluralistic nature of identity. Furthermore, they do not treat seriously arguments that tie divestiture processes to lower innovation and creativity (cf. Van Maanen & Schein, 1979) or, I would argue, to the alienation of people from their work. There is considerable evidence attesting to the importance of self-verification in individuals' lives and thereby to identity negotiation agreements that encourage people to invest themselves in their lives and work. Identity negotiation processes can support such agreements. Creating an environment within which men can enact their masculinities in a collectively responsible way arguably enhances feelings of self-worth, intrinsic motivation, and community. Individualistic rewards of self-expression, self-efficacy, and self-consistency ensue, along with benefits associated with an enhanced sense of relationship, as people feel valued for who they are and extend the same acceptance to others. Both individuals and their organizations thereby benefit.

Initially, I was reluctant to write a chapter focusing on alternative masculinities. My first reaction: "Me—*but*—I am a woman—I am a feminist—How could I?" And I think therein lies the point—How could I not? In confronting my hesitancy, I came to realize that—as a social scientist, as an organization scientist, as a human being, and as a woman—I am arguing for a nonhegemonic rather than a neohegemonic social order.

Acknowledgments

I wish to thank William Swann, Camille Buckner, Cliff Cheng, Jeffrey Polzer, and two anonymous reviewers for their generous comments on earlier drafts of this work. I am also indebted to Paul Mang for helping me refine my conceptualization of cooperation and to both Cary Booker and Saurabh Gupta for their input into examples of various masculinities. To Cliff Cheng, I express particular gratitude; his support as an editor and as colleague has been invaluable.

Notes

1. As Kimmel (1994) elaborates, this masculinity defines white, middle-class, early middle-aged, heterosexual men. It is important, however, to remember that we often use demographic categories as proxies for "characteristics," for instance, "hyper-masculine, competitive, Rambo types," and that any demographic category is unlikely to be monolithic. Thus, it is a mistake to lump all men within any demographic category into the stereotype of hegemonic male. It is fair to say, however, that the hegemonic masculine gender construction is dominant and has become normative and that, at a particular point in history, its profile may be more closely aligned with some groups of men rather than with others. The degree of alignment can be empirically assessed.

2. The terms verification and self-verification are used interchangeably within this chapter.

3. It is important to note that the tendency to seek negative feedback does not appear to be the result of a masochistic personality. Research has found, for example, that people with low self-esteem sought unfavorable information with respect to their limitations, but they sought positive information about their other strengths (Swann, Pelham, & Krull, 1989). Erickson (1960) argued that "social confirmation of *some* identity, even a negative one, is often preferable to a lack of confirmation and the uncertainty and confusion that results" (p. 62).

4. The idea that the reactions of others provide the basis of self-views is widely accepted in the social sciences. It has been theoretically argued (Cooley, 1902; Mead, 1934; Swann, 1983) and empirically demonstrated (Felson, 1989; McNulty & Swann, 1994). Theoretical and empirical evidence that reflected appraisals' moderate appraisal effects is outlined in Shrauger and Schoeneman (1979).

5. Consider, for example, a man trying to enact his gay masculinity at work. As Buchbinder (1994) points out, "since dominant notions of masculinity assume heterosexuality to be the norm in men, homosexuality may be interpreted as a failure of masculinity" (p. 62). Whether it is construed as a curable ailment or as an irreversible disease, it is seen as a subversion of the normal. Society often responds by discriminating against gays or targeting them for ridicule, violence, and moral and legal coercion. Such is the reality that often confronts a man trying to validate his homosexual masculinity at work.

6. Refer to Trice and Beyer (1993) for a related discussion with respect to relationships between occupational subcultures.

7. Whether cooperation is mutual, helping, or altruistic, cooperation is not the same thing as consensus; people may disagree and experience conflict and yet still cooperate. In fact, it has been strongly argued that constructively processing conflict is one of the main characteristics of cooperative and highly functioning groups (Golembiewski & Kiepper, 1988); group-think is not an inevitable outcome of cooperation.

8. The connection between self-verification and cooperation within organizations (or elsewhere) has not been explicitly studied. To date, empirical studies of self-verification have focused on verification of abilities and characteristics (e.g., intellectual and academic ability, social skills and social competence, artistic ability, athletic ability, and physical attractiveness). Research has also tended to focus on social and intimate (including dating and marriage) relationships within dyads. In this chapter, I extend a self-verification argument beyond these self-attribute and skill identities to the masculinities that men define themselves through. In other work, I apply a verification argument to social identities (Milton, 1995).

9. This observation was based on unpublished data that was cited in Swann, 1987.

10. This is true for a number of reasons that are related to a verification argument. Pragmatically, behaving in a fashion that is consistent with one's self-view requires the least effort (see both Gilbert, Krull, & Pelham, 1988, and Sutton, 1991, for empirical support and Hochschild, 1983, for a related theoretical argument). It also fits well within the premises of cognitive dissonance (Cooper & Fazio, 1984; Festinger, 1957; Festinger & Carlsmith, 1959), self-perception (D. J. Bem, 1972), and symbolic interactionist (Cooley, 1902; Mead, 1934; Shrauger & Schoeneman, 1979; Stryker, 1987) theories. The arguments of self theorists who support the importance of coherent mental and social lives that were cited earlier within this chapter also bolster the argument.

11. McNulty and Swann (1994) argue for the need for this type of research.

12. For a related discussion on a multifactorial theory of gender identity, refer to Spence and Buckner, 1995.

References

Abrams, D., & Hogg, M. (1988). Comments on the motivational status of self-esteem in social identity and intergroup discrimination. *European Journal of Social Psychology, 18,* 317-334.

Angle, H. L., & Perry, J. L. (1981). An empirical assessment of organizational commitments and organizational effectiveness. *Administrative Science Quarterly, 26,* 1-14.

Argyle, M. (1991). *Cooperation: The basis of sociability.* London: Routledge.

Axelrod, R. (1984). *The evolution of cooperation.* New York: Basic Books.

Batson, C. D. (1991). *The altruism question: Toward a social-psychological answer.* Hillsdale, NJ: Lawrence Erlbaum.

Bem, D. J. (1972). Self-perception theory. In L. Berkowitz (Ed.), *Advances in experimental social psychology* (Vol. 6, pp. 1-62). New York: Academic Press.

Bem, S. L. (1974). The measurement of psychological androgyny. *Journal of Consulting and Clinical Psychology, 42,* 155-162.

Bennett, J. (1977). Transition shock: Putting culture shock in perspective. *International and Intercultural Communication Annual, 4,* 45-52.

Berger, P. L. (1963). *Invitation to sociology: A humanistic perspective.* Garden City, NY: Anchor.

Berger, P. L., & Luckmann, T. (1967). *The social construction of reality* (2nd ed.). Garden City, NY: Anchor.

Blumer, H. (1969). *Symbolic interactionism: Perspective and method.* Englewood Cliffs, NJ: Prentice Hall.

Brewer, M. B. (1979). In-group bias in the minimal intergroup situation: A cognitive-motivational analysis. *Psychological Bulletin, 86,* 397-324.

Brewer, M. B. (1991). The social self: On being the same and different at the same time. *Personality and Social Psychology Bulletin, 17,* 475-482.

Brod, H. (Ed.). (1987). *The making of masculinities: The new men's studies.* New York: Routledge.

Browning, L. D., Beyer, J. M., & Shelter, J. C. (1995). Building cooperation in a competitive industry: SEMATECH and the semiconductor industry. *Academy of Management Journal, 38,* 113-151.

Buchbinder, D. (1994). *Masculinities and identities.* Carlton, Victoria, Australia: Melbourne University Press.

Carrigan, T., Connell, R. W., & Lee, J. (1985). Toward a new sociology of masculinity. *Theory and Society, 14,* 551-604.

Chatman, J. A., & Barsade, S. G. (1995). Personality, organization culture, and cooperation: Evidence from a business simulation. *Administrative Science Quarterly, 40,* 423-443.

Connell, R. W. (1987). *Gender and power: Society, the person and sexual politics.* Oxford, UK: Polity Press.

Cooley, C. H. (1902). *Human nature and the social order.* New York: Scribner.

Cooper, J., & Fazio, R. H. (1984). A new look at dissonance theory. *Advances in Experimental Social Psychology, 17,* 229-266.

Deutsch, M. (1993). Educating for a peaceful world. *American Psychologist, 48,* 510-517.

Dutton, J. E., Dukerich, J. M., & Harquail, C. V. (1994). Organization images and member identification. *Administrative Science Quarterly, 39,* 239-263.

Eccles, R. G., & White, H. C. (1988). Price and authority in inter-profit center transactions. *American Journal of Sociology, 94,* S17-S51.

Erickson, E. (1960). The problem of ego identity. In M. R. Stein, A. J. Vidich, & D. M. White (Eds.), *Identity and anxiety: Survival of the person in mass society* (pp. 37-87). Glencoe, IL: Free Press.

Felson, R. B. (1989). Parents and the reflected appraisal process: A longitudinal analysis. *Journal of Personality and Social Psychology, 56,* 965-971.

Festinger, L. (1957). *A theory of cognitive dissonance.* Evanston, IL: Row, Peterson.

Festinger, L., & Carlsmith, J. M. (1959). Cognitive consequences of forced compliance. *Journal of Abnormal and Social Psychology, 58,* 203-211.

Franklin, II, C. W. (1988). *Men and society.* Chicago: Nelson-Hall.

Gecas, V. (1982). The self-concept. In R. H. Turner & J. G. Short, Jr. (Eds.), *Annual review of sociology* (Vol. 8, pp. 1-33). Palo Alto, CA: Annual Reviews.

Gilbert, D. T., Krull, D. S., & Pelham, B. W. (1988). Of thoughts unspoken: Social inference and the self-regulation of behavior. *Journal of Personality and Social Psychology, 55,* 685-694.

Gilmore, D. D. (1990). *Manhood in the making; Cultural concepts of masculinity.* New Haven & London: Yale University Press.

Goffman, E. (1955). On face work: An analysis of ritual elements in social interaction. *Psychiatry, 18,* 213-221.

Goffman, E. (1959). *The presentation of self in everyday life.* New York: Doubleday.

Golembiewski, R. T., & Kiepper, A. (1988). *High performance and human costs: A public-sector model of organization development.* New York: Doubleday.

Gramsci, A. (1971). *Selections from the prison notebooks.* London: Lawrence & Wishart.

Granovetter, M. (1985). Economic actions and social structure: The problem of embeddedness. *American Journal of Sociology, 91,* 481-510.

Greenwald, A. G. (1980). The totalitarian ego: Fabrication and revision of personal history. *American Psychologist, 35,* 603-618.

Hamilton, D. L., & Trolier, T. K. (1986). Stereotypes and stereotyping: An overview of the cognitive approach. In J. F. Dovidio & S. L. Gaertner (Eds.), *Prejudice, discrimination, and racism* (pp. 127-163). Orlando, FL: Academic Press.

Hawes, F., & Kealey, D.J. (1981). An empirical study of Canadian technical assistance. *International Journal of Intercultural Relations, 5,* 239-258.

Hochschild, A. R. (1983). *The managed heart.* Berkeley & Los Angeles: University of California Press.

Hoffman, D. M. (1990). Beyond conflict: Culture, self, and intercultural learning among Iranians in the U.S. *International Journal of Intercultural Relations, 14,* 275-299.

James, W. (1890). *Principles of psychology.* New York: Holt.

John, O. P., & Robbins, R. W. (1994). Accuracy and bias in self-perception: Individual differences in self-enhancement and the role of narcissism. *Journal of Personality and Social Psychology, 66,* 206-219.

Katz, D., & Kahn, R. L. (1978). *The social psychology of organizations* (2nd ed.). New York: Wiley.

Kimmel, M. S. (1994). Masculinities as homophobia: Fear, shame, and silence in the construction of gender identity. In H. Brod & J. Kaufman (Eds.), *Theorizing masculinities* (pp. 119-141). Thousand Oaks, CA: Sage.

Kohn, A. (1992). *No contest: The case against competition* (2nd ed.). New York: Houghton Mifflin.

Kramer, R. M. (1991). Intergroup relations and organizational dilemmas: The role of categorization processes. In L. L. Cummings & B. M. Staw (Eds.), *Research in Organizational Behavior* (Vol. 13, pp. 191-228). Greenwich, CT: JAI.

Lecky, P. (1945). *Self-consistency: A theory of personality.* New York: Island.

Markus, H. R., & Kunda, Z. (1986). Stability and malleability of the self-concept. *Journal of Personality and Social Psychology, 51,* 858-866.

McCall, G. L., & Simmons, J. L. (1966). *Identities and interactions: An examination of human associations in everyday life.* New York: Free Press.

McGrath, J. E. (1984). *Groups: Interaction and performance.* Englewood Cliffs, NJ: Prentice Hall.

McNulty, S. E., & Swann, W. B., Jr. (1994). Identity negotiation in roommate relationships: The self as architect and consequence of social reality. *Journal of Personality and Social Psychology, 67,* 1012-1023.

Mead, G. H. (1934). *Mind, self, and society.* Chicago: University of Chicago Press.

Meyer, J. P., & Allen, N. J. (1991). A three-component conceptualization of organizational commitment. *Human Resource Management Review, 1,* 710-720.

Meyer, J. P., Allen, N. J., & Smith, C. A. (1993). Commitment to organizations and occupations: Extension and test of a three-component conceptualization. *Journal of Applied Psychology, 78,* 538-551.

Miller, L., & Hamblin, R. (1963). Interdependence, differential rewarding, and productivity. *American Sociological Review, 28,* 768-778.

Milton, L. (1995, August). *Taking the self seriously: Encouraging cooperation within work groups.* Paper presented at the annual meeting of the Academy of Management. Vancouver, BC, Canada.

Morgan, G., Frost, P. J., & Pondy, L. R. (1983). Organization symbolism. In L. R. Pondy, P. J. Frost, G. Morgan, & T. C. Dandridge (Eds.), *Organization Symbolism* (pp. 3-39). Greenwich, CT: JAI.

O'Reilly, C., Caldwell, D., & Barnett, W. P. (1989). Work group demography, social integration, and turnover. *Administrative Science Quarterly, 34,* 21-37.

O'Reilly, C., & Chatman, J. (1986). Organizational commitment and psychological attachment: The effects of compliance, identification, and internalization on prosocial behavior. *Journal of Applied Psychology, 71,* 492-499.

O'Reilly, C., Chatman, J., & Caldwell, D. (1991). People and organizational culture: A profile comparison approach to assessing person-organization fit. *Academy of Management Journal, 34,* 487-516.

Rafaeli, A., & Sutton, R. I. (1987). Expression of emotion as part of the work role. *Academy of Management Review, 12,* 23-37.

Rosenberg, M. (1979). *Conceiving the self.* New York: Basic Books.

Rubin, G. (1975). The traffic in women: Notes on the "political economy" of sex. In R. R. Reiter (Ed.), *Toward an anthropology of women* (pp. 157-210). New York: Monthly Review.

Scott, W. R. (1992). *Organizations: Rational, natural, and open systems.* Englewood Cliffs, NJ: Prentice Hall.

Secord, P. F., & Backman, C. W. (1965). An interpersonal approach to personality. In B. Maher (Ed.), *Progress in experimental personality research* (Vol. 2, pp. 91-125). New York: Academic Press.

Shibutani, T. (1961). *Society and personality: An interactionist approach to social psychology.* Englewood Cliffs, NJ: Prentice Hall.

Shrauger, J. S., & Schoeneman, T. J. (1979). Symbolic interactionist view of self-concept: Through the looking glass darkly. *Psychological Bulletin, 86,* 549-573.

Spence, J. T., & Buckner, C. (1995). Masculinity and femininity: Defining the undefinable. In P. J. Kalbleisch & M. J. Cady (Eds.), *Gender, power, and communication in human relationships* (pp. 105-138). Hillsdale, NJ: Lawrence Erlbaum.

Spencer, S. J., & Steele, C. M. (1994). *Under suspicion of inability: Stereotype vulnerability and women's math performance.* Unpublished manuscript, State University of New York at Buffalo and Stanford University.

Steele, C. M. (1988). The psychology of self-affirmation: Sustaining the integrity of the self. In Leonard Berkowitz (Ed.), *Advances in experimental social psychology* (Vol. 21, pp. 261-302). New York: Academic Press.

Steele, C. M., & Aronson, J. (1995). Stereotype threat and the intellectual test performance of African Americans. *Journal of Personality and Social Psychology, 69,* 797-811.

Stryker, S. (1987). The vitalization of symbolic interactionism. *Social Psychology Quarterly, 50,* 83-94.

Stryker, S., & Gottlieb, A. (1981). Attribution theory and symbolic interactionism. In J. Harvey, W. Ickes, & R. Kidd (Eds.), *New directions in attribution research* (Vol. 3, pp. 425-458). Hillsdale, NJ: Lawrence Erlbaum.

Sutton, R. I. (1991). Managing norms about expressed emotion: The case of bill collectors. *Administrative Science Quarterly, 36,* 245-268.

Swann, W. B., Jr. (1983). Self-verification: Bringing social reality into harmony with the self. In J. Sulsand & A. G. Greenwald (Eds.), *Psychological perspectives on the self* (Vol. 2, pp. 33-66). Hillsdale, NJ: Lawrence Erlbaum.

Swann, W. B., Jr. (1984). Quest for accuracy in person perception: A matter of pragmatics. *Psychological Review, 91,* 457-477.

Swann, W. B., Jr. (1987). Identity negotiation: Where two roads meet. *Journal of Personality and Social Psychology, 53,* 1038-1051.

Swann, W. B., Jr. (1990). To be adored or to be known: The interplay of self-enhancement and self-verification. In E. T. Higgins & R. M. Sorrentino (Eds.), *Handbook of motivation and cognition: Foundations of social behavior* (Vol. 2, pp. 408-448). New York: Guilford.

Swann, W. B., Jr. (in press). *Self-traps: The elusive quest for higher self-esteem.* New York: Freeman.

Swann, W. B., Jr., de la Ronde, C., & Hixon, J. G. (1994). Authenticity and positivity strivings in marriage and courtship. *Journal of Personality and Social Psychology, 66,* 857-869.

Swann, W. B., Jr., Pelham, B. W., & Krull D. S. (1989). Agreeable fancy or disagreeable truth? How people reconcile their self-enhancement and self-verification needs. *Journal of Personality and Social Psychology, 57,* 782-791.

Swann, W. B., Jr., & Predmore, S. C. (1985). Intimates as agents of social support: Sources of consolation or despair? *Journal of Personality and Social Psychology, 49,* 1609-1617.

Swann, W. B., Jr., Wenzlaff, R. M., Krull, D. S., & Pelham, B. W. (1992). The allure of negative feedback: Self-verification strivings among depressed persons. *Journal of Abnormal Psychology, 101,* 293-306.

Tajfel, H. (1982). Social psychology of intergroup relations. In M. R. Rosenzweig & L. W. Porter (Eds.), *Annual review of psychology* (Vol. 33, pp. 1-39). Palo Alto, CA: Annual Reviews.

Tajfel, H., & Turner, J. C. (1985). The social identity theory of intergroup behavior. In S. Worchel & W. G. Austin (Eds.), *Psychology of intergroup relations* (Vol. 2, pp. 7-24). Chicago: Nelson-Hall.

Taylor, S. E., & Brown, J. D. (1988). Illusion and well-being: Some social psychological contributions to a theory of mental health. *Psychological Bulletin, 103,* 193-210.

Tom, V. (1971). The role of personality and organizational images in the recruiting process. *Organization Behavior and Human Performance, 6,* 573-592.

Trice, H. M. (1993). *Occupational cultures in the workplace.* Ithaca, NY: ILR.

Trice, H. M., & Beyer, J. M. (1993). *The cultures of work organizations.* Englewood Cliffs, NJ: Prentice Hall.

Van Maanen, J., & Schein, E. J. (1979). Toward a theory of organizational socialization. *Research in Organization Behavior, 1,* 209-59.

Zaharna, R. S. (1989). Self-shock: The double-binding challenge of identity. *International Journal of Intercultural Relations, 13,* 501-525.

8

Unwrapping Euro-American Masculinity in a Japanese Multinational Corporation

TOMOKO HAMADA

International competition and foreign direct investment in the United States have brought forth a new model of corporate arrangements from Japan to this country.[1] This research sets an anthropological lens within Takachiho USA Corporation (pseudonym), a Japanese multinational in the United States, where decision-making power is largely in the hand of the often invisible and abstract Tokyo headquarters. It explores how Japanese control and its culturally defined power asymmetry relate to the socially *invented* category of being a Euro-American, middle-class, college-educated, heterosexual, male manager.[2]

The first part of this ethnographic study illustrates the body politics of Takachiho Company, where locally hired Euro-American male managers meet Japanese male managers sent from the Japanese headquarters. The second part describes the Euro-Americans' responses to the perceived blocked opportunities in their career aspirations. The Euro-Americans believe that there is an artificial barrier to advancement for non-Japanese employees of Takachiho Company. This phenomenon has been labeled by social scientists as the "rice-paper ceiling," or the "bamboo ceiling"

AUTHOR'S NOTE: This research was made possible by the Abe Fellowship funded by the Japan Center for Global Partnership and administered by the Social Science Research Council.

(Kopp, 1994). The bamboo ceiling refers to human resource problems of Japanese multinationals that involve (a) the exclusion of local employees from key decision making and information, (b) the lack of career paths for locally hired employees, (c) the existence of a dual salary structure and working conditions between those dispatched from the headquarters and those hired locally, (d) a high level of stress and mutual distrust between expatriates and local employees, (e) and difficulty in retaining high caliber local managers (cf. Fucini & Fucini, 1990; Kidahashi, 1990; Kopp, 1994; March, 1992; Pucick, Hanada, & Fifield, 1989; Shibuya, 1990).

Heated political debates on the bamboo ceiling[3] suggest a large gap in expectations, assumptions, and incentives between Japanese top management and Euro-American staff that often results in cross-cultural frictions and organizational problems. Gender and race politics are often considered the results of cultural clashes and normative differences. However, this researcher argues that the bamboo ceiling has little to do with Japanese "culture," and that it has more to do with the highly centralized patriarchal system of international management. This researcher concludes that the institutional patriarchy of the multinational firm demands "feminized" behavioral responses from male managers (regardless of their nationalities or sexual orientations), who in turn contextualize immediate power situations in their pursuit of political and economic agenda in practice. This study points to the creativity of individual male managers who interpret and respond to unequal social relationships, changing ideals, and political alliances over time. In doing so, these managers use available political labels and boundary markers, and they "invent" stories about their maleness, "Americanness," or both against their cultural others' "non-masculine" traits or their "non-Americanness." This case study pays special attention to the representations of "new" American masculinities in the international power asymmetry.

It may sound ironic to emphasize the perceived disempowerment of Euro-American managers, when their corporatism and the aggregate of their "white male" power control a large amount of world resources and people. And yet, we need deeper sociopolitical analyses of subjective masculinities across space and time that are theoretically distinct from hegemonic masculinity as a collective force.

A growing volume of literature describes the social construction of reality and organizational cognition (for literature review, see Collinson, 1992, and the introductory chapter of this volume). The present anthropological approach is to investigate a chronological sequence of social dramas at local sites and to analyze heterogeneous definitions of masculinities as manifestations of organizational power politics. Giddens (1979, 1984) argued that power relations are always two-way and to some extent interdependent and reciprocal. Individual actors, such as Euro-American males in this firm, often create and re-create their own intersubjective, psychic lives, social relations, local knowledge, and skills, despite (and because of) the opposing, prevailing, and contending influence of dominant structures and practices.

In the next section, Takachiho's storytellers will describe how they constructed their underlying masculine logic for territorial claims and entitlement. These men will give statements about how they felt entitled to occupy certain ecological space and how and when they felt they should be touched, gazed at, or both. They will describe organizational incidents when their ideas and values were challenged by alternative rationale presented by the Japanese male management. The organizational folklore about the male body and the hegemonic masculinity presented below will clarify how one's gender as a sociopolitical marker ties directly to changing schematic relationships between self and others that are mutually constitutive and interactively represented. The dominant discourse and counter-argument about gender becomes central to the global control of the multinational organization.

The Masculine Body and Its Ecological Space at Work

Individual masculinities are often translated not only into sexual fantasies and body images but into postures, positions, and the feels and textures of human bodies in concrete place, time, and occasion (Connell, 1987). For example, there are patterned and meaningful ways to place the male body in front of other males, females, or some other symbolic objects in the environment. In business firms, there are organization-specific ways to interpret the position of the male body. Seating arrangements, office sizes, locations, and layouts of built environment all have meanings. Different norms dictate how men and women case their bodies in immediate surroundings and how the body claims a territory.[4]

The first incident of the organizational body politics took place when Takachiho Company put all managers, technicians, and clerks in an open common space with no partition between their desks, and gave each of them the same type of furniture. This "egalitarian" locational arrangement was modeled after the Tokyo headquarters' practice, where space is a primary cost factor. President Ohno of Takachiho USA mentioned that the open office would encourage interpersonal communication and the corporate spirit of teamwork.

The newly hired Euro-American male managers, on the other hand, resented this setting and stressed their need for private space to hold confidential information and meetings. They said that the open office layout demeaned the value of their work as managers, as decision makers, and continued to complain much about the noise level, the lack of privacy, and general difficulties in conducting quality work in open space. Finally, the Takachiho management compromised and added several conference rooms. However, the middle managers, Euro-American and Japanese, were still left to work in the open area with their clerical staff, who happened to be females at that time.

Only the president had a separate office in this new building. Ohno was also a senior board member of Takachiho Kaisha in Tokyo, and he visited the Euro-American subsidiary regularly, once every 2 months. The empty office of the president began to symbolize the abstract power held by someone far away from the immediate work environment of middle managers.

Another key marker of the traditional Euro-American managerial authority that was missing from Takachiho was a group of female secretaries. Kanter (1977) discussed the cultural significance of the secretary-manager relationship in the Euro-American company. She noted the following:

> For bosses, the traditional secretarial system offered something many of them found nowhere else in their work. It was a pocket of personal privilege in a setting where few areas of completely individual discretion and control were allowed. Secretaries offered an arena of power and control—and sometimes adoration—for bosses who were otherwise rendered powerless and not very important by the routinization of their own job or the numerous constraints on bureaucratic action. In the person of the secretary was someone over whom bosses could claim at least partial "ownership" and to whom they could give orders that rarely had to be justified to anyone else. (Kanter, 1977, p. 101)

In Takachiho, the managers were told that nobody, not even the president, had a secretary. Managers should be able to send out their own mail, create their documents, and perform other "secretarial" tasks, using the latest computerized equipment. When one Euro-American male manager asked another Euro-American female invoice clerk to type some documents for him, she replied, "I am not your secretary." Thus, the last Euro-American "repository of Gemeinschaft emotion-laden relations of individual loyalty" (Kanter, 1977, p. 101) was gone in the contractual and instrumental involvements of Takachiho USA.

Euro-American managers also relayed stories about who should sit next to whom. Not having their own offices, "management" furniture, nor secretaries, and having to sit next to female invoice clerks who refuse to type for them, for example, were interpreted as a "put-down." The Euro-Americans evaluated their relative value to the organization based on where their bodies were located in the company building.

Open-Door: Lack of Occupational Boundary

The office of the president was rarely occupied. When Ohno visited the local operation, he seldom stayed in his elegantly furnished office. He put on a factory worker's uniform and moved straight to the plant floor. He learned the names of individual workers and paid close attention to the production processes and technological issues. The president's "open door policy" broke down the spatial distinction between the blue collar and the white collar. "The office" now had a different meaning to Takachiho plant workers[5] who welcomed the Japanese style of participatory management. However, it did "threaten" the acknowledged chain of command and the power of white-collar middle management. Individual workers at the bottom of the organization now had direct access to the president who knew them personally, and they used every opportunity to make critical comments on the performance of the middle management, especially in the human resources area.

Touching a Male Body

The masculine body is a tangible entity that can touch and be touched. In Euro-American business dealings, only certain body parts are allowed to connect—shaking hands is allowed, but hugging is not. There are organizational rules and rituals that define a permissible boundary of bodily contact between a man and a woman and between a man and a man.

After the business operation started, interactions intensified between Japanese and Euro-American male engineers who worked together for the company's technological transfer. Soon different modes of body touching began to surface. Some Japanese men seemed to enjoy holding another man or be touched or held by another man. Japanese engineers slapped each other's back as a friendly or congratulatory gesture, and they sometimes leaned casually against each other. A Japanese engineer named Toru Ueno, who was a martial arts champion, actually liked to touch Japanese and Euro-American men to show his friendliness. Toru stated that his fraternal love toward fellow males had been nurtured through his sports activities. He said that touching was a positive thing that would intensify the feeling of connectedness among coworkers and help convey positive feelings, particularly when there was a linguistic barrier. Toru's English was not fluent. When a job was well done by his mates, he tapped their shoulders, touched their backs, and sometimes tried to put his arm around their shoulders.

Euro-American male engineers, on the other hand, became very uptight about such bodily contact in business settings. Whenever Toru touched one of them, the Euro-American's whole body stiffened, his shoulders tightened, and an expression of acute embarrassment or anger surged on the Euro-American's face. Many jokes and changes of topics suddenly became necessary to ease their tension. A rumor began concerning Toru's "homosexual" tendency[6] among Euro-American managers.

It is understandable how Euro-American male managers of Takachiho felt threatened by being touched by another (Japanese) male, because "being touched" implied to them power inequity and possible violation of their heterosexual, Euro-American male body. Homophobia and the subordination of marginalized masculinities have been constituting a significant ideological base for Euro-American hegemonic masculinity. Toru's "homosexual" touching challenged and invaded the categorical base of Euro-American hegemonic heterosexual power over their "sexually marginal" men, over their woman, and over their cultural others.

Three months into the operation of Takachiho, a big fist fight erupted on the plant shop floor, between Tom Murphy, a Caucasian engineer, and Toru Ueno. When a machine broke down, Tom was the first one to get to the scene and he struggled to fix it, as the test run was temporarily halted. Toru, who was more experienced with this particular machine, wanted to help Tom but he could not communicate well in English. Tom was too busy fixing the machine to notice Toru's approach from behind. In his frustration from not being able to get Tom's attention, Toru grabbed Tom's upper arm and tried to pull him away from the machine. Tom jumped up and punched Toru in the face. A fist fight broke out. I was later called in to explain the possible sexual connotations of bodily contact in the middle-class Euro-American male culture to Toru, who was still furious about Tom's violent and "irrational" behavior, especially because Toru's intention had been only to help his buddy. Tom, on the other hand, felt insulted by Toru's "disgusting way of grabbing me."

Male Gaze

Manners of glancing, gazing, or simply looking constituted another set of cultural meanings, either to uphold or defy power authority in this Japanese firm. According to the general eye ritual in Euro-American middle-class men, direct eyeline indicates straightforwardness and personal integrity: An honest man should look straight in the eye of the other. According to the Japanese norm, however, subordinates are supposed to avert their gaze after having returned the supervisor's for a brief time. The dominance hierarchy and turf consciousness in male behavior are very much at issue here. A Euro-American middle manager who continued to look straight into the eye of his Japanese superior was surprised when the Japanese supervisor began evading his eyes. As he tried to refocus and reconnect the eyeline between them, he unwittingly started an uneasy game of chasing his boss's gaze that also affected their speech patterns. The Japanese boss suddenly halted the conversation and fell into silence, which annoyed the Euro-American, who began imagining all sorts of possible reasons for this boss's evasiveness. Obviously, the Japanese did not share the behavioral norms held by Euro-American managers for appropriate code switching and recognition rituals for supportive interchanges (Goffman, 1971, pp. 62-94).

Japanese executives talked about "aggressive" Euro-American men, as they interpreted their direct gaze as a form of defiance against their authority. "Why are they so combative?" was a question raised by a Japanese executive who inquired about the Euro-American communication pattern. The Euro-American managers, on the other hand, considered the Japanese executives as being "wishy-washy" and "sissy."

The Bamboo Ceiling and Ideology for Domesticity

Over the years, it became clear that the corporate ideology of Takachiho Company was for teamwork and collaboration among different departments. Direct expression of individual competitiveness was regarded as a sign of poor interpersonal skills in this firm. Likewise, claiming individual credit for achievements and forgetting the infrastructure that helped make their achievements possible was considered as being politically unwise and personally immature. There was no room for a Marlboro Man in Takachiho. Those who exhibited traditional Euro-American masculine traits, such as strong individuality, directness, and competitiveness, began to leave the company, whereas the top management repeatedly stressed the significance of corporate familism, nurturance, and, in short, "gentler and kinder" ways of managing people.

The Euro-American managers in Takachiho had mixed feelings about and different reactions toward their positions under the bamboo ceiling. They felt that their career advancement opportunities were limited and that they were regarded only as "hired guns" by the Japanese simply to provide the knowledge and capabilities that the expatriates lacked. American managers also felt that they were not included in the process of vital decision making and information dissemination, which was often conducted in the Japanese language. One manager, David Menkin, summarized their frustration:

> I was brought into this company to deal with issues that the Japanese managers did not have experience with. I am continually amazed at the resistance to concepts that the Japanese culture does not accept but that are normal, common practices here—this included U.S. standards of hiring, affirmative action compliance, job assignments, etc. They have been ignored or modified to fit Japanese world-views. Decisions on local issues are taken over by Tokyo. In the long run, this is not productive.

In many ways, David's perception of being ignored in Takachiho echoed the experiences of people of any kind who work for an organization that is sociologically different. Kanter (1977) described the negative environment of saleswomen in the highly male-dominated organization called Indsco. She concluded that it was rarity and scarcity rather than femaleness per se that shaped their negative experiences.

It is not the numerical scarcity but rather the cultural scarcity and rarity of particular sociological characteristics that estrange people from the dominant discourse and resource allocation of an organization. The Euro-Americans in Takachiho were numerically dominant but they were culturally scarce. Their sense of alienation became more acute, because the perceived differences between the insiders and themselves were compounded by linguistic, cultural, and other differences. Here, domination no longer needs to be exerted in a direct, personal way, because it is entailed in the possessions of the means—linguistic and cultural capital of appropriating the economic and political mechanisms of resource allocation.

Euro-American managers in Takachiho, if they were to stay in the workplace, had to enact their new status of being a cultural minority, and many of them incorporated the new work roles into their job performances. An ideal Euro-American manager who could survive and prosper in this system was a cooperative and friendly expert consultant, who was thoughtful, competent, professional, dedicated, modest, and psychologically "mature enough" not to show "raw" emotions nor to insist that he be the final decision-making authority.

Powell and Kido (1994), in their study of stereotypes of American and Japanese managers, discovered that their American subjects preferred masculinity over femininity, whereas Japanese subjects preferred femininity over masculinity as their stereotypical images of a good manager (p. 224). My research in Takachiho Corporation also points to a similar conclusion that Japanese prefer nonmasculine managers. It casts a challenge to the findings of Hofstede's study (1980) that rated Japanese culture as the highest in masculinity among the 40 cultures he surveyed and American culture as the 13th highest in masculinity.

Meanings of Masculine Self

The Euro-American managers who stayed in the firm accepted their new social roles, not necessarily because they endorsed them but because they had to provide for others, namely their families. These male managers believed in a sense of altruism in that they had "to put up with some crap" for the sake of their wives and children and the resultant enhanced image of their own masculinity. Gender in this mind-set represented a particular historical response to human reproductive biology, because these men continued to believe that it was the male's primary role to provide for his family. Although these managers put a new wrapping over their masculinity by becoming more sensitive, gentle, cooperative, and efficient Takachiho men, and by suppressing their "traditional" Euro-American maleness, they nevertheless collectively tried to secure themselves as being "manly men," by emphasizing their productive contribution and breadwinner status in the domestic household.

The Japanese and Euro-American managers were similar in that they both believed that their livelihood was directly linked to their employment that was, in turn, linked to their family's survival and to the "humane" existence of those they love. Thus, women, men, and work all became linked in the dynamics of global capitalistic production and reproduction. They seemed to accept the "paternalistic" principle and corporate "familism" of this firm, where the authority and masculinity of the *father* demands the meekness and obedience of the son and the daughter in the organization. Where the power was taken away from individuals and shifted to a center a thousand miles away, the ideal manager became a person very much like the ideal 19th-century middle-class woman—motivated by duty and loyalty, subservient, and other-directed (Kwaleck-Folland, 1994).

Nationalism and Masculinity

Some Euro-Americans mystified and sometimes demonized the Tokyo headquarters as the source of oppression and trouble. Others criticized the autocratic aspects of the corporate patriarchy of Takachiho Japan-Takachiho USA that forces men's devotion first and foremost to the company. In relaying their stories, these Americans' discursive strategies seemed to position Euro-American nationalism against the Japanese ownership. For example, manager John Davidson took a particularly "Euro-American" stance, when he stated the following:

> It seems to me that pressure applied from the top in Tokyo has at times been too strong and not necessary. There has been a strong sense of management by intimidation.
>
> I think that some of the Japanese managers, engineers and technicians here are able to see clearly where some Japanese cultural views or ways of doing things are wrong, and that the Euro-American standards should be applied. When a decision is handed down from Tokyo that is contrary to U.S. practices, these managers, engineers and technicians are trapped. I as an Euro-American

> manager have the option to simply say, "I will not work here anymore," and I leave to find work elsewhere. The Japanese here cannot do that and I believe this makes even more pressure on them.

In dichotomizing the "trapped" Japanese and the "free" Euro-American manager, John drew a circle with a big "J" in the middle of it, then drew another smaller circle right beneath the first one and wrote "me" in it. The small circle stood alone, proudly. His self-image of being a liberated, rugged individual, who "has the option . . . to leave to find work elsewhere," opposed the image of his Japanese colleagues who could not afford such an option. In this narrative, John's espoused Euro-American values for individuality and self-reliance were placed against the meek submission of his cultural others and the "organizational slavery" of this firm. In dichotomizing self and others in this way, he kept silent about his own estrangement and "otherness" in this top-down Japanese organization.

Male Nurturance, Male Sacrifice

Several Japanese expatriate managers had school-aged children whose education in Japan was vital to them, and these fathers had chosen not to bring their families to the United States. Such men on *tanshin-funin* (a transfer without the accompaniment of family members) stayed in the United States for several years, providing money for their women and children back home, while living and working in the foreign country. This Japanese practice was, for better or worse, the ultimate form of masculine nurturance, that is, "sacrifice-to-feed," and is related to the larger social gender relations in Japan and the symbolic masculinity of the absent "father" played out by Japanese wives (Cohen, 1993; Ishii-Kuntz, 1993).

The Euro-American male managers did not approve of this practice of *tanshin-funin,* their usual reaction being, for example, "Don't they love their families? I would rather quit the company." When plant manager Kazuo Konishi's father passed away and Konishi chose not to go back to Japan for the funeral, Euro-American manager Timothy Deetz described him as being a workaholic "organization man." However, the socially entrenched "sacrificing father" image also existed in the Euro-American mind-set. A few weeks later, Tim himself refused to rest at home, despite his doctor's diagnosis that the cause of his recent physical problem was work stress-related. Tim said that he had a project to finish and could not afford to take a day off. Then, on the following day, Tim fell and hit his head in the company parking lot. An ambulance was called in. Tim insisted that it was not a big deal, and he endured the pain without a single complaint as he was rushed to the hospital. His supervisor ordered him to take 1 week off, but he showed up to work within 3 days. Tim said that he needed the job to "feed" his family. "I'm OK," he insisted. "Don't worry about me. I can handle it." This sacrifice-to-feed is a male form of nurturance, and Tim was committed in important and engendered ways to his wife and children.

Male Domesticity

Japanese institutions, such as religious establishments, political parties, and business organizations, are so totally patriarchal that admitting the institutional domination of individuals (male or female) and accepting the effeminization of males within such organizations may not be news to these Japanese men. University-educated male managers have been the vanguards of Japan's post-World War II corporate expansion. They have accepted and worked for the highly gendered system and its masculine ideology—with its fundamental exclusivity of Japanese women, its sexual division of labor, its ideology of industrial familism, and its domestication of males for life-long labor—and they have produced Japan's phenomenal postwar economic miracle.

Japanese managers privately talked about their role as a husband as being a *gekkyu haitatsu-nin* (a delivery man of the monthly pay check). They deliver money to their wives who are full-time housewives and who hold domestic power, particularly as consumers in postindustrial Japan. Unlike the popular image of the corporate samurai warriors, the situation these men recognized was that the Japanese household is "fatherless."[7] One high-powered senior director of Takachiho, Yoichiro Takanashi, jokingly stated that after he retires, he would become a *sodai-gomi* (oversized disposable waste) and *nure-ochiba* (a wet fallen leaf). All these self-defacing terms were used in the colloquial Japanese language to describe the lives of *sararii man* (salaried men).

Japanese managers have also created culturally loaded metaphors to convey their personal sense of male disempowerment at work—by calling themselves *shachiku* (domesticated cattle of the company), and *miyazukae* (servants of the Lord). It is perhaps less stigmatizing for the Japanese to compare themselves to overworked cattle, as their culture tends to admire the nobility of failure and self-sacrifice. In describing themselves as subhumans, however, these men were actually affirming their fundamental belief that work should be for "human" dignity and respect—that people, men or women, have a basic human right to some measure of control over their own destiny and livelihood. It calls to mind a distinction made by Najita between efficient, impersonal structures and oppositional, caring, humane communities—an axis constituted by "bureaucratism" (*kanryoshugi*) on the one hand and "purity of human spirit" (*ningensei* or *kokoro*) on the other (Najita, 1974; Turner, 1994).

Some managers talked about recent newspaper articles about Japanese managers who died or were "killed in action" because of overwork. There was a word for it—*karoshi* or death caused by an abnormal load of work. Japanese *enka* songs that *tanshin-funin* managers sang in *karaoke* bars were about their unfulfilled dreams, broken hearts, and longing for love—similar to some blue-grass songs of the American South, a culture that also admires fallen heroes like Robert E. Lee. Now the economic miracle is over, and some of these middle-aged male managers are becoming redundant in the current economic recession. They are the first to admit their personal disillusionment about the system.

In contrast, perhaps because of their strong "masculine" values for equating managerial position, money, and male power, and because of their masculine ethics for independence and individuality, Euro-American businessmen lack linguistic terms to describe their personal dependence, domesticity, and weakness. In creating their neocolonial discourses about being white, heterosexual, and male, they continue to paint themselves as being individual heroes who serve and protect their wives and children.

The ambivalent and contradictory attitudes of American males toward unpaid work at home and paid employment (Bronstein & Cowan, 1988; Pleck, 1981, 1985) were nevertheless noticeable in the twisted discourses of Euro-American male managers. Although they talked lovingly and proudly about their independent-minded, strong, working wives and their willingness to accept increased domestic responsibilities at home, at the same time, as the business expanded, their overtime (without pay) increased, and many of them worked for more than 50 hours per week for the company. In their double talk about "strong males/domesticated males," there were subtle and paradoxical turns, as many managers also felt pressure to earn more money and keep up with the financial demands of their consumer families. They were, however, not complaining nor asking for help for themselves. Nor did they employ counter-cultural macho forms of resistance against the corporate patriarchy[8] that has been observed among blue-collar male workers under Western managerial domination (cf. Burawoy, 1979, 1985; Collinson, 1992).

Takachiho's Euro-American managers, although producing sharp critiques of Japanese (male) chauvinism, do not seem to recognize the fact that in the postindustrial world, power has been taken away from individual males and shifted into the hands of more controlling collective institutions, such as the government, the military, and the multinational business organization. Colloquial business English has not produced apt expressions for this new reality of individual masculine subservience and victimization and individual male domesticity.

Conclusion

There is currently a definite disjunction in individual Euro-American and Japanese middle-class men's experience—a contradiction—between the facts of their collective dominance over the rest of the world population and resources *and* the feelings of personal powerlessness and sense of ambivalence and alienation as individual males. The present study has illustrated that male managers' stories about their families, their work, their bosses, and their companies are becoming increasingly polysemic, dialogical, and diverse over time. Although Euro-American managers struggle to uphold their traditional "masculine" values for individual independence, freedom of choice, and male nurturance as bread-winners, they are also facing logical contradictions inherent in the effeminized masculinities required by the rapidly spreading, international, corporate, hegemonic patriarchy, where transnational corporations are attempting to rediscipline managers and professionals.

This case study has paid special attention to "new" multiple Euro-American masculinities in the emerging global patriarchy and has revealed that the institutional patriarchy of the multinational firm demands "feminized" behavioral responses from male managers (regardless of their nationalities or sexual orientations), who in turn contextualize immediate power situations in their pursuit of a political and economic agenda in practice. The Japanese multinational's bamboo ceiling has much to do with the highly centralized hegemonic masculinity of late 20th-century capitalism that has been growing at a tremendous speed.

The current study of masculinities in a multinational firm indicates that the psychological conceptualization of masculinities as manifested forms of an individual subjectivity, or of any other autonomous, stable unitary entity, no longer has much theoretical utility for transnational organizational analysis. The stable dichotomy, such as the one between public and private, male and female, work and leisure, production and reproduction, individual and society, becomes increasingly problematic in late, postindustrial capitalism, where everything consists of the global-local recombination of discourse, structure, categories, and semiotics. Individual masculinities and hegemonic masculinity must be analyzed according to this new reality.

Notes

1. About a quarter-million Japanese businessmen and their families have been transplanted to the United States since 1975 (Hamada, 1991, 1992).

2. I am a native Japanese female academic who is married to an American male. My particular social characteristics and my anthropological perspectives clearly influenced my ethnographic search of the natives' viewpoints.

3. The "rice-paper ceiling" or "the bamboo ceiling" debate began with a number of lawsuits filed by Americans in the 1980s, who alleged discrimination by Japanese firms, that led to the 1991 Congressional hearings chaired by Congressman Tom Lantos (D-California). The hearings prompted a great deal of criticism from the public that Lantos was engaged in another form of Japan-bashing and a "witch-hunt inquisition" reminiscent of McCarthyism. To me, this was another form of culture clash. See U.S. House Committee on Government Operations, Employment Discrimination by Japanese-Owned Companies in the United States: Hearings Before the Employment and Housing Subcommittee of the Committee on Government Operations, 102 Cong., 1st session, 1991. See also the criticism of the Lantos hearings by Yoshino Tsurumi (1991).

4. As an anthropologist, I do not support the sharp division between humans and animals. Research in primatology, communication, and cognition indicates that differences between monkeys, apes, and hominids are gradual, not qualitative (see King, 1995).

5. In general, the production area of American manufacturers physically and symbolically forms a distinct unit, separate from the office area. American blue-collar workers do not regularly visit the office area, unless there are specific problems concerning such issues as discipline, attendance, annual merit evaluation, insurance, and payroll. In this company, factory workers freely moved in and out of the area for offices and conference rooms, and they chatted with top managers who welcomed them. The Japanese executives' frequent meetings with blue-collar workers ironically limited their time for interacting with middle managers.

6. Homophobia is often expressed by American men. It is also noteworthy that there is a historical practice of white heterosexual males to label minority men (Afro-Americans, Asians, and others) as being more like females, boys, beasts, or manipulatable objects. On the other hand, the Japanese historical categorization of the *gaijin* (the outsider-foreigner) depicts the beastlike, demonic, threatening, or polluting figure of a Caucasian male, but it does not have a gender connotation of "sissyness." Japanese

derogatory terms such as *keto* (the hairy monster-savage-Westerner) imply a beastlike image, but they do not connote the weakness or the exploitability associated with images of femininity or boyhood.

7. Personal interview with Hiroshi Wagatsuma, UCLA, 1979. See also Ishii-Kuntz,1993.

8. Many historical and ethnographic studies analyzed Japanese workers' class consciousness, collective actions, or both (cf. Cole, 1979; Gordon, 1988, 1993; Ishida, 1984; Smith, 1988; Turner, 1994). However, relatively little attention has been given to the resistance of Japanese middle management, who individually make choices about speaking out in opposition, remaining silent, or accommodating themselves to the corporate hierarchy. The lack of data on the subjectivity of Japanese management has led to an uncritical assumption about the satisfied passivity of Japanese male managers. The linguistic representations and behavioral manifestations described in the present research refutes the image of passivity, that Japanese managers devise a wide variety of individual oppositional politics, ranging from open resistance to informal sabotage, toward the organizational hierarchy of power, status, and authority.

References

Bronstein, P., & Cowan, C. (Eds.). (1988). *Fatherhood today: Men's changing role in the family.* New York: John Wiley.

Burawoy, M. (1979). *Manufacturing consent.* Chicago, IL: University of Chicago Press.

Burawoy, M. (1985). *The politics of production.* London: Verso University Press.

Cohen, T. F. (1993). What do fathers provide? In E. S. Krauss, T. P. Rohlen, & P. G. Steinhoff (Eds.), *Conflict in Japan* (pp. 1-22). Honolulu: University of Hawaii Press.

Cole, R. (1979). *Work, mobility, and participation: A comparative study of Euro-American and Japanese industry.* Berkeley, CA: University of California Press.

Collinson, D. L. (1992). *Subjectivity, masculinity and workplace culture.* New York: Walter de Gruyter.

Connell, R. W. (1987). *Gender and power: Society, the person, and sexual politics.* Stanford, CA: Stanford University Press.

Fucini, J., & Fucini, S. (1990). *Working for the Japanese: Inside Mazda's American auto plant.* New York: Free Press.

Giddens, A. (1979). *Central problems in social theory.* London: Macmillan.

Giddens, A. (1984). *The constitution of society.* Cambridge, MA: Polity.

Goffman, E. (1971). *Relations in public.* New York: Harper & Row.

Gordon, A. (1988). *The evolution of labor relations in Japan: Heavy industry 1855-1935.* Cambridge, MA: Harvard University Press.

Gordon, A. (Ed.). (1993). *Postwar Japan as history.* Berkeley: University of California Press.

Hamada, T. (1991). *American enterprise in Japan.* Albany: State University of New York Press.

Hamada, T. (1992). Under the silk banner: The Japanese company and its overseas managers. In T. S. Lebra (Ed.), *Japanese social organization* (pp. 135-164). Honolulu: University of Hawaii Press.

Hofstede, G. (1980). *Culture's consequences: International differences in work-related values.* London: Sage.

Ishida, T. (1984). Conflict and its accommodation: Omote-Ura and Uchi-Soto relations. In E. S. Krauss, T. P. Rohlen, & P. G. Steinhoff (Eds.), *Conflict in Japan.* (pp. 45-67). Honolulu: University of Hawaii Press.

Ishii-Kuntz, M. (1993). Japanese fathers: Work demands and family roles. In J. C. Hood (Ed.), *Men, work, and family.* (pp. 45-67). Newbury Park, CA: Sage.

Kanter, R. M. (1977). *Men and women of the corporation.* New York: Basic Books.

Kidahashi, M. (1990). *Dual organization: A study of a Japanese-owned firm in the United States.* Unpublished doctoral dissertation, Columbia University, New York.

King, B. (1994). *The information continuum: Evolution of social information transfer in monkeys, apes, and hominids.* Santa Fe, NM: School of Euro-American Research Press.

Kwaleck-Folland, A. (1994). *Engendering business: Men and women in the corporate office 1870-1930.* Baltimore, MD: Johns Hopkins University Press.

Kopp, R. (1994). *The rice-paper ceiling: Breaking through Japanese corporate culture.* Berkeley, CA: Stone Bridge Press.

March, R. M. (1992). *Working for a Japanese company: Insight into the multicultural workplace.* New York: Kodansha International.

Najita, T. (1974). *Japan: The intellectual foundations of modern Japanese politics.* Chicago, IL: University of Chicago Press.

Pleck, J. H. (1981). *The myth of masculinity.* Cambridge: MIT Press.

Pleck, J. H. (1985). *Working wives/working husbands.* Beverly Hills, CA: Sage.

Powell, G. N., & Kido, Y. (1994). Managerial stereotypes in a global economy: A comparative study of Japanese and American business students' perspectives. *Psychological Reports, 74,* 219-226.

Pucick, V., Hanada, M., & Fifield, G. (1989). *Management culture and the effectiveness of local executives in Japanese-owned U.S. corporations.* Ann Arbor: University of Michigan Press.

Shibuya, K. (1990). *How do the Japanese companies grow in the American soil?* Unpublished doctoral dissertation. Columbia University, New York.

Smith, T. (1988). *Native sources of Japanese industrialization.* Berkeley: University of California Press.

Tsurumi, Y. (1991, Summer/Fall). The ghosts of McCarthyism haunts Japanese firms. *Pacific Basin Quarterly,* p. 15.

Turner, C. L. (1994). *Japanese workers in protest: An ethnography of consciousness and experience.* Berkeley: University of California Press.

9

"We Choose Not to Compete"

The "Merit" Discourse in the Selection Process, and Asian and Asian American Men and Their Masculinity

CLIFF CHENG

In an earlier work, I reported on my ethnographic study that extended the "Good Manager" research by combing gender *and* race attributions (Cheng, 1996). In that study, I examined 215 (113 female, 102 male) undergraduate and graduate students at five different universities of differing types in Organizational Behavior courses in each of which a mini-assessment center was used to select student Team Managers. The mini-assessment centers were conducted over a 5-year period. The participants, through their role as Assessors, made selections that reproduced the "Good Manager" ideal type. Good managers are hegemonically masculine (Cheng, 1996; Powell, 1992; Powell & Butterfield, 1979; Powell & Kido, 1994; Schein, 1992). This ideal type was extended from the sociopsychologically oriented organizational behavior literature into the profeminist sociological men's studies literature and founded to be what Connell (1987, 1995) and Kimmel (1994) call "hegemonic masculinity," the *current* definition of masculinity that is the ideal on which it *depends on* the subordination of femininity *and* the marginalization (and colonialization) of *other forms* of masculinity. In all six mini-assessment centers, none of the 13 Asian or Asian American male Candidates were chosen, whereas almost all (23 of 25) the Euro-American males, and Euro-American females who performed hegemonic masculinity, were selected.

"Many fewer organizational studies have been done with Asian American, Hispanic, or native American samples than with African American or white females" (James, 1996). Existing studies in the organizational literature that include Asian Americans tended to include them *in comparison* to other groups rather than to specifically study them as a group. There is little in the way of studies dedicated specifically to Asian Americans, besides Khoo's (1988) unpublished senior thesis. My earlier study, and this one as well, hopes to contribute to the literature by examining the discourse of discrimination against Asian and Asian American men in the selection process.

This chapter first summarizes my earlier empirical study (Cheng, 1996). Then, it further examines how Assessors resisted examining their biased selections after making the racial and gender attributions that Asian and Asian American male Candidates were "nerds." These studies were delimited to Asian and Asian American men, because their metatheoretical goal of these papers is to show that gender is socially constructed and not always synonymous with biological sex. The dominant attribution is that Asian and Asian American men are not hegemonically "masculine." Their gender role performance is not socially appropriate for their biological sex. Asian and Asian American women are attributed by the dominant culture as performing gender roles appropriate to their sex.

Summary of the Earlier Study

A new instructional design called the Classroom as High-Involvement Organization (CHIO) was used (Cheng, 1993a, 1993b, 1993c, 1993d, 1993e) by the six Organizational Behavior classes studied. The metapurpose of the CHIO design was to give participants an experience of the stages of group development, so they could double-loop learn (Argyris, 1990, p. xi; Dewey, 1922) from their own self-generated behavior data (Cheng, 1993d). The CHIO entails a long-term "simulation," in which the class is broken up into semiautonomous work teams that were told *what* to do: Task 1—case studies and Task 2—processing the team's work process. *How* they did this was up to them. Becoming aware and more effective in *how* they did what they did, along with self-correcting errors, was a metalearning objective of the CHIO design.

A mini-assessment center was used at the beginning of the term to select Team Managers (Cheng, 1993b). At the beginning of the first class, interested students volunteered to become Candidates in the mini-assessment center. The remaining students were given assessment training and served as Assessors. After selecting Team Managers, the Assessors became the employees of the new Team Managers.

The Assessors and Candidates in the assessment center were a diverse group of students. In four of the six classes, they were traditional undergraduate and graduate students: young and lacking work experience. In two classes, the students were nontraditional, older students, with significant work experience. Student racio-ethnicity was self-categorized. Of the 215 students in the 6 classes, 112 were minority group members. At one church-affiliated teaching university, only 3 of the 33 students were minority group members. At an inner-city public teaching university, on the other hand, only 3 of the 43 students in a class of evening undergraduate students were Euro-Americans. None of the students chose to anonymously or otherwise disclose that they were gay or lesbian.

The schools in which they attended were also diverse: (1-2) undergraduate and MBA classes at a suburban public research university that is a member of the American Association of Universities (AAU), (3) undergraduate class at an inner city private research AAU member university, (4) a graduate class at a suburban state teaching university, (5) an undergraduate class at an inner-city state teaching university, (6) and an undergraduate class at a suburban church-affiliated teaching university.

Findings

There were seven data points in the earlier study. First, value statements were made by the entire class as part of a team building process. The values stated across the 6 mini-assessment centers were humanistically oriented, for example, fairness, equality, merit, value differences, honesty, listening to one another, resolving conflict immediately and interpersonally, and so on.

Second, the "Good Manager" ideal type was identified by students in a brainstorming process, as shown in Table 9.1.

The two subsets of good-manager characteristics directly and compositely related to Bem's (1974) masculinity characteristics on the Bem Sex Role Inventory (BRSI). Assessors' definition of the good manager as hegemonically masculine was consistent with previous studies in the good-manager literature (Powell, 1992; Powell & Butterfield, 1979; Powell & Kido, 1994; Schein, 1992; for a review, see Powell, 1993).

Hegemonic masculinity refers to the *current* dominant form of masculinity that is constructed *in relation* to femininity *and* subordinated and

TABLE 9.1 Classes' Ideal of the Characteristics of "The Good Manager"

First Subset

Directly includes 11 of Bem's (1974) 20 masculine characteristics:
- Aggressive and assertive
- Ambitious
- Analytical (good problem solver, rational, logical)
- Athletic
- Competitive
- Decisive (makes decisions easily)
- Independent and self-reliant
- Individualistic and strong personality.

Second subset

Indirectly includes five of Bem's (1974) masculine characteristics:
- Being in control (defending own beliefs, dominance, forcefulness, and willing to take a stand)
- Fairness

marginalized masculinities (Connell, 1987, pp. 183-188). Kimmel (1994) elaborates with the following:

> All masculinities are not created equal; or rather, we are all *created* equal, but any hypothetical equality evaporates quickly because our definitions of masculinity are not equally valued in society. Once definition of manhood continues to remain the standard against which other forms of manhood are measured and evaluated. Within the dominant culture, the masculinity that defines white, middle-class, early middle-aged, heterosexual men is the masculinity that sets the standards for other men, against which other men are measured and, more often than not, found wanting. . . .
>
> The hegemonic definition of manhood is a man *in* power, a man *with* power, and a man *of* power. We equate manhood with being successful, capable, reliable, in control. The very definitions of manhood we have developed in our culture maintain the power that some men have over other men and that men have over women.
>
> Our culture definition of masculinity is thus several stories at once. It is about the individual man's quest to accumulate those cultural symbols that denote manhood, signs that he has in fact achieved it. (pp. 124-125)

What ran consistently through the 6 mini-assessment centers was a definition of hegemonic masculinity as the social construction and repro-

TABLE 9.2 Assessors' Ranked Order Attributions of Most Frequently Discussed Characteristics of Selected Team Managers

Being in control (defends own beliefs, dominance, forcefulness, and willing to take a stand)
Decisive (makes decisions easily)
Aggressive and assertive
Ambitious
Analytical (good problem solver, rational, logical)
Competitive
Athletic
Independent and self-reliant
Individualistic and strong personality.

duction of the ideal type. The ideal exists in relation to that which is purportedly not feminine or effeminate. In management, hegemonic masculinity is what Kanter (1977) calls a traditionally "masculine ethic" (p. 22).

Third, the Assessors' attributions of the Candidates reinforced the Good Manager ideal type and hegemonic masculinity, as shown in Table 9.2. The Assessors reported directly observing eight of Bem's (1974) 20 characteristics of femininity in the Asian and Asian American male Candidates, as shown in Table 9.3: Cheerful, Gentle, Naive (Gullible), Shy, Quiet (Soft-Spoken), Too Nice, Not Tough Enough (Sympathetic), Understanding, and Passive (Yielding).

The second subset in Table 9.3 on Assessors' attributions included Dependence, Unathleticness, Being unsure of himself (indecisive), and Having a weak personality—all low in masculinity in relation to Bem's (1974) masculine characteristics. The third subset consisted of analytical ability, the area where Asian and Asian American male Candidates converged with Euro-American males. The last subset consisted of behaviors that the Assessors perceived as negative: Deferent, Too Polite, Too Respectful, and Too Traditional (Non-risk-taker).

Fourth, the selections reinforced the Good Manager ideal type and hegemonic masculinity, as shown in Tables 9.4, 9.5, and 9.6.

Males were selected at a higher 1.958:1 ratio, compared to a 2.7:1 ratio for females. When race *and* gender were examined together, Euro-American males and Euro-American females had the highest selection ratios. Minority females were selected at a higher ratio (3.2:1) than minority males (21:1). Of the 25 Euro-American males who applied, 23 were selected (1.087:1). Following more distantly were the 11 Euro-American

TABLE 9.3 Assessors' Observations of Nonselected Asian Male Candidates

First subset[a]
Cheerful
Gentle
Naive (gullible)
Shy
Quiet (soft-spoken)
Too nice, not tough enough (sympathetic)
Understanding
Passive (yielding)
Second subset[b]
Dependent
Unathletic
Unsure of himself (indecisive)
Weak personality
Third subset[c]
Analytical (good problem solver, rational, logical)
Fourth subset[d]
Deferent
Too polite
Too respectful
Too traditional (non-risk-taker)

a. Directly includes 8 of Bem's (1974) 20 feminine characteristics.
b. Low masculinity, in relation to Bem's (1974) masculine characteristics.
c. High masculinity characteristic on Bem's (1974) scale:
d. Behaviors perceived as feminine.

females who applied, of whom 5 (who observably performed hegemonic masculinity) were selected (2.2:1). African American females had a similar ratio, whereby 7 applied and 3 (who observably performed hegemonic masculinity) were selected (2.333:1). Of the 3 Asian American males who applied, 1 was selected (3:1). Trailing farther behind were Hispanics: females had a 6:1 ratio, whereas males had a 7:1 ratio. Far behind them were African American males who had a 2:0 ratio. Finally, none of the 13 Asian and Asian American men who applied were selected (13:0).

Fifth, in the private debriefings of the selected Candidates, most of whom where Euro-American males and females who performed hegemonic masculinity, almost without exception they said they were selected due to "merit," "qualifications," "skills," or "experience," or a combination thereof. Yet, on examination of their job applications, a

TABLE 9.4 Racio-Ethnicity and Gender of Candidates

No.	*Euro-American* *M*	*F*	*African American* *M*	*F*	*Hispanic* *M*	*F*	*Asians (All)*[a] *M*	*F*	*Total Candidates* *M*	*F*	*Total*
1.	1	1	0	0	0	0	1	0	2	1	3
2.	3	1	0	0	0	1	2	0	5	2	7
3.	4	2	1	3	3	2	2	1	10	8	18
4.	5	1	0	2	3	2	3	1	11	6	17
5.	6	0	0	1	0	0	1	0	7	1	8
6.	6	6	1	1	1	1	4	1	12	9	21
Total	25	11	2	7	7	6	13	3	47	27	74

a. None of the applicants in the other or unknown categories applied for the position of team manager.

pattern of a lack of qualifications emerged. Many had never held a paid off-campus job. Most of the off-campus work experience they had was in non-career-track jobs, for example, waiter/waitress, fast food worker, retail sales clerk, and so on, that did not develop managerial skills. Comparatively, many of the nonselected Candidates were quantitatively more experienced. In the mini-assessment centers in which fraternities and sororities were dominant—the undergraduates at the church-affiliated teaching university and the undergraduate class at the public AAU university in particular—most of the Candidates selected were members of fraternities or sororities.

TABLE 9.5 Racio-Ethnicity and Gender of Selected Candidates

No.	*Euro-American* *M*	*F*	*African American* *M*	*F*	*Hispanic* *M*	*F*	*Asians (All)* *M*	*F*
1.	1	1	0	0	0	0	0	0
2.	3	1	0	0	0	0	0	0
3.	4	1	0	2	0	1	0	0
4.	5	0	0	1	0	0	0	0
5.	5	0	0	0	0	0	0	0
6.	5	2	0	0	1	0	0	1
Total	23	5	0	3	1	1	0	1

TABLE 9.6 Racio-Ethnicity and Gender and Applicant-to-Selection Ratios (in descending order)

1. Euro-American males—25:23. 1.087:1.
2. Euro-American females—11:5. 2.2:1.
3. African American females—7:3. 2.333:1.
4. Asian American females—3:1.
5. Hispanic American females—6:1.
6. Hispanic American males—7:1.
7. African American males—2:0.
8. Asian American males—13:0.

Total males—47:24. 1.958:1.
Total females—27:10. 2.7:1.
Total minority females—16:5. 3.2:1.
Total minority males—21:1.

Sixth, in confidential debriefings of the nonselected Candidates, the group as a whole reported an internalized sense of inadequacy for not being "good enough" to become Team Manager. The inadequacy self-attribution reveals a "buy-into" the status quo, rather than an examination of the status quo, given the clear pattern of a selection bias favoring Euro-American males and females who perform hegemonic masculinity.

Finally, in debriefings of the Assessors, without the Candidates present, Assessors overwhelmingly said that they picked the most qualified Candidates. Dissenting remarks were squelched by other class members. I shall return to these findings later in this chapter.

Analysis and Discussion

The selections reinforced the contradiction between the espoused theory of diversity and hegemonic masculinity theory in use. Clearly, Assessors favored selecting males at a 1.958:1 ratio, compared to females at a 2.7:1 ratio (see Tables 9.4, 9.5, and 9.6). Because reductionism occurs when gender alone is viewed in isolation, gender *and* race must be examined together (Cheng, 1995). Whenever possible, which is not the case here, other aspects of diversity must be simultaneously explored, for example, sexual identity, religion, class, colonialism, and physical disability. Euro-American males were selected at 1.087:1 ratio, followed by Euro-American males at a 2.2:1 ratio. Behind them were minority females who were selected at a 3.2:1 higher ratio. Minority males fared worst at a 21:1 ratio. It is striking to note that when job applications were compared with job descriptions, most Candidates were clearly unqualified for lack of applicable or, in some cases, any work experience. Yet, Assessors rejected the few Candidates with work experience in favor of Candidates more consistent with their hegemonically masculine ideal type of the Good Manager.

Process Analysis

In the rest of this chapter, I will report on the process analysis of process consultation (Beckhard, 1971) efforts to reveal and change the pattern of discrimination that occurred in these 6 mini-assessment centers. In the CHIO design, classes had two tasks: Task 1—Work together *interdependently* to do case studies as a team—and Task 2—Process the development of *how* a team works together or fails to work together. Because the case teams were semiautonomous, my role was nontraditional. Grading was done by formula, using objective criteria to minimize the authoritarian attributions that students applied to authority figures such as myself. As the consultant to the teams, I offered process observations and training on topics such as group dynamics (Beckhard, 1971), team building (Dyer, 1987), double-loop learning (Argyris & Schon, 1978), and so on, rather than top-down control. When requested, I intervened and provided consulting services, such as leadership coaching, third-party conflict resolution, and so on.

Organizational Defensiveness

All the mini-assessment centers reacted defensively to process consultation attempts to raise and facilitate a dialogue on why the ideal type of the Good Manager and selections contradicted the value statements. The class at the church-affiliated suburban teaching university was the most defensive of all, refusing to discuss the contradiction on three occasions when I mentioned it in class and dozens of other times when I attempted to raise the issue with Team Managers and commented on it in their learning journals. What was encountered in these classes is what Argyris (1993) calls organizational defensiveness:

> Skills most individuals, groups, intergroups, and organizations use to solve . . . problems are learned early in life. They are protected and rewarded by the culture. Yet they are counterproductive because they fail to produce effective actions—that is, actions that achieve the intended result of reducing problems. . . . Any change that does not first change the meaning of effective action cannot persist because it continues to expose individuals to potential embarrassment or threat. This causes them to resort back to their old actions because a sense of competence and esteem are largely based on personal values and skills consistent with the old status quo. This individual embarrassment or threat is what has led to the organizational embarrassment and threat that has resulted in limiting genuine organizational learning. (p. 2)

Effective behavior would entail engaging in Task 1 and in examining how people are working together to accomplish Task 2. If this was done, and the selections analyzed, an inconsistency between the values statements and action would be found.

The theory the students used to act with is what Argyris and Schon (1978, pp. 110-127) called Model I; that is, to use advocacy, unilateral control, suppression of emotions and negative feelings (such as those surrounding discrimination), withholding information, and privately testing one's theory of action. This theory did not test the validity of whether or not those (preferably Euro-American males) who display hegemonic masculinity are good managers. There was little Task II individual, group, and organizational learning going on that could have been used to detect, test and correct this ineffective, sexist, and racist theory of action.

The "Merit" Discourse, Organizational Justice, and Privilege

The argument of organizational defensiveness that the Assessors made was a "merit" discourse. They said they followed their espoused value of "equality"—which in these classes' theory-in-use meant sameness or undifferentiation. At every opportunity that the teams and classes had to deal with their conflicts over differences, they either ignored the issue or glossed over it by affirming their "equality" (i.e., sameness). Color blindness is racist and sexist (Calvert & Ramsey, 1992), for sameness denies the differences between women, minorities, and other diverse peoples and hegemonic masculinity. Although equal opportunity denies nepotism, birth rights, and patronage (Bell, 1973, pp. 424-425), the fact is that there already are competitive differentials based on personality, cognitive abilities, physical abilities, family and social economic status, and so on. The idea that everyone starts equal is false. Sexism, racism, classism, homophobia, ageism, and so on render starting points unequal. "Merit" is the governing value of a theory-in-use that is incompetent, because the action produced fails to result in the intended action of "equality" and merely suppresses prejudicial attitudes by framing the denial as a success of meritocracy.

As I facilitated a dialogue on the Assessors' definition of "merit," I noticed a pattern develop throughout the 6 mini-assessment centers. An underlying issue was a resentment of others who are perceived or actually treated as *different* or *special*. Interestingly enough, almost all the diverse peoples in the mini-assessment centers did not report perceiving themselves as different or special. On the whole, they did not want to upset the status quo and claim difference or specialness, even though the status quo was biased against them.

Further questioning revealed the untested assumption that acknowledging differences would lead to a "competitive advantage." The governing value, beneath their untested assumptions (Argyris & Schon, 1978, p. 30), was that Assessors, even the diverse ones, saw difference as threatening to the status quo of hegemonic masculinity. On the level of the collective unconscious, this fear is the same that produced the backlash against affirmative action by "angry white men" (Lynch, 1989). From an intrapsychic reading, the intergroup conflict may be based on unresolved sibling rivalry.

Assessors claimed that "the selections are made based on qualifications." Most of the women and minority Assessors bought into this discourse. My observation that almost all fraternity and sorority members voted for their fellow members was denied or justified by members saying that voting for fellow members was based on merit. Merit, or more specifically work experience, at students' early stages of career development, was by and large disregarded in the selections. Better qualified *Candidates who did not perform hegemonic masculinity were not selected.* The fraternities or sororities represented in these classes, except for the MPA and evening undergraduate class at the teaching university, tended to be homogenous (i.e., Euro-American) and homosocial (single-sexed) organizations. A key differentiation between these two types of organizations is gender roles. Hegemonic masculinity differentiates itself from emphasized femininity that pleases hegemonically masculine males (Connell, 1987, pp. 183, 185-188). Another key in and out group distinction is race, or more specifically Euro-American in-groupers and peoples of color as out-groupers.

For the Assessors, *merit* refers to *input equity* or equal opportunity. Their argument is that every student had an equal chance to apply. This is an argument based solely on input. The skewed output favoring Euro-American males is accounted for under this argument as the "Candidates not chosen were not good enough." This argument obscures the standards used in the process and the imputing phase. As Bellah, Madsen, Sullivan, Swidler, and Tipton (1985, p. 26) put it, "our available moral traditions do not give us nearly as many resources for thinking about distributive justice as about procedural justice, and even fewer for thinking about substantive justice."

In interviewing students who did not self-select and apply to become Team Manager, I learned that students would not have likely applied if they thought they did not stand a reasonable chance of being selected (Pettigrew & Martin, 1987, p. 51). "I'm not what they are looking for" was a common response. Knowledge of the hegemonically masculine standard of the good manager is diffused throughout the society in which the students live. It is likely, given the exercise that visioned what the characteristics of a good manager are, that many students did not self-select and apply, because they perceived themselves as inconsistent with a hegemonically masculine ideal type of the Good Manager.

It is necessary to examine what group benefited from the dominant definition of *merit,* and what group defined merit. Merit is a social construct, a product of methodology that produces culture, not some abstract concept of "truth" (Calas, 1992). Eurocentric methodology is socially constructed by the ruling class (i.e., Euro-American, middle-upper class, college educated, capitalist, imperialist, heterosexualist, and patriarchal) to maintain its own power and exclude others, such as third-world (colonized) people, people of color, women, gays and lesbians, the economically disadvantaged classes, the physically challenged, and so on.

For Rawls (1971), meritocracy is "democratic" but unfair. Because people start off in unequal starting places, due to talent, background, and so on, "equal opportunity" actually means an equal chance to leave the less fortunate behind. In America, equality was originally defined by Pilgrim settlers amongst their own kind: Protestant, male, and Euro-American (Bell, 1973, p. 424). Bell further echoes Rawls (1971) by saying that equal opportunity does not mean equality of result (Bell, 1973, pp. 427-433). Equality of opportunity preserves status quo by giving to those who are starting ahead due to inherited intelligence or inherited class privilege. Merton (1968) elaborates with the following:

> Our egalitarian ideologies denies by implication the existence of noncompeting individuals and groups in the pursuit of pecuniary success. Instead, the same body of success symbols is held to apply for them all. Goals are held to transcend class lines, not be bound by them yet the actual social organization is such that there exist class differentials inassessibility of the goals. (pp. 146-147)

"Equality of opportunity is the mask of social Darwinism—the survival of the fittest. It doesn't speak to the problem or the worth of the unfit and the socially disempowered" (Maguire, 1980). The "merit" (p. 23) discourse is a universalism forced on all by the ruling class to maintain dominance and privilege. Members of more communitarian and noncompetitive cultures, such as Confucian-influenced Asians and Asian Americans, as well as women, are disadvantaged by the imposition and enforcement of hegemonically masculine standards.

Buying-In, Self-Oppression, and Defining Masculinities

Having asked Assessors and selected Candidates why the selections were made as such, and having run into resistance to double-loop learning, I proposed that same question to the nonselected Candidates. Most of them bought into the merit discourse. *Buying in* means believing in one's inferiority and the superiority of hegemonically masculinity.

Gender Attributions, Inferiorization, and "Nerd" Attribution

The gender attributions used by Assessors characterized the Asian and Asian American male Candidates as feminine, with the exception of analytical ability (see Table 9.3). This gender attribution supports the notion that gender is socially constructed rather than tied to biology (Kessler & McKenna, 1978). Femininity can be performed or attributed (or both) to men *as well as* women. Masculinity can be performed or attributed (or both) to women (such as the selected female Candidates) *as well as* men. In the case of the Asian and Asian American male Candidates, Assessors constructed them as "feminine" and, therefore, unfit for the hegemonically masculine-defined job of Team Manager. However, the finding that women who performed hegemonic masculinity were more likely to become selected as Team Manager was consistent with Baril,

Elbert, Mahar-Porter, and Reavy's (1989) finding that successful women supervisors perform hegemonically masculine behaviors, whereas unsuccessful ones perform feminine behavior.

One Euro-American male Assessor at the church-affiliated teaching university bluntly summed up what he and others at other universities said indirectly about the Asian and Asian American male Candidates: "We don't pick nerds. It's not that they are Asians. We don't want nerds. We want real managers." This statement extends the Assessors' attribution that in effect said that Asian and Asian American men are not masculine (see Table 9.3). This direct statement and other less direct ones revealed how race and gender intersect in the "nerd" attribution. When race is examined *with* gender, masculinity can become separated from sex and becomes plural. *Masculinity* in the hegemonic sense is *not necessarily synonymous* with sex. The Asian and Asian American men in the assessment center are of the male sex. They did not perform hegemonically *real masculinity* as emically defined by the Assessors, although they acknowledged that Asian and Asian American men can perform such a role (only by violating the Confucian norms of their heritage cultures). In social science (i.e., etic) terms, Assessors wanted hegemonic masculinity, the current dominant form of masculinity that they defined in the Good Manager ideal type. They want *man*agers (preferably by Euro-Americans males), a display of hegemonic masculinity. However, as the case of the Asian and Asian American men reveals, *hegemonic masculinity is only one type of masculinity.*

I strongly admonished the Assessors during assessment training for not presuming dichotomies from their ideal type and what they observed and further suggested that they separate their Good Manager ideal from individuals who do not have those characteristics or whom they perceive as "bad." I asked them to think in terms of functional and dysfunctional *with respect to specific jobs* rather than to personalities. Yet, all 6 mini-assessment centers engaged in dichotomous gender attributions. To the Assessors, the hegemonically masculine Good Manager ideal type would be "good," whereas the Candidates who did not meet their ideal type would be "bad" managers. The Assessors did in practice lump feminine, androgynous, and undifferentiated behaviors into the "bad" category (Bem, 1974).

The gender dichotomy used by Assessors polarizes two good-manager characteristics. Analytical ability was attributed to both nonselected Asian and Asian American men and selected Euro-American men. Athletic ability was often attributed to many of the selected Euro-American Candidates. It is stereotypical to attribute analytical ability to both Asian females and males. Analytical ability is often perceived as dichotomous to athletic ability. Asian and Asian American men are gender-attributed as archetypal nerds who, among other characteristics, exhibit brains with underdeveloped (i.e., weak and feminine) bodies.

The social construction of a nerd is one of deeper implications, because it illustrates Morgan's (1992, p. 44) point that men may be or, in this case, are perceived as either masculine or feminine, heterosexual or homosexual. The nerd construction is dependent on the analytical ability attribution. This dimension distinguishes Asian and Asian American men (feminine, heterosexual) from gay men (feminine or masculine, homosexual), acknowledging there are gay Asian and Asian American men, none of whom were out of the closet in these classes. It should be noted that the nerd construction is in opposition to the "samurai" or "Bruce Lee" (the late Chinese kung fu action movie hero) construction. Kimmel's (personal communication, 1996) concept of the "Goldilocks dilemma" informs us that hegemonic masculinity must define other masculinities as either insufficiently masculine, such as nerds, or too masculine, such as samurais or Bruce Lees.

Nerd is an attribution that signifies difference and inferiority, flawed masculinity, passiveness (Chin, 1972, p. 67), weakness, "good natives" (Wong, 1992, p. 112) who are subservient to Euro-Americans (Woo, 1981, pp. 144-145), and desexualization (Wong, 1993, p. 68) or, in a pejorative sense, femininity (Chin & Chan, 1972, p. 68), homosexuality (Chan, Chin, Inada, & Hsu, 1991, p. xiii), or both. *Masculinity* is an achievement, an earned status. Those who are unable to earn, are unwilling to earn, or do not know how to achieve this status are positioned nerds as a subordinated masculinity.

Self-Perceptions and the Confucian Influence on Masculinity

I asked the Asian and Asian American men how they viewed their behavior at the assessment center, as it seemed that this was what the Assessors gave more weight to than the job applications. As shown in Table 9.7, their most frequent responses were that they acted differently, humbly, politely, respectfully, and like a team player, as opposed to acting like a competitive individual.

The Assessors viewed these behaviors as a liability, whereas the Asian and Asian American men regarded them as an asset. The Asian and Asian

TABLE 9.7 Most Frequently Mentioned Asian Males' Perspectives of Their Behavior at the Assessment Center

Deferent
Humble
Polite
Respectful
Team player (noncompetitive and nonindividualistic)

American men thought they were behaving in a way that mature adult males and managers should, according to their cultural upbringing. Cultural norms of modesty and humility prevent Asian Americans from "selling themselves" or even from accepting praise (Khoo, 1988, pp. 134-137).

Although negotiation researchers report numerous differences between Chinese, Japanese, and American negotiation styles (Chen, 1993; Graham & Sano, 1984, p. 29; Moran, Allen, Wichmann, Ando, & Sansano, 1994, p. 48; Pye, 1982; Tung, 1984), these differences may also affect perceptions of leadership ability. I interpret the self-attributions of the Asian and Asian American male Candidates and those made of them by the Assessors to be in etic terms, in varying degrees, to manifest a Confucian cultural influence. All these 13 Asian males were either from or descended from China, Japan, and Korea, countries that, as Chen (1995) points out, are heavily influenced by Confucian ethics. In behavioral terms, this manifests as conformity, piety, cooperation, collectivism, an absence of open ego displays that may invite criticism, harmony and consensus, an honor of tradition, an emphasis on rituals and strict role adherence, standardized behavior, relationship-centered capitalism, patriarchal paternalism, mistrust of out-groupers, a belief that mistrust is reciprocal, long-term orientation, thrift, and *guanxi* (connections, obligations, and social exchange) (Chen, 1995, pp. 29-30, 41; Hall & Hall, 1987, pp. 65-94; Hofstede & Bond, 1988; Redding, 1990, pp. 59, 208; Weber, 1916/1951, pp. 152-159, 244). Many of these behaviors were visible at the assessment center to Assessors (see Table 9.3), Candidates (see Table 7), and myself.

The antagonism between Western capitalism, which most of the Assessors were or are in training to be a part of, and those influenced by Confucianism is deep, historical, and significant. In Japan after World War II, the American occupational authority regarded Confucianism and paternalism as blocks to "democratic" (i.e., Eurocentric) reforms (Kawai, 1960). Weber (1916/1951, pp. 86-100, 237) wrote that the *sib,* kinship networks that Confucianism gave rise to, blocked rational, Western-styled capitalism. It is no wonder that Assessors ethnocentrically judged Asian men and their Confucian influence as unmanagerial. However, it may be unreasonable and ethnocentric to expect international students and in particular Asian American students socialized as Asians to know or at least have much practice in performing hegemonic masculinity.

One Asian male student whom I interviewed stated, "We choose not to compete with the Americans in such a manner [hegemonic masculinity]." Note that he said "we." This man is from a collectivistic, Confucian-influenced culture. His behavior during the rest of the term, as was that of the other Asian and Asian American men who were rejected, was consistent with a collectivistic orientation. In a later interview, this student viewed aggressive competitiveness, which was how he described the hegemonically masculine behaviors of the Euro-American males (and females who adopted them) as antisocial, selfish, and morally wrong. The punishment for not wishing to use such behavior was to be branded a nerd and to be considered feminine, even by women. "Not wanting to compete" threatens the hegemonically masculine system by presenting an option that undermines the seeming naturalness of the dominant order. To change hegemonic masculinity, therefore, rewards must be put in its place instead of punishments.

Orientalism, the Post-Colonial Discourse, Race, Representation, and Masculinities

The nerd attribution is an ethnocentric and Eurocentric cultural representation by the dominant group: heterosexual, capitalist, racist, patriarchal Euro-American males and their female agents. Race has been either unstated or treated as irrelevant in organization behavior (OB) research (Cox & Nkomo, 1990; Nkomo, 1992, pp. 488-489). Most Americans who deny race and racism as significant probably consider race and colonialism to be unrelated. However, if one is to critically examine race in OB, then one must address the postcolonial discourse and the effects of colonialism embedded in race relations. Racism has its roots in America's "manifest destiny," that is, its capitalist imperialism (Wood, 1990).

In academia, the postcolonial discourse is Orientalist in nature. As Said (1978, pp. 5-6, 20-21) notes, the Oriental, who in his definition includes Arabs and Indians, as well as Asian Pacific Islanders, do not speak for themselves. "The tradition in much of American social research . . . has been largely dominated by white men" (Alderfer, 1982, p. 126). "For the native, objectivity is always directed against him" (Fanon, 1963, p. 77). Europeans speak for them and present their own culturally imperialist models of the Orient (Said, 1978, pp. 5-6, 20-21). hooks (1981, p. 10) notes that funding agencies finance white women's research on black women but not black women's research on white women. Asians in Asia and in the United States are a problem to be studied in the Orientalist discourse. The problem is actually that of postcolonial domination by one group over another, that historically has been imposed by Western, Caucasian, capitalist, imperialist patriarchs (and the white and other women who collude with them) on Third World people.

Orientalists are existentially and morally outside the Orient. The authority of Euro-American writers is the representation, the surface level rather than what is hidden in the text (Said, 1978, pp. 5-6, 20-21). Orientalism is neither merely representational nor a reflection of culture, scholarship, and institutions by complex scholarly, economic, historical, sociological interests. Its intent is to understand, control, manipulate, incorporate, or any combination thereof (Said, 1978, p. 12).

The Orientalism of the Euro-American Assessors and their agents, who may have been born as diverse peoples but who are now functionally hegemonized into the dominant discourse, is built on the following:

> The deprecation of the cultural integrity of non-Western people appears to be the result of specific values and emphasis within the Western ethos, not just a matter of ignorance, arrogance, and ill will. The leading concepts of Western culture, intensified in Protestantism, include control and dominance, property and appropriation, competition and individualism. These values have worked well in support of racial oppression and cultural domination: equalitarian and democratic themes have been weak countertrends at best. Particularly important has been the conflict between Western technological orientation or engineering mentality and the more organic, harmonious notions of the relation between man and nature that were held by the societies dominated by non-Western styles of life are contributed to the white man's depreciation of peoples of color. (Blauner, 1972, p. 114)

Orientalism is a colonial, neocolonial, and postcolonial discourse in which race *and* gender intersect with other aspects of diversity that my classes did not wish to deal with or may not have known of.

As the Asian and Asian American men and other nonselected diverse peoples believed that they "were not good enough" to be Team Managers, they were really saying to themselves and others that they believe they are inferior to the hegemonically masculine Good Manager ideal type. The cultural domination of Third-World peoples, including African Americans, Asians and Asian Americans, and many others, demands their self-negation (hooks, 1992, p. 19), such as the Asians and Asian Americans Candidates who bought into their own inferiority, despite having comparable or, in some cases, superior qualifications to the Euro-American males (and Euro-American females who performed hegemonic masculinity).

When race relations and other forms of diversity are considered, the mini-assessment center, contrary to its intentions, was turned into an assimilating institution. Writing about black-white race relations, West (1982, p. 125) states that blacks have to believe they are inferior to whites in order to assimilate. Assimilation is based on self-hatred, shame, and fear. Fanon (1964, pp. 38-40) explains the racial shaming process of neocolonialism:

> The oppressor, through the inclusive and frightening character of his authority, manages to impose on the native new ways of seeing, and in particular a pejorative judgment with respect to his original forms of existing. . . .
>
> The inferiorized group had admitted, because the force of reasoning was implacable, that its misfortunes resulted directly from its racial and cultural characteristics.
>
> Guilt and inferiority are the usual consequence of this dialectic. The oppressed then tries to escape these, on the one hand by proclaiming his total and unconditional adoption of the new cultural models, and on the other, by pronouncing an irreversible condemnation of his own cultural style. . . .
>
> Having judged, condemned, abandoned his cultural forms, his language, his food habits, his sexual behavior, his way of sitting down, of resting, of laughing, of enjoying himself, the oppressed *flings himself* on the imposed culture with the desperation of a drowning man. . . .
>
> It is not possible to enslave men without logically making them inferior through and through. And racism is the only emotional, affective, sometimes intellectual explanation of this inferiorization.

The oppressors' perceived authority comes through the methodology of positivism and the organizations that produce and reproduce it rather than through racial, intellectual, religious, or moral superiority. The technology and power of the dominant class that includes co-opted diverse peoples self-justify their morality only for those who buy into it.

"Men of color, poor and working-class men, and gay men are often in very contradictory positions at the nexus of intersecting systems of domination and subordination" (Messner, 1993, pp. 733-734). By definition, hegemonic masculinity requires the subordination and marginalization of alternative forms of masculinities.

> Hegemonic masculinity is constructed in relation to women and subordinated masculinities. These other masculinities need not be as clearly defined—indeed, achieving hegemony may consist precisely in preventing alternatives gaining cultural definition and recognition as alternatives, confining them to ghettos, to privacy, to unconscious. (Connell, 1987, p. 186)

Men who have been subordinated and marginalized are shamed into inferiorization by the dominant discourse for not being a Euro-American, heterosexual, middle-upper-class, able-bodied, First World, Christian male, and so on; yet their sex renders them the object of hegemonically masculine projections of the control, domination, and power that they lack but may not even desire. Economic discrimination, such as that simulated in the mini-assessment centers, is not the only form of subordinating men. The social systems of the West subordinate and marginalize men, *as well as* women (Connell, 1987). Studying masculinities need not detract from feminist studies of sexism.

Conclusion

At the end of the selection process's term, when we debriefed the selections made for Team Managers with them out of the room, the Assessors, who had since spent a term being managed by the Team Managers whom they helped to select, almost uniformly attributed personal defects to Team Managers with whom they were dissatisfied. The team members and Assessors held the Team Managers accountable to an ideal type of the Good Manager. Yet in hindsight, they did not realize that they did not select a good manager. They accounted for this by claiming that the applicants were personally inadequate, or the assessment center was too short. Although the assessment center was indeed short, it did take up an entire week of the term. The length of the assessment center was adequate for its metalearning objective of indoctrinating the participants into the process of experiential learning.

What they did not recognize was that their "rationality" in insisting that their ideal type be lived up to was a defectively espoused theory, something that I pointed out. This is a metalesson of the CHIO design. The participants in the CHIO needed to learn that excessive "rationality" leads to defective theories-of-action, in this case producing racial discrimination and cultural imperialism. These theories-of-action are misaligned with theories-in-use.

Another metalesson here is that most individuals believe that they are being rational. Their theory-of-action is an act in self-interest (Culbert & McDonough, 1980). When this self-interest is viewed from the individual level of analysis, the action is rational. However, when individuals all pursue their self-interest based on theories-in-use in a group or organizational context or both, they often conflict and appear to be irrational within the broad unit of analysis of the group, organization, or both. Some participants learn this; on the other hand, rigid thinkers insist on conformity to their "rationality," failing to appreciate the fact people will act out of self-interest to pursue individual goals that conflict with groups and organizations. The answer, then, is not more control, as authoritarians would prefer but, rather, to test and correct defectively espoused theory—that is, the ideal types of the good, hegemonically masculine manager.

The result that I would like to see out of this is not the establishment of Confucian masculinity in the modernistic organizations of the West. Confucian masculinity, although perhaps in many ways less severe than the current version of Western capitalist hegemonic masculinity, is still patriarchal. I would like to see research and interventions into modernistic organizations and Western society (i.e., for practical purposes, almost the entire world) that value the diversity of groups and individuals. Men (and women who have adopted hegemonic masculinity) need to be free to, and even encouraged and rewarded to, act nonhegemonically and in prosocial ways in the workplace, with their families, and in social settings.

References

Alderfer, C. P. (1982). Problems of changing white males' behavior and beliefs concerning race relations in the United States. In P. Goodman (Ed.), *Change in organizations* (pp. 122-165). San Francisco: Jossey-Bass.

Argyris, C. (1990). *Overcoming organizational defenses: Facilitating organizational learning*. Boston, MA: Allyn & Bacon.

Argyris, C. (1993). *Knowledge for action: A guide to overcoming barriers to organizational change.* San Francisco: Jossey-Bass.

Argyris, C., & Schon, D. A. (1978). *Organizational learning: A theory of action perspective.* Reading, MA: Addison-Wesley.

Baril, G., Elbert, N., Mahar-Porter, S., & Reavy, G. (1989). Are androgynous managers really more effective? *Group & Organizational Studies, 14*(2), 234-249.

Beckhard, R. (1971). Helping a group with planned change. In H. A. Hornstein et al. (Eds.), *Social intervention: A behavioral science approach.* New York: Free Press.

Bell, D. (1973). *The coming of post-industrial society: A venture in social forecasting.* New York: Basic Books.

Bellah, R. N., Madsen, R., Sullivan, W. M., Swidler, A., & Tipton, S. M. (1985). *Habits of the heart: Individualism and commitment in America.* Berkeley: University of California Press.

Bem, S. L. (1974, April). The measurement of psychological androgyny. *Journal of Consulting and Clinical Psychology, 42*(2), pp. 155-162.

Blauner, R. (1972). *Racial oppression in America.* New York: Harper & Row.

Calas, M. B. (1992). An/other silent voice?: Representing "Hispanic woman" in organizational texts. In A. J. Mills & P. Tancred (Eds), *Gendering organizational analysis* (pp. 201-221). Newbury Park, CA: Sage.

Calvert, L. M., & Ramsey, V. J. (1992, March). Bringing women's voice to research on women in management. *Journal of Management Inquiry, 1*(1), pp. 79-88.

Chan, J. P., Chin, F., Inada, L. F. & Hsu, S. (Eds.). (1991). *The big aiiieeee: An anthology of Chinese American and Japanese American literature.* New York: Meridian.

Chen, M. (1993, March/April). Understanding Chinese and Japanese negotiating styles. *International Executive, 35*(2), pp. 147-159.

Chen, M. (1995). *Asian management systems: Chinese, Japanese and Korean styles of business.* London: Routledge.

Cheng, C. (1993a). *Classroom as high-involvement organization: An extension of the classroom-as-organization instructional design.* Unpublished manuscript, John E. Anderson Graduate School of Management at UCLA.

Cheng, C. (1993b). *Mini-assessment centers and team selection in group based instructional designs.* Unpublished manuscript. John E. Anderson Graduate School of Management at UCLA.

Cheng, C. (1993c). *Improving team member commitment with a participatively designed multi-rater, multi-leveled performance appraisal sequence.* Unpublished manuscript, John E. Anderson Graduate School of Management at UCLA.

Cheng, C. (1993d). *Integrating task and process with self-generated behavioral data: Teaching and facilitating team-based instructional designs using ethnographic journaling and a theory of action approach.* Unpublished manuscript, John E. Anderson Graduate School of Management at UCLA.

Cheng, C. (1993e). *Participative job and course design, teambuilding and organizational commitment.* Unpublished manuscript, John E. Anderson Graduate School of Management at UCLA.

Cheng, C. (1995, November). Multi-leveled gender conflict analysis and organizational change. *Journal of Organizational Change Management, 8*(5).

Cheng, C. (1996). *"Nerds" need not apply: Masculinity and racial discrimination against Asian and Asian American Men in an assessment center laboratory.* Manuscript in preparation, University of Southern California, Los Angeles.

Chin, F. (1972, Fall). Confessions of the Chinese cowboy. *Bulletin of concerned Asian scholars, 4*(3), pp. 58-70.

Chin, F., & Chan, J. P. (1972). Racist love. In R. Kostelanetz (Ed.), *Seeing through shuck* (pp. 65-79). New York: Ballantine.

Connell, R. W. (1987). *Gender and power: Society, the person and sexual politics.* Stanford, CA: Stanford University Press.

Connell, R. W. (1995). *Masculinities.* Berkeley: University of California Press.

Cox, T., & Nkomo, S. M. (1990). Invisible men and women: A status report on race as a variable in organizational behavior research. *Journal of Organizational Behavior, 11,* 419-431.

Culbert, S., & McDonough, J. J. (1980). *The invisible war: Pursuing self-interests at work.* New York: Wiley.

Dewey, J. (1922). *Democracy and education: An introduction to the philosophy of education.* New York: Macmillan.

Dyer, W. G. (1987). *Team building: Issues and alternatives.* Reading, MA: Addison-Wesley.

Fanon, F. (1963). *The wretched of the Earth* (C. Farrington, Trans.). New York: Ballantine.

Fanon, F. (1964). *Toward the African revolution* (H. Chevalier, Trans.). New York: Monthly Review.

Graham, J. L., & Sano, Y. (1984). *Smart bargaining: Doing business with the Japanese.* Cambridge, MA: Ballinger.

Hall, E. T., & Hall, M. R. (1987). *Hidden differences: Doing business with the Japanese.* Garden City, NY: Anchor.

Hofstede, G., & Bond, M. (1988). The Confucius connection: From cultural roots to economic growth. *Organizational Dynamics, 16,* 4-21.

hooks, b. (1981). *Ain't I a woman: Black woman and feminism.* Boston: South End.

hooks, b. (1992). *Black looks: Race and representation.* Boston: South End.

James, K. (1996, August). *Dealing within diversity.* Paper presented at the annual meeting of the Academy of Management, Vancouver, Canada.

Kanter, R. M. (1977). *Men and women of the corporation.* New York: Basic Books.

Kawai, K. (1960). *Japan's American interlude.* Chicago: University of Chicago Press.

Kessler, S. J., & McKenna, W. (1978). *Gender: An ethnomethodological approach.* New York: Wiley.

Khoo, G. P. S. (1988). *Asian Americans with power and authority in the corporate world: An exploratory investigation.* Unpublished senior thesis, University of California, Santa Cruz.

Kimmel, M. S. (1994). Masculinities as homophobia: Fear, shame, and silence in the construction of gender identity. In H. Brod & M. Kaufman (Eds.). *Theorizing masculinities* (pp. 119-141). Thousand Oaks, CA: Sage.

Lynch, F. R. (1989). *Invisible victims: White males and the crisis of affirmative action.* New York: Praeger.

Maguire, D. C. (1980). *A new American justice: Ending the white male monopolies.* Garden City, NY: Doubleday.

Merton, R. K. (1968). *Social theory and social structure.* Glencoe, IL: Free Press.

Messner, M. A. (1993). "Changing men" and feminist politics in the United States. *Theory and Society, 22,* 723-737.

Morgan, D. H. J. (1992). *Discovering men.* London: Routledge.

Moran, R. T., Allen, J., Wichmann, R., Ando, T., & Sansano, M. (1994). Japan. In M. A. Rahim & B. A. Blum (Eds.), *Global perspectives on organizational conflict* (pp. 33-52). Westport, CT: Praeger.

Nkomo, S. M. (1992, July). The emperor has no clothes: Rewriting "race in organizations." *Academy of Management Review, 17*(3), pp. 487-513.

Pettigrew, T. F., & Martin, J. (1987). Shaping the organizational context for Black American inclusion. *Journal of Social Issues, 43*(1), 41-78.

Powell, G. N. (1992). The good manager: Business students' stereotypes of Japanese managers versus stereotypes of American managers. *Group & Organizational Studies, 17*(1), 44-56.

Powell, G. N. (1993). *Women and men in management* (2nd ed.). Newbury Park, CA: Sage.

Powell, G. N., & Butterfield, D. A. (1979). The "good manager": Masculine or androgynous? *Academy of Management Journal, 22,* 395-403.

Powell, G. N., & Kido, Y. (1994). Managerial stereotypes in a global economy: A comparative study of Japanese and American business students' perspectives. *Psychological Reports, 74,* 219-226.

Pye, L. (1982). *Chinese commercial negotiation styles.* Cambridge, MA: Oelgeschler, Gunn & Hain.

Rawls, J. (1971). *A theory of justice.* Cambridge, MA: Harvard University Press.

Redding, S. G. (1990). *Spirit of Chinese capitalism.* Berlin: De Gruyter.

Said, E. W. (1978). *Orientalism.* New York: Pantheon.

Schein, V. E. (1992, August). *Sex role stereotyping.* Paper presented at the annual meeting of the Academy of Management, Las Vegas, NV.

Tung, R. L. (1984). *Business negotiations with the Japanese.* Lexington, MA: Lexington.

Weber, M. (1951). *The religion of China: Confucianism and Taoism* (H. H. Herth, Trans.). Glencoe, IL: Free Press. (Original work published 1916)

West, C. (1982). *Prophesy deliverance: An Afro-American revolutionary Christianity.* Philadelphia: Westminster.

Wong, S. W. (1992). Ethnizing gender: An exploration of sexuality as sign in Chinese immigrant literature. In S. G. Lim & A. Ling (Eds.), *Reading the literature of Asian America* (pp. 111-130). Philadelphia: Temple University Press.

Wong, S. W. (1993). Subverting desire: Reading the body in the 1991 Asian Pacific Islander men's calendar. *Critical Mass, 1*(1), 63-74.

Woo, M. (1981). Letter to ma. In C. Moraga & G. Anzaldúa (Eds.), *This bridge called my back: Writings by radical women of color* (pp. 140-147). Watertown, MA: Persephone.

Wood, F. G. (1990). *Arrogance of faith: Christianity and race in America from the colonial era to the twentieth century.* New York: Knopf.

Author Index

Subject Index

About the Contributors

Judi Addelston, PhD, obtained her doctorate in Social/Personality Psychology from the City University of New York Graduate Center in 1996. Her research interests focus on the social construction of gender, masculinities, and women's studies, with an emphasis on the development and performance of masculinities in multiple settings. She is now working with an elite, independent, all-boys high school, investigating the construction of a masculinity privileged by race and class. With Michelle Fine, PhD, she has published several articles on the construction of whiteness and masculinity. Additionally, she is writing a textbook on the psychology of prejudice. She is currently a Visiting Assistant Professor of Psychology and Women's Studies at Rollins College in Winter Park, Florida.

Sharon Bird is a PhD candidate in sociology at Washington State University. Her doctoral research focuses on the salience of stereotypical gender characteristics among work unit members, workers' perceptions of similarity, and the effects of these factors on workers' job satisfaction and organizational commitment. She is also interested in the social construction of masculinities and gender inequality.

Cliff Cheng, PhD (Policy and Organization, University of Southern California), has held research and teaching appointments at the John E. Anderson Graduate School of Management at the University of California, Los Angeles (UCLA), University of Southern California, and the University of California at Irvine. He has 45 publications and papers on organizational change, organizational diversity, Asian American and leadership, Chinese family businesses, and so on. Cheng recently coedited special issues on diversity, gender, and Asian transplant management for *Journal of Organizational Change Management.* He is currently coediting with Tojo Joseph Thactchenkery a special issue of *Journal of Applied Behavioral Sciences* on Asian Americans and organizational diversity. (ccheng@lmumail.lmu.edu)

Tomoko Hamada is Associate Professor and Chairperson of the Department of Anthropology at the College of William and Mary. Born in Yokosuka, Japan, she received her PhD from University of California, Berkeley, in 1980. She is an industrial ethnographer and has conducted studies of multinational companies in the Republic of South Africa, the People's Republic of China, Japan, and the United States. Her recent publications include *American Enterprise in Japan* (1995, 2nd ed.) and *Anthropological Perspectives on Organizational Culture* (1994).

Martin Kilduff is Associate Professor of Organizational Behavior at Pennsylvannia State University. He received his doctoral training at Cornell University and taught at INSEAD before joining Penn State. His research interests include social networks, postmodernism, individual identity, and personality. Recent publications have appeared in *Academy of Management Journal, Academy of Management Review, Journal of Personality and Social Psychology,* and *Journal of International Business Studies.* He is on the boards of *Administrative Science Quarterly, Academy of Management Review,* and *Journal of Management Inquiry.*

Ajay Mehra is a doctoral student in management at Pennsylvannia State University. His research interests include social networks, sense making, and social cognition. Current projects include a social network study of race and gender relations, and an examination of identity processes in a Japanese factory.

James W. Messerschmidt is Professor of Sociology and Chair of the Criminology Department at the University of Southern Maine. His research interests focus on the interrelation of gender, race, class, and crime. He has authored *The Trial of Leonard Peltier* (1983), *Capitalism, Patriarchy, and Crime: Toward a Socialist Feminist Criminology* (1986), *Criminology* (with Piers Beirne, 1995, 2nd ed.), and *Masculinities and Crime: Critique and Reconceptualization of Theory* (1993).

Jennifer Pierce, PhD, is Assistant Professor of Sociology at the University of Minnesota. She is also an affiliate with the Center for Advanced Feminist Studies (CAFS) and the American Studies Program. She is a former associate editor of *Signs: Journal of Women in Culture and Society.* Her current book, *Gender Trials: Emotional Lives in Contemporary Law Firms,* examines the gendered emotional division of labor in law offices by considering the experiences of paralegals and trial lawyers. She is currently coediting an anthology with the CAFS editorial collective, titled *Social Justice, Feminism and the Politics of Location.* She has also published articles in *American Sociological Review, Signs, Berkeley Journal of Sociology,* and *Explorations in Ethnic Studies.*

Michael Stirratt, PhD candidate, City University of New York Graduate School, is currently a research assistant in the Evaluation of Fighting Back, a substance abuse prevention program funded by the Robert Wood Johnson Foundation. His research focuses on workplace and employment issues facing lesbian, gay, and bisexual workers with a special interest in developing and promoting work environments that respect and support these workers. His current work examines the effects of workplace climates and sexual orientation policies on lesbian, gay, and bisexual employees. The work was supported by an Applied Issues Internship from the Society for the Psychological Study of Social Issues (SPSSI). He also shares an interest in gender dynamics and the social construction of gender roles, especially in organizations and work environments.

Laurie Telford, MBA, MSc, is a doctoral candidate in Organization Science at the University of Texas at Austin. From 1987 to 1993, she was a faculty member at Mount Royal College, Canada. She received her undergraduate degree in Family Studies and her master's degree in Consumer Studies from the University of Alberta. She earned her MBA at the University of Calgary. Her research interests include identity and identity negotiation, social interaction and relationships in organizations, resource allocation in nested social dilemmas, cooperation within and between organizations, and emotional display. Prior to entering academia, she worked for ten years as a manager in evaluation and public policy research. In one of her positions, she directed research in the Alberta Legislature.

Amy Wharton is Associate Professor of Sociology at Washington State University. She has published articles on the causes and consequences of gender segregation at work, the effects of emotional labor on workers' orientations to their jobs, and work-family relations among service workers. Her current research interests include service work, work-family relations, and the social construction of "difference" in organizations.

Rosemary Wright, PhD, is Assistant Professor of Social Sciences and History at Fairleigh Dickinson University in Madison, New Jersey. She received her PhD in sociology from the University of Pennsylvania in 1994. She is in the process of turning her dissertation, *Women in Computer Work: Controlled Progress in a Male Occupation,* into a book. She has published in the *American Sociological Review, Gender and Society, Computers and Society, Contemporary Sociology,* and two edited collections, *Gender Inequality at Work* and *Minorities and Women in American Professions.* Prior to her current career in sociology, she earned degrees in mathematics at UCLA and the Courant Institute of Mathematical Sciences at NYU and has spent sixteen years as a computer professional, manager, and consultant. Her computer experience spans engineering and information services positions at Bell Laboratories and AT&T, as well as computer and management consulting for a number of corporate and government clients with American Management Systems and with her own consulting firm. Her research interests lie at the intersection of the sociology of work, technology, and gender.